County Map of Scotland

1. Shetland Islands
2. Orkney Islands
3. Hebrides
4. Sutherland
5. Caithness
6. Ross and Cromarty
7. Nairn
8. Moray
9. Banff
10. Aberdeen
11. Inverness
12. Kincardine
13. Angus
14. Perth
15. Argyll
16. Fife
17. Kinross

18. Clackmannan
19. Dumbarton
20. Stirling
21. West Lothian
22. Midlothian
23. East Lothian
24. Berwick
25. Renfrew
26. Peebles
27. Lanark
28. Bute
29. Ayr
30. Selkirk

31. Roxburgh
32. Dumfries
33. Kirkcudbright
34. Wigtown

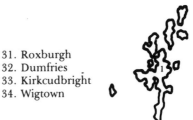

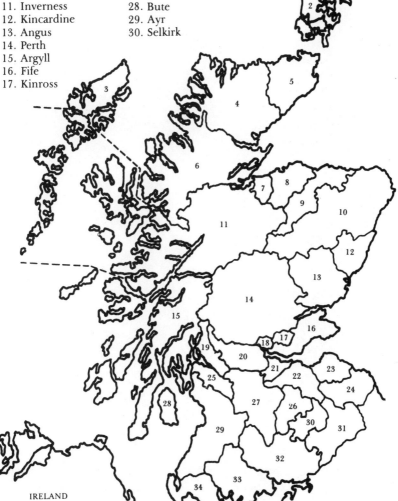

IRELAND

ENGLAND

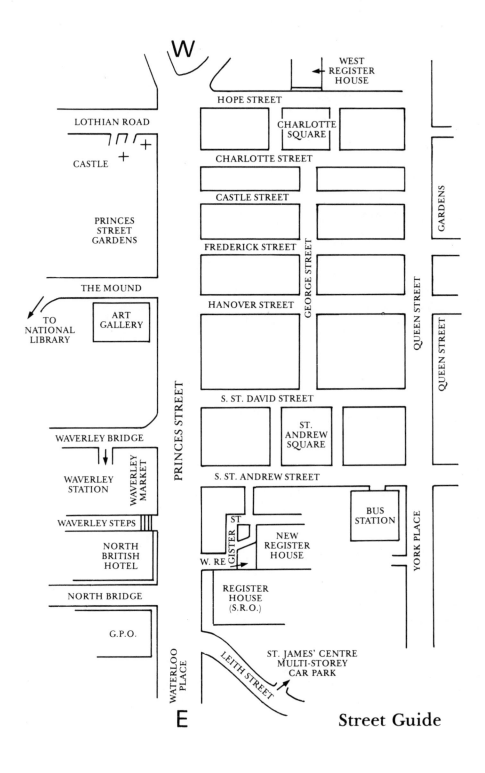

Street Guide

Tracing Your Scottish Ancestry

Tracing Your Scottish Ancestry

Kathleen B. Cory, FSA Scot.

Polygon
EDINBURGH

© Kathleen B. Cory 1990
Foreword © Gordon Donaldson 1990
Polygon
22 George Square, Edinburgh

Set in Baskerville by Polyprint, Edinburgh
and printed and bound in Great Britain by
Bell and Bain Limited, Glasgow

Reprinted 1991 (twice)

British Library Cataloguing in
    Publication Data
Cory, Kathleen B.
    Tracing your Scottish Ancestry
    1. Scotland. Genealogy. Research
    I. Title
    929′.1′0720411

ISBN 0 7486 6054 2 (limp)

Contents

Foreword

BY PROFESSOR EMERITUS GORDON DONALDSON, CBE
HM Historiographer in Scotland

Ancestor hunting has been very much a growth industry in recent years and is by no means confined to Scotland. Yet its scale may have been exceptional there, perhaps because of the enormous emigration from Scotland which began on some scale in the seventeenth century and reached its peak after World War II. Scattered in every part of the globe there are many millions – several years ago the figure was put by a wild guess at 20,000,000, which would now surely be an under-estimate of people of Scottish extraction. Therefore numbers alone are enough to explain the vast amount of activity related to Scottish ancestry.

Yet searching for ancestors has a long history behind it. We hear plenty about searchers of records in the nineteenth century – many of course engaged for legal purposes in connection with property, but sometimes pursuing pedigree simply to satisfy people's curiosity about their ancestry. In the late nineteenth and early twentieth centuries two Edinburgh families earned their bread and butter for three successive generations by searching records, mainly for genealogical purposes.

There was something of a slump just after World War II, and some searchers gave up at that point because they saw no future in the business. How wrong they were. Private searchers have multiplied in the second half of the twentieth century and there are assuredly far more now than ever before. Nor are they confined to the traditional centre in Edinburgh, for modern methods of reproduction of record material have made it possible for genealogists to operate successfully even in remote parts of the country. But the business has gone far beyond private searchers and has extended into corporate activities of various kinds. The Scottish Genealogy Society was founded in 1953, the Scots Ancestry Research Society in 1945, and several local family history groups have sprung up, one of which has been so enterprising as to open a shop in a main street of a Scottish city.

Apart from the private searchers and the societies, the business has been taken up in another way. Ancestry hunting has become something like 'part of the package' for visitors from overseas. Facilities are offered at a popular recreation centre and in at least one well-known hotel. If all this means that there is much competition, it also makes it the more important that anyone proposing to trace his family line must be well equipped and not attempt searching without first learning from the experience of those practised in the work.

The emphasis of the searcher has changed in recent times. In the nineteenth century and perhaps after it a lot of people sought ancestors because they were optimistically looking for a link with some noble family or the bearer of some famous name. A lot of searching was specifically aimed at establishing a right to property or to a title. Cases heard in the House of Lords, involving a claim to a peerage or a dispute over a peerage, proliferated in the nineteenth century and have not been entirely rare in the twentieth. Some of them involved vast research. Indeed, anyone who thinks that it is easy to pursue pedigree, even among the relatively well-documented members of a noble family, might glance at the complexities of a case like that of the Dudhope Viscountcy in 1952: the last holder of the title had died in 1668 and the claimant had not only to prove his descent, generation by generation, from a common ancestor who was killed at the battle of Harlaw in 1411, but also to demonstrate that the many intermediate lines had died out.

More recently the seeking of title, property or even distinguished ancestry has become less important, and most people who search for their ancestors do not much mind – indeed they may be positively pleased, if only in a kind of inverted snobbery – should their search lead to humble or even disreputable characters.

Some of the searcher's problems are the same whether his ancestor be noble or humble. In earlier records there are inevitable difficulties of handwriting and language (often Latin or old Scots). I was amused at the understatement of someone who was looking with puzzled bewilderment at an early record and remarked, 'It must need something of a flair to read that'. Perseverance and practice are all-important.

But much hard work is necessary before one ever sees an original document or record. The searcher has to identify material which might be relevant, to discover what guides in the way of indexes and lists are available, to learn where the records are preserved. On such matters Mrs Cory not only furnishes wise guidance but gives the appropriate 'class references' which are necessary to direct the searcher to and through the multitudes of record volumes. She reminds her readers of certain sources which are far from obvious and which have been ignored by other writers on the subject. She gives examples of how to set about a search, but it is not only beginners who will learn a lot from her pages, containing as they do so many hints and tips drawn from her extensive experience.

When you have discovered which records are relevant to your search, when you have found where those records are, when you have used an index – if there is an index – to lead you to the entry or entries in which you are interested, when you have at last reached the original document, have read the entry and deciphered it, with its handwriting and spelling, you still have the problem of interpreting it. What deductions can be made about matters on which the record itself is not explicit?

It is in this field that many of the more subtle pitfalls are awaiting, some of them peculiar to Scottish genealogy and arising from common presuppositions, errors or myths, often simply from ignorance of the origins and development of surnames. Names ending in '-son' or beginning with 'Mac-' reflect old practice whereby people were designated not by surnames but by patronymics. Thus Robert's son John was John Robertson, his son might be Andrew Johnson, his son Peter Anderson and so on. Likewise, Neil, son of Donald, was Neil MacDonald. At some stage, we must suppose, a son of a John Robertson decided to call himself not Andrew Johnson but Andrew Robertson, and from that generation Robertson became a surname. The same applied with most of the 'Mac-' names, though some of them appear from an early stage to have carried the connotation 'descendant of' rather than literally 'son of'.

Some indication of a fundamental misunderstanding is perhaps given by the very way in which Scots are apt to speak of their surnames. A man says, 'I'm a Robertson', almost as if Robertsons constitute some unique sub-species of humankind. That at once suggests an assumption that every Robertson is related to other bearers of that name. This is preposterous. The very most that a bearer of the name Robertson can deduce from his surname is that in some generation or other in the past he probably had an ancestor called Robert. It is no more than *probable*, for men changed their surnames because they moved from one part of the country to another, because they changed landlords or employers, perhaps even because they changed their occupation. To believe even that there was necessarily ever an ancestor called Robert is going beyond what the evidence warrants.

To assume that there is necessarily any kinship among 'Robertsons' is to be carried beyond rational thinking. But it is on such irrationality that a great deal which passes in common currency is based. Not only do Robertsons seem to believe that they constitute a sub-species: they also believe that they all came from a little place in Perthshire called Struan. Which at once summons up the picture of the most tremendous industry at Struan over the centuries, in the manufacture and export of Robertsons. Generation by generation, we must suppose, they marched out, kilts no doubt waggling and pipes skirling, to take possession of other parts of the country which meantime had obligingly remained empty awaiting their arrival. This is the kind of belief by which Scots bring down ridicule on their heads. Yet people who are otherwise quite rational seem to believe that kind of thing.

So while many people who engage in ancestor-hunting in Scotland seek no more than to learn what reliable records reveal about their ancestry, a good many are misled into other quests on which records give no information. They want to be connected with some kind of 'clan'. Now, clans (which were military, economic and social communities) ceased to be a reality generations ago: when they were realities few of their members had surnames at all, and members who had a surname did not necessarily share it with other members of the clan. There is of course no reason why people of the same surname should not form an association if it gives them any satisfaction to do so, but that association should not be confused with an historic clan. The idea that anyone, just because he chances to have a particular name, is automatically a member of a particular organisation is absurd. Some people want to argue some connection with a 'chief' – and some 'chiefs' are not averse from having 'clansmen', whose contributions can sometimes be relied on to patch up the roof of the 'chief's' ancestral home. Some want a 'clan connection' because they believe that 'entitles' them to wear cloth of a particular pattern, a so-called 'clan tartan'. Experience shows that the only qualification for the acquisition of a 'clan tartan' (nearly always a nineteenth-century invention) is the same qualification as for the acquisition of any other piece of cloth, namely, ability to pay for it. That is where the emphasis should be laid, because of course the whole tartan cult is a commercial enterprise – it is business, big business, for the tartan-makers, and no doubt it yields many a fee to hard-working genealogists. It is a sobering thought that anyone turning up in the Lowlands four hundred years ago clothed in anything recognisable as 'Highland dress' would probably have been shot on sight!

Our Robertson may be lucky enough to trace his own original Robert, the descent from whom gave him his name – but even so he should remember that had the change to a surname come a generation earlier or later his name might have been not Robertson but, say, Anderson or Johnson. However, as the adoption of a fixed surname may have taken place as far back as the fifteenth century the chances of a twentieth century Robertson identifying his 'Robert' are not very good. Sometimes, though, the change took place more recently. It did so in my own case. I was aware that in Shetland (whence my paternal ancestry derives) there were Donaldsons who had arrived from Scotland, already with that name, before 1600, and that there were also Donaldsons or Danielsons who had used patronymics until, in some generation or other, an individual's patronymic Danielson was retained by his family as a surname. I thought I belonged to the first category, and indeed I did, but only through the curious coincidence that one of my patronymic ancestors happened to marry a Donaldson descended from Scottish immigrants. What mattered more was the discovery that my great-great-grandfather, William Donaldson or Danielson (baptized 1770), was the son of Daniel Theodoreson, who was the son of Theodore Danielson, and so back in patronymic succession to Matthew Thomasson about 1600. Readers of those pages will appreciate that I have good reasons to be thankful for skilled genealogical research.

Yet some would say that I am 'a Donaldson'. Worse than that, they might say that I am 'a MacDonald', that I am a member of 'The Clan Donald' and no doubt 'entitled' to wear the 'MacDonald Tartan'. What a load of nonsense! Of course the financial interests keep coming in. I recall some years ago receiving a request for funds for some object under the patronage of 'The Clan Donald'. I replied: 'If you can prove (a) that there is such a thing as The Clan Donald and (b) that I am a member of it, I shall gladly subscribe; but until you do I shall continue to deplore the way you distort historical truth for financial gain.' I heard no more.

Be warned!

Few people would be so foolish as to believe that all 'the Smiths' are descended from one and the same blacksmith or that all 'the Littles' are descended from one and the same Little Richard or Richard Little, but when patronymics come in common sense flies out of the window.

These remarks are not intended to depreciate the historical importance of the surname or family name in Scottish society and politics, but the name was often used as a badge of party allegiance or affiliation rather than as proof of descent or kinship. I emphasise the numerous complexities to indicate the great danger of relying on casual assumptions about kinship and descent, based on nothing more than the surname. The case for serious study is strengthened, not weakened, because assumptions or guesses are no substitute for thorough research in original sources, for which Mrs Cory, who is well aware of all the manifold pitfalls, provides comprehensive guidance.

Fife, 1989   Gordon Donaldson

Acknowledgements

Extracts from the Statutory Registers, Indexes of Births, Marriages and Deaths, and Census Returns, held in New Register House, Edinburgh, are reproduced by permission of the Controller of Her Majesty's Stationery Office. Government Emigration Regulations are reproduced with the approval of the Keeper of the Records of Scotland. The 'C H' extracts are taken from the originals in the Scottish Record Office by permission of the Principal Clerk of the General Assembly of the Church of Scotland. The chart of the divisions and reunions of the Scottish Church 1690–1929 is from Professor J. H. S. Burleigh's *A Church History of Scotland,* and it is reproduced by kind permission of John K. Burleigh, Esq.

On a more personal note, I wish to thank Margaret Dudgeon Young and her brother Archibald Henderson Young who allowed me to search and use their family line as the example in Part II of this book.

I would also like to thank Selina J. Corkerton, Alison E. Denholm and Daniella Shippey for checking dates and the index. I am very grateful to Professor Gordon Donaldson for all his invaluable advice and information; to Sir Malcolm Innes of Edengight K.C.V.O., Lord Lyon King of Arms, for allowing me to use information from the heraldry leaflet and for approving the chapters on Heraldry and Clans and Tartans; to Dr Athol Murray, Keeper of the Records of Scotland, for his help with matters relating to the 'Old House', and to Dr John Shaw, Mrs Jackie Ross and Mrs Margaret Whyte for their help in the 'New House'.

I am grateful too to my daughters, Elizabeth S. B. Cory, Alison C. B. Kozowyk, and Margaret D. B. Murray for 'keeping me at it' and checking my spelling – no easy task on either count! – as well as for the constructive comments they made.

Lastly, on a good biblical precedent that the last shall be first, I must thank Charles J. Burnett, Ross Herald, who provided me with the opportunity of writing this book, which I had threatened to do for some years!

K.B.C.

Part I

A GUIDE TO GENEALOGY IN SCOTLAND

Introduction

'Is it upon record, or else reported successively from age to age?' asked the Prince of Wales in Shakespeare's *Richard III*. Pooh Bah, the Lord High Everything Else, in Gilbert and Sullivan's *Mikado* had no such doubts. He knew his background: 'I can trace my ancestry back to a protoplasmal primordial atomic globule. Consequently, my family pride is something inconceivable. I cannot help it. I was born sneering.'

To whichever category you may feel you belong, I hope you will find this book interesting, informative and, in parts, entertaining.

Several books have been written about Scottish genealogy and record searching, but none, so far as I know, has combined a thorough explanation of the complexities of the records with step-by-step instructions on completing a search of your family history, using all the resources available, principally in Scotland.

While lecturing on genealogy in the United States I was often asked if my notes existed in book form. At the time they did not, but this book is based on the experience gained from these lectures. I believe that it will succeed in answering most, if not all of the questions which have come my way in the past fifteen years.

The great advantage to be gained from working with post-1854 birth, marriage and death records in New Register House in Edinburgh, is that you may view each entry, and so determine its relevance to your own search. This is very different from working in St Catherine's House, London, where each certificate has to be purchased, with no possibility of viewing it beforehand to establish its relevance.

1855 is the important date to remember as far as Scottish genealogy is concerned. It was in 1854 that Parliament decided to introduce statutory (or civil) registration of births, marriages and deaths in Scotland. This Act (17 & 18 Vict. c.80), was to take effect from 1 January 1855, and since that date it has been compulsory, by law, to register all births, marriages and deaths which take place in Scotland.

1

I stress *Scotland* because statutory or civil registration had been introduced in England in 1837, some eighteen years earlier.

It is not clear why Scotland lagged behind on this issue, but it certainly gave the Scottish authorities time to take note of the short-comings in the English recording system. When statutory registration was eventually introduced, then the information required was far and away more detailed and more comprehensive than that found in English records. For example, a Scottish marriage certificate from 1855 onwards records the age of the bride and bridegroom, whereas an English certificate often merely states 'of full age'. A Scottish certificate also records the maiden surname of the mother of both bride and groom, as well as their fathers' names and occupations, whereas the English equivalent records only the names and occupations of the fathers. At present (1989) there is a proposed alteration to the form of the marriage certificate for future use in England.

The greatest difference in the system can be seen in death certificates. A Scottish death certificate, unlike its English counterpart, gives a wealth of genealogical information, such as the name of the deceased's mother, her maiden surname and the name and occupation of the father, as well as, in most cases, the name of the spouse.

When it comes to searching census returns, again we are lucky in Scotland, as we have access to these from 1841–91 inclusive, while in England the 100-year closure rule holds, and only recently have the 1881 census returns become available to the public. Unfortunately, however, Scotland is about to fall into line with England, and to observe the 100-year closure rule, so that the 1901 census return will not be available for public inspection until the year 2001, which may be a little late for some of us!

Census returns hold a wealth of interesting material. By reading them carefully you can determine the lifestyle of the people. For example, you can discover how many families lived in a block of flats, and how many, or how few rooms each family had. Census returns also record occupations, as well as stating whether or not an individual was employed, unemployed, or employing servants.

Searching through Old Parish Registers (births, marriages and deaths prior to 1855), and kirk session minute books, you will come across many socially and historically interesting comments, such as this birth entry in Dunfermline in July 1690: 'The 12 day about 9 hours in the morning being a saturday John Christie precentor had ane manchild born to him of his wife Joan Finlay baptized ye 15 instant by Mr. Simon Cowper and called James. The Godfayers was James King of Great Britain, France, and Ireland, defender of ye Faith, and James Finlay Grandfather to the Child'. Genealogically speaking, the nugget of gold in that entry is that Joan Finlay was the daughter of James Finlay, and that James Finlay was still alive in 1690. He may have even left a will!

Before you start your search you may like to read about Scotland's interesting social and local history, which would help you to understand why, and how, families moved around as much as they did. To this end I have appended a list of useful books (see book list in Appendix IV).

In the text I have tried to describe the best method of approaching and questioning members of your family who may not be very cooperative. You should try to stir their memories of days and times gone by; and always remember that there is more to geneaology than just dates and places.

Bearing this in mind, and trying to learn something of the background of my own family, I tape-recorded a conversation I had with my mother when she was ninety-one. She talked of her childhood in Buriton, Hampshire, with her two sisters and her only brother, William King, who emigrated to Australia, returned with the Australian Army, and died of wounds in 1917. My uncle Bill, who died long before I was born, left behind in Australia a young wife and baby daughter. I am in touch with Barbara Edgar, his granddaughter, and have been able to supply her with photographs and information about her great-grandparents.

My mother remembered what London was like on armistice night in 1918 at the end of World War I, and I recorded her impressions of the early motor-cars, the airships, and the Royal Flying Corps before the Royal Air Force existed.

This recording will be played to my grandchildren, who, although they may not remember their great-grandmother, will have photographs of her, and will be able to hear her voice; then 1895, the year of her birth, will not seem such a remote and meaningless date, and they will have listened to somebody whose memory ranges from the first car in her village (with a man walking in front, holding a red flag), to the first landing of a man on the moon!

I now invite you to turn the pages, and enter, or re-enter, the fascinating world of genealogy; I strongly recommend you to be like the pedlar Autolycus – 'a snapper-up of unconsidered trifles' – you never know when they might be useful in bringing to life the facts you have found.

Good luck and happy hunting!

Kathleen B. Cory
Edinburgh, 1989

1

Searching records in New Register House

New Register House, the General Register Office for Scotland, is in Princes Street, Edinburgh, adjacent to the Scottish Record Office. The end-papers of this book show a street plan of central Edinburgh, from which you can see where the main repositories are situated. New Register House holds the indexes to, and registers of births, marriages and deaths from 1855 to the present day. It also holds the Old Parish Registers (OPRs) of births, marriages and deaths to 1854 from the earliest extant date (this date varies from parish to parish, see Appendix III); as well as census returns for 1841–1891 inclusive; some Army, Navy, and Air Force registers; and a selection of miscellaneous records.

Most of these pre-1855 records, and all the census returns, are on microfilm. Index books are in process of being transferred to computers. The records are available to the public for inspection only on payment of a search fee. *No searching is free:* this includes searching the index to statutory registers of births, marriages and deaths from 1855, and searching census returns. Once you have bought a search pass, it is only for your own use; you may not share it with anybody. For example, you may not use it in the morning, and hand it to somebody to use in the afternoon. New Register House is open from 9.00 a.m. until 4.30 p.m. from Monday to Thursday, and from 9.00 a.m. until 4.00 p.m. on Friday. It is closed on Saturdays and on some local and public holidays, so you are advised to write or telephone in advance to check this.

Accommodation is limited, therefore, during the holiday months, when there is an influx of visitors to Edinburgh, you should always write or telephone in advance to book yourself a seat/desk. If you are unable to do this, then you should arrive at least half an hour early to be sure of being admitted. It is important to arrive complete with a large pad, preferably A4 size, on which to write out all the information you find, and at least two *lead pencils*. The use of biros or pens is prohibited and smoking or eating in any of the search rooms is forbidden. There are lavatories, but no cafeteria, though there are

4

several small eating places nearby. Prior arrangements can be made to assist wheelchair searchers, and there is a lift available.

SEARCHING THE RECORDS FROM 1855 ONWARDS

From 1855 onwards, registers of births, marriages and deaths are indexed. At the time of writing the *birth* index books are bound in *red,* the *marriage* index books in *green,* and the *death* index books in *black,* each volume showing the year on the spine; so it is not difficult to spot at a glance which one you need. However, this system is being changed, and the index books are in the process of being put on computer, starting with present-day records, and working back to 1855. This should be completed by 1993.

Each yearly index is like a telephone directory, arranged by surname, followed by Christian or forename; male and female entries are separate, and from 1855 you will find the male entries at the front of the book, and the female entries at the back. From 1914 male and female entries are in separate books, and this is indicated on the spine. Events are generally to be found indexed in the year when they were registered, and not in the year when they occurred. For example, a birth, marriage or death which took place on 31 December 1870 is most likely to be found in the index for 1871. Over the years the layout of the indexes has altered, and the amount of information shown has increased.

Indexes to Births, Marriages and Deaths after 1854

I have set out below what you may expect to find in the various index years.

Birth index: Male and female

1855–65   Photocopies of handwritten indexes. Arranged chronologically in alphabetical order of surname and Christian name. Show the parish or district of birth and the entry number in the birth book for that parish or district.

1866–1905   Printed indexes comparable with those of 1855–65.

1906–present   On computer, and comparable with those of 1855–65. *Except* from 1929 the mother's maiden surname (M/S) is shown, and from 1966 there is the additional advantage of finding the registration number of the parish or district as well as the entry number of the birth.
Note: Registration numbers may be different from those in previous years.

Marriage Index: Male

1855–65   Photocopies of handwritten indexes. Arranged
                 chronologically in alphabetical order of surname and
                 Christian name. Show the parish or district of
                 marriage and the entry number in the marriage book
                 for that parish or district.

1866–1965   Printed indexes comparable with those of 1855–65.
                 Except from 1929 the surname of the spouse is
                 indexed.

1966–present   On computer, showing the name of the spouse and the
                 printed registration number of the parish or district as
                 well as the entry number of the marriage.
                 Note: Registration numbers may be different from
                 those in previous years. No ages are recorded in
                 marriage indexes.

Marriage Index: Female

1855–63   Photocopies of handwritten indexes. Arranged
                 chronologically and in alphabetical order of surname
                 and Christian name. Show the parish or district of
                 marriage and the entry number in the marriage
                 register.
                 Note: The name in the index is the *maiden surname*; the
                 married surname is written in brackets beside it, for
                 example, Hutton (or Wallace) Anne . . . Peebles 14. If
                 a widow remarried, then all her surnames are indexed,
                 for example:
                         Hutton (or Brown,
                             (f. Wallace,) Anne . . . Peebles 14.
                         Wallace (or Brown,
                             (m.s. Hutton) Anne . . . Peebles 14.
                     So this index entry reads: 'Anne Hutton, married (1)
                 Wallace; (2) Brown'; 'f' stands for formerly; 'm.s.' for
                 maiden surname.
                     If a woman married a husband of the same
                 surname, the index would only show this once, for
                 example:
                         Craig, (   ) Sarah . . . Perth 12.
                 The blank does not mean that they did not know the
                 married surname!

1864–65   Photocopies of handwritten indexes, comparable with those of 1855–63. *Except* the married surname is not recorded.

1866–1965   Printed indexes comparable with those of 1864–5 i.e., no married surname recorded. *Except* from 1929 the surname of the spouse is indexed.

1966–present   On computer, showing the name of the spouse, and the printed registration number of the parish or district, as well as the entry number of the marriage. *Note:* Registration numbers may be different from those in previous years. No ages are recorded in marriage indexes.

Death Index: Male

1855–65   Photocopies of handwritten indexes. Arranged chronologically and in alphabetical order of surname and Christian name. They show the parish or district of death and the entry number in the death book for that parish or district. *Note:* No ages are shown in the index for this period.

1866–1965   Printed indexes comparable with those of 1855–65. *Except* age at death is shown from 1866 onwards.

1966–present   On computer, comparable with 1866–1965. *Except* the maiden surname of the deceased's mother is shown from 1974, and from 1966 the printed registration number of the parish or district as well as the entry number for the death register. *Note:* Registration numbers may be different from those in previous years.

Death Index: Female

1855   Photocopies of handwritten indexes. Arranged chronologically and in alphabetical order of surname and Christian name. They show the parish or district of death and the entry number in the death book for that parish or district. *Note:* A married woman is indexed under her married name, and beside this is shown her maiden surname.

1856–58   Photocopies of handwritten indexes, comparable with those of 1855. *Except* no maiden surname is recorded for a married woman.

1859–65   Photocopies of handwritten indexes. A married woman is now indexed (1) Under her married surname with her M/S shown beside it; (2) Under her maiden surname, but with no mention of her married name.
                 Note: No ages are shown in the index 1855–65.

1866–1965   Printed indexes.
                 Note: Age at death is shown from 1866 onwards. A married woman is indexed twice: (1) Under her maiden name; (2) Under her married name or her married names, if she had been married more than once. Each entry shows the same parish or district, and entry number. A widow may sometimes revert to her M/S and not be indexed under her married name at all.

1966–present   On computer, comparable with those of 1866–1965. *Except,* the maiden surname of the deceased's mother is shown from 1974, and from 1966 the printed registration number of the parish or district, as well as the entry number of the death.
                 Note: Registration numbers may be different from those in previous years.

A few points to remember when using an index

Names starting with Mc or Mac are indexed separately; if your search is for McLeod, for example, remember to search under MacLeod as well as McLeod.

Although your ancestor may have always used a middle name, he or she was not necessarily baptised with this middle name; so do not despair if the entry you hope to find is not seen instantly. Look again at the index, this time ignoring the entries with middle names, but bearing in mind the parish of birth if this is known.

If you are not searching in New Register House in Edinburgh, you may be making use of Mormon microfiche held in a local library or hired from Salt Lake City. At the time of writing the latest Mormon IGI (International Genealogical Index) is 1988. This microfiche index contains some post-1854 entries, and although it is by no means a complete record of all the births and marriages registered in Scotland, it can be a useful tool. You may pick up baptism and marriage dates for some, if not all, members of your family.

Whenever you are using a Mormon microfiche index it is most important to search under all spelling variations and also to note that on some IGI microfiche you will find all the spelling variations are together under one agreed spelling.

For example, the surname Caroline and all variations such as Carline, Carolan etc., are to be found all together under Carlin. There is more detailed information on names and how to find them in Chapter 4.

What can I expect to find from a Birth Certificate from 1855 onwards?

The information found in an 1855 certificate of birth, marriage, or death is the most detailed, as this was the first year of Statutory (Civil) Registration in Scotland.

Unfortunately, the years 1856–60 contain much less information, but thereafter things improve, from the point of view of the genealogist.

An 1855 birth certificate contains:

1. Full name of the child and its sex
2. Date and time of birth
3. Address at birth
4. Name, age, place of birth (and if registered there), and occupation of father
5. Name, age, place of birth (and if registered there), and maiden surname of mother
6. Usual address of parents (if this differs from the place of birth)
7. Date and place of parents' marriage
8. Number and sex of children born prior to the registration of the baby in 1855; and if these children were still living or if they had died. No names of siblings were recorded
9. Name of the informant and relationship of the informant to the child (if any).

Birth certificates for the years 1856–60 inclusive take the form of the 1869 example (see Part II, p. 164) but do *not* show the date and place of the parents' marriage. From 1860 onwards this information *is* shown which makes the search much easier. Once again, remember that the information, although nearly always accurate, is not unfailingly so. Sometimes, because of illiteracy, 'his X mark' or 'her X mark' was written beside the name of the informant, indicating that the name had been written by the registrar or by a witness, and was not the signature of the informant. Naturally, if the informant could not write his or her name, nor read what had been written, then the information supplied may well be suspect.

As well as the civil registers of births recorded since 1855, there are the following:

Register of adopted children (from 1930)

A record of persons adopted under orders made by Scottish courts; there are no entries relating to anyone born before 1909. There is no general index showing natural parents available to the public. Confidential information about the natural parents is given only to the adopted person concerned if he or she has reached the age of seventeen years.

Register of still-births (1939)

Records of still-births which occur in *Scotland* are compiled by district registrars but are not open for public search. Extracts are issued only in exceptional circumstances, such as for legal purposes.

The following registers may be useful, but they tend to be 'patchy', so do not rely on them absolutely:

Marine register of births (from 1855)

Certified returns received from the Registrar-General for Shipping and Seamen in respect of births on British-registered merchant vessels at sea if the child's father was a Scottish subject.

High Commissioners' returns of births (from 1964)

Returns from certain Commonwealth countries relating to persons of Scottish descent or birth. Some early returns are available for India, Pakistan, Bangladesh, Sri Lanka and Ghana.

Register of births in foreign countries (1860–1965)

A record compiled by the General Register Office until the end of 1965. It relates to the births of children of Scottish parents, and the entries were made on the basis of the information supplied by the parties concerned, after due consideration of the evidence of each event.

Air register of births (from 1948)

A record of births in any part of the world in aircraft registered in the United Kingdom, where it appears that the child's father was usually resident in Scotland. The Civil Aviation (Births, Deaths and Missing

Persons) Regulations 1948, state that illegitimate births can be registered in the Air Register. In such cases the mother's usual residence should be in Scotland. The question of the mother's usual residence being taken into account would not normally arise if the child were legitimate and the parents were living together.

Service records (from 1881)

These include (1) The Army returns of births of Scottish persons at military stations abroad during the period 1881–1959; (2) The service departments' registers which, since 1 April 1959, have recorded births outside the United Kingdom relating to persons ordinarily resident in Scotland, but who are serving in, or employed by, HM Forces, including the families of members of the Forces.

Consular returns of births (from 1914)

Certified copies of registrations by British consuls relating to persons of Scottish descent or birth.

What can I expect to find from a Marriage Certificate from 1855 onwards?

An 1855 marriage certificate contains:

1. Date and place of the marriage
2. Denominational rites (Church of Scotland, Free Church, Episcopal Church in Scotland, Roman Catholic, etc.)
3. Bridegroom's name, rank and occupation; Birth place; Where and when registered; Age and marital status (single or widower); Whether second or third marriage; Children by each former marriage; Living/Deceased; Relationship of parties (if any); Usual residence or residence at time of marriage; Name and occupation of father and if he was deceased at the time of the marriage; Name and maiden surname (M/S) of mother and if she was deceased at the time of the marriage
4. Bride as for the bridegroom
5. Name of officiating minister or priest
6. Names (and sometimes addresses) of witnesses.

Marriage certificates from 1856 to 1921 contain the same information as those registered in 1855, except that information concerning previous marriages and birthplace is omitted. From 1922 onwards, the words 'or divorced' are added to the marital status.

Note: Very often, on a marriage certificate you will find only the initials, and not the full Christian or forenames for the bride and/or groom. This occurs because the certificate available to the public (which is also the one used when you order an official copy) is a copy of the original marriage schedule. This copy has been produced in different form, and the *signatures* of the bridal couple have been copied; if the groom or the bride signed with initials and not with their full name, then this is what will be found on the certificate. I have sometimes found the full names in the index, but only initials on the certificate, indicating that the index was made from the original marriage schedule.

This is a point to bear in mind when comparing signatures. On a birth or a death certificate the signature of the informant is just that, but on a marriage certificate the signature is a copy written by the clerk who was copying out the marriage schedule.

As you will see from the copy of the 1979 marriage certificate of my daughter Alison and Ned Kozowyk, the amount and type of information have not changed much over the years (Figure 1). Reading the certificate carefully, you will find a great many pointers to direct you to further searching in different countries.

1. The marriage took place in an Episcopal Church in Edinburgh.

2. The bride was born in Bermuda. Her date and place of birth, her occupation, her parents' names and her usual residence are recorded.

3. The bridegroom is Canadian. His date and place of birth, his occupation, his parents' names and where he was living in Canada are recorded.

4. The bride's father was deceased by 1979, and he had been a Clerk in Holy Orders. This means he had been ordained, and as the marriage took place in an Episcopal Church he was likely to have been a priest in either the Episcopal Church in Scotland, or the Church of England. 'Crockford', the register of clergy in the Anglican Church could be examined and from this could be found where the family had lived.

5. The marriage service was taken by Kenneth Riches, Retired Bishop of Lincoln . . . (what was the connection . . . search 'Crockford' again?).

As well as the civil registers for marriages recorded since 1855 there are the following marriage registers which, like birth registers, tend to be 'patchy'.

High Commissioners' returns of marriages (from 1964)

Following the Foreign Marriage Act in 1892, a marriage was allowed to take place in any foreign country, solemnised by or before a designated marriage officer (Consul, High Commissioner, or Army Chaplain), as long as one of the parties was a British subject, and a marriage warrant had been given to the marriage officer by the Secretary of State. The marriage warrants are issued and withdrawn according to the circumstances and needs of individual posts, and they were retained after the Foreign Marriage Order 1970 only in those countries where the local facilities are inadequate; for example, because of a restriction on the marriage of divorced persons or the lack of a civil or a monogamous form of marriage.

In the following countries marriage warrants are held by consular marriage officers, as at May 1984, the latest available date:
Afghanistan, Bahrain, Burma, Egypt, Greece, Iran, Iraq, Israel, Jerusalem, Jordan, Morocco, Nepal, Oman, Qatar, Saudi Arabia, Senegal, Somalia, Spain, Sudan, Syrian Arab Republic, United Arab Emirates, Yemen Arab Republic, Yemen People's Republic.

Note: Greece and Spain were due to be removed from this list shortly after its compilation.

Register of marriages in foreign countries (1860–1965)

This record was compiled by the General Register Office up until the end of 1965. It related to the marriages of Scottish subjects, and the entries were made on the basis of information supplied by the parties concerned and after due consideration of the evidence of each event.

Service records (from 1881)

These contain (1) The Army returns of marriages of Scottish persons at military stations abroad during the period 1881–1959; (2) The service department registers which, since 1 April 1959, have recorded marriages outside the United Kingdom relating to persons ordinarily resident in Scotland who are serving in, or employed by, HM Forces, including the families of members of the Forces, and certified copies of entries relating to marriages solemnised outside the United Kingdom by army chaplains since 1892, where one of the parties to the marriage is described as Scottish and at least one of the parties is serving in HM Forces.

The Foreign Marriage Act 1947 extended the provision for military personnel to be designated marrying officers, to include the Royal Navy, the Army and the Royal Air Force. As stated above, military marriages by those officers could only be conducted if one party was a member of the Forces.

Consular returns of marriages (from 1917)

Certified copies of registrations by British consuls relating to persons of Scottish descent or birth.

Foreign marriages (from 1947)

These are certified copies of certificates (with translations) relating to marriages of persons from Scotland in certain foreign countries according to the laws of these countries, without the presence of a British consular officer.

Register of Divorces (from 1984)

A central register of divorces granted in Scotland has been kept by the Registrar General since May 1984. Extracts from the register show the names of the parties, the date and place of marriage, the date and place of divorce and details of any order made by the court regarding financial provision or custody of children. The headings on the microfiche index are: Name; Spouse's name; Date of marriage; Divorce Reference.

The index of divorces recorded in the Central Register Office since 1984 is on microfiche, and is available for inspection on request by the general public. Provisions for searching this index and for the issue of extracts of entries in the register are the same as for the statutory indexes and registers of births, marriages and deaths. From 1855 to 1984 divorces were recorded in Scotland by writing the words 'divorce RCE' (Register of Corrected Entries) against the marriage entry. However, when the index of divorces was introduced in May 1984, the practice of stamping divorce (through the RCE) on the Scottish marriage entry was discontinued. If a divorce was granted outwith Scotland, and documentary evidence to that effect was produced to the General Register Office, then the Scottish marriage entry would be annotated. However, this practice was also discontinued in May 1984.

As there is no general index available to the public prior to 1984, the only way to find out if a couple obtained a divorce is to look up the original marriage entry and see if it has been annotated. If the divorce was later than 1984, or if it was granted outside Scotland, and the General Register Office had not been notified, then the marriage entry would not record the fact.

What can I expect to find in a Death Certificate from 1855 onwards?

An 1855 death certificate contains:

1. The names of the deceased
2. Date and time of death

3. Address at time of death and usual residence, if not the same
4. Age and occupation
5. Name of spouse (if married)
6. Names of any issue; their ages at the time of the death, and their ages and when they died, if prior to the death in 1855
7. Name and occupation of the deceased's father, and if he was deceased by this date
8. Name and M/S of the deceased's mother, and if she was deceased by this date
9. Cause of death, and name of medical attendant (if any)
10. Burial place, and name of the undertaker
11. Signature of the informant, and relationship to the deceased (if any).

An example of an 1855 death certificate, and how best to make full use of the information it contains, may be found in Part II, p. 178).

Death certificates from 1856–60 contain the same information as in 1855 *except* that the marital status (single/widow/widower) of the deceased is shown, although no name of spouse is recorded; no names of issue are recorded.

Sometimes the informant was the spouse, which is one of the ways a certificate can be identified as being correct for your search.

Death certificates from 1861–65 contain the same information as above *except* that the name of the spouse is now recorded; burial place is no longer recorded.

Death certificates from 1866 onwards contain the same information as above *except* that from 1967 the date of birth of the deceased is recorded.

As well as the copy of the 1855 death certificate for Jane Dudgeon (Figure 19), I have included here a copy of the more modern death certificate of my father in 1947 (Figure 2). This is an example of having to trace a line back through Army and Navy records. Charles Hubert Reed died aged 54. He was a captain in the Army, and his father, William Reed, had been a naval officer; searching for the birth entry of Charles Reed *circa* 1893 should therefore put you on the track of William Reed and his naval career. For these service records it will probably be necessary to go to the Public Record Office at Kew, Surrey.

Additional to the civil registers of deaths recorded since 1855 there are the following, but like their birth and marriage counterparts, these registers tend to be 'patchy' and incomplete.

Marine register of deaths (from 1855)

Certified returns received from the Registrar General for Shipping and Seamen in respect of deaths on British registered merchant vessels at sea if the deceased person was a Scottish subject.

High Commissioners' returns of deaths (from 1964)

Returns from certain Commonwealth countries relating to persons of
Scottish descent or birth. Some earlier returns are available for India,
Pakistan, Bangladesh, Sri Lanka and Ghana.

Register of deaths in foreign countries (1860 to 1965)

A record compiled by the General Register Office until the end of
1965. It related to the deaths of Scottish subjects, and the entries were
made on the basis of information supplied by the parties concerned,
after due consideration of the evidence of each event.

Air register of deaths (from 1948)

A record of deaths in any part of the world in aircraft registered in the
United Kingdom where it appears that the deceased person usually
resided in Scotland.

Service records (from 1881)

These include: (1) The Army returns of deaths of Scottish persons at
military stations abroad during the period 1881–1959; (2) The service
department registers which, since 1 April 1959, have recorded deaths
outside the United Kingdom relating to persons ordinarily resident in
Scotland, and who are serving in, or employed by, HM Forces,
including the families of members of the Forces.

Consular returns of deaths (from 1914)

Certified copies of registrations by British consuls relating to persons
of Scottish descent or birth.

War Registers (from 1899)

There are three registers:
1. South African War (1899–1902), which records the deaths of
   Scottish soldiers.
2. World War I (1914–18), which records the deaths of Scottish
   persons serving as warrant officers, non-commissioned officers or
   men in the Army, or as petty officers or men in the Royal Navy.
3. World War II (1939–45), which consists of incomplete returns of
   the deaths of Scottish members of the armed forces.
   These registers, listed among the Minor Records (Ref. Min.), are
arranged in chronological and alphabetical order.

World War I Army returns

These include the following regiments for the period 1914 to 1919:

Argyll and Sutherland Highlanders; Cameronians; Cameron Highlanders; Gordon Highlanders; Highland Light Infantry; King's Own. Scottish Borderers; Black Watch; Royal Scots; Royal Scots Fusiliers; Seaforth Highlanders; 'various regiments'.

Extracts from Navy returns, including Navy and Marines
In two volumes, surnames A–L and L–Y (1914–1920). *Precognitions:* US Transport/*Tuscania*/Islay (February 1918); US Transport/*Otranto*/ Islay (February 1918).

World War II returns

Extracts from Army returns (1939–48)
Officers; other ranks.

Extracts from Navy returns (1939–48)
In two volumes, surnames A–Mac and Mac–Y.

Extracts from RAF returns (1939–48)
In three volumes, surnames A–G, G–M, M–Z.

Scotland did not have a regular army until the Union of the Parliaments in 1707. Before that date, only a small standing army existed. Forces were raised when necessary, and disbanded once the wars or skirmishes were over. The Scottish Record Office holds some army records, the most useful probably being the muster rolls. These date mainly from about 1680, although there are some earlier ones. (See chapter on 'Other Sources'.)

As time is always an important factor, whether searching in New Register House, where you have to pay a search fee for each day you are there, or working from hired microfilm, you may like to prepare blank mock-up forms of birth, marriage and death certificates from the examples found at the end of this book (Appendix V); it is so much quicker if you only have to fill in details as you find them. Do make sure you *copy all the information* contained on the certificates. I cannot stress this too strongly. People imagine they are saving time by taking notes in brief, and in a 'shorthand' they think they will understand when they get home; but more often than not they misinterpret what they have written, and mistakes creep in.

Official copies (extracts) of birth, marriage and death certificates may be bought from New Register House by post or in person.

CENSUS RETURNS

Census returns are undoubtedly the most useful records for you to search. They are particularly necessary for bridging the gap between statutory (or civil) registers which start in 1855, and the Old Parish Registers (OPRs) which end in 1854 as they give place of birth.

Unless you are quite certain that you know the name of the parish, or at least the name of the county of origin of your family, you will be in deep trouble when it comes to searching through Old Parish Registers, as you will have over 900 from which to choose!

Censuses of the population are taken every ten years. In Scotland such censuses have been taken since 1801, but only statistical reports are preserved for 1801–31. Returns for individual households are available to the public for the years 1841–91 inclusive, but they vary greatly in content. Sets can be viewed on microfilm at New Register House on payment of the appropriate fee.

Increasingly, local libraries and family history societies are acquiring microfilm copies pertaining to their own parts of the country. It is worthwhile to check this if you are visiting your family's old home, if you do not have time to go to Edinburgh, of if you are conducting your own search by letter. However, do remember that unless your family lived in a small village where there were not many inhabitants, searching through a census return may take several hours, as they are *not indexed by inhabitants' names*, and only the larger towns and cities have a street index.

The street index, as it names implies, lists all the streets and roads and some large houses in a town or city; as well as the names of farms and hamlets in rural areas. It gives a reference number to be used to obtain the census you require, and also a reference number to guide you to the correct enumeration book within the census, for the road of your choice.

Although the first available population census return is for 1841, there are a few parishes where returns are extant for 1821 and 1831, or even earlier. However, these are usually lists of people, and, like the 1841 census, they do not show kinship. These pre-1841 returns were taken by church ministers and schoolteachers. Some of these lists are to be found in the Old Parish Registers in New Register House, and some in the Kirk Session Records in the Scottish Record Office. Very few have been published, and they are therefore difficult to locate, but a letter, enclosing a stamped addressed envelope or postal coupons, to the local archivist or librarian, might lead you to your goal. Access would depend on the policy of the County Archivist.

A useful list of parishes with communion rolls and census lists, compiled by Mrs A. Rosemary Bigwood, is to be found in the June 1988 edition of the *Scottish Genealogist*.

Other early 'census' sources are lists which were made for military purposes, such as muster rolls, as well as poll and hearth tax lists. These are to be found among various papers which have been deposited in the Scottish Record Office in Princes Street, and in the National Library of Scotland on George IV Bridge, Edinburgh (see Chapter 3). To enable a search to be made through these records, it would be necessary to have a fair amount of detail about the family concerned, and where they had lived.

On the whole, these pre-1841 census returns are only useful to establish whether or not the family (often naming only the head of the house) was living in a particular parish at a particular time. They were part of a 'last ditch' search for early information.

The 1841-91 census returns were recorded by district or parish, each district or parish having its own registration number. These were subdivided into enumeration books, each book having its own number. At the start of each enumeration book you will find the names of the streets and roads contained within the particular book, and, in a country parish, names of farms and the area covered by the enumeration book.

Beware! No census returns are indexed by occupants' names, so it is essential for you to have noted in full all the addresses you may have found in birth, marriage and death entries during the search in statutory (after 1854) records. Without this information, particularly in a large parish, you may take days, not just hours, reading through names looking for the one you need. If your search is in a large town or city, and you do have an address, always refer to the street index. Remember, however, that people moved around, so spend a little time reading the names in the nearby streets if you have not found your family at the address you noted.

If you took the address from a marriage certificate, bear in mind that this address was probably the home address; when the census was taken, your person may have been away working somewhere, and the address given at the time of marriage may have been that of the parents or some other relative. Looking broadly at the census you may find a brother or sister who had remained near the parents, even if you do not find your immediate ancestor.

It is advisable to obtain a map of the place to see where the street is, and from that you should decide how far to extend your search. Again, use the street index for reference numbers.

Make a note of when each census return was taken and bear this in mind when looking for an entry. If great-grandfather George died on 7 April 1861, you cannot expect to find him in the 1861 census which was taken on 8 April, although, if he died before his wife and the death certificate stated 'married to' and not 'widower of' Mary Brown then you may well find her there, or nearby, living with some other members of the family.

Note whether or not the informant on the death certificate was a relation, and if the informant gave an address, as great-grandmother Mary may well have gone there to live.

Similarly, you cannot expect to find a child listed in the census unless he or she was born before the date on which the census was taken, even if born in a census year, i.e. in 1841, 1851, 1861, 1871, 1881 or 1891.

When reading a census return, look at the headings at the top of each page, which indicate the contents of the vertical columns. Be sure to write down, in full, all the information you find there, particularly people's ages. From 1851 to 1891 be sure to note marital status (if the subject was unmarried, married, widow or widower) and place of birth.

Beware! The enumerator could only record what he thought he had been told. In many instances he was dealing with illiterate people who could not check what was being written on their behalf. Furthermore, he was sometimes unfamiliar with the local accent, and he was apt to have his own peculiarities of spelling. For example:

1841/651/18/9 at Gardensquer, Airdrie, New Monkland, Co. Lanark

James	Couk	40	Col.M.	I
Mrs	"	35		I
Teen	"	16		N
David	"	14	Do.	N
Enouch	"	12		N
Sarouch	"	10		N
Meggey	"	7		N
Heney	"	4		N
Esebelau	"	1		N

Of all these wildly original spellings I think I prefer Esebelau – a wonderful variation on Isabella! This is a good example of an entry in which the Irish brogue defeated the enumerator, whose own spelling was slightly suspect, as you can see from the address, and from the occupation. James Couk/Cook was a coal-miner.

This would be an infuriating entry to find if it involved your own family. The information does not really get you any further in the search, except to tell you the names of the children, the fact that the parents were both born in Ireland, and that none of the children was born in the County of Lanark. Unless you were to find them in the 1851 census, which would tell you their places of birth in Scotland, you would still have a long search on your hands.

The information concerning the subject's place of birth may vary from census to census; it may then be necessary to find more than one census entry before searching the Old Parish Registers for births and marriages prior to 1855. If the subject was born out of Scotland then the precision of the information depends on the accuracy and/or knowledge of the census enumerator. If the subject was born anywhere else in the UK (England, Wales or Ireland), it was seldom that the enumerator recorded, or even knew of, the actual parish. Those born abroad sometimes fared better, and more detail may be found.

Beware! If you are searching in Orkney, you may find several people recorded as having been born in Ireland, because Ireland is the name of a place in the parish of Stennes, in the County of Orkney. You must be careful to read the whole entry. If the place of birth was recorded as Ireland, then it means just that. If the place of birth was recorded as Ireland, Co. Orkney, then it means Ireland in Orkney, and most probably in Stennes parish. This cautionary note applies to all census reading. Do make a note of the *county*, as well as the *parish*.

It is important to realise that a census return included the names, and details of *everybody* residing in the place on the night before the census was taken. It is therefore possible that persons born before 1855 who, for one reason or another, had never been recorded in the Old Parish Register, may well be listed in a census return, and their place of birth recorded.

When working on registers after 1854, you should make full use of the census returns in order to cut down on the time taken to search the index of births, marriages and deaths. If you know that the family lived in a certain place, and you find them there in the 1861 census return, then look for them in the same place in the census returns for 1871, 1881 and 1891. You may find that during these years either the man or his wife had died, leaving a widower, or widow; or that a son or a daughter had married, and grandchildren were living at that address. Using this kind of information you can cut down on the years to be covered when searching for a death or a marriage or a birth in the index to the statutory registers.

When listing a husband and wife and their children, pay attention to the ages of the children, for example:

1871 census (for a fictitious family in Galston, Co. Ayr)

Rich^d	Murray	Head	married	40	Farmer	Born	Kilmarnock, Co. Ayr
Margt.	"	wife	"	39		"	Irvine	"	"
Alex.	"	son	unmar	19	"	"	Galston	"	"

Willm	"	"	"	17	"	Born	Galston,	Co.	Ayr
Charles	"	"		11	Scholar	"	"	"	
Sarah	"	daur.		9	"	"	"	"	

There you will see William, aged 17, (born *circa* 1854), and Charles, aged 11 (born *circa* 1860); so it is likely that there was at least one child born between 1854 and 1860. As all the other children were born in Galston, you may well find the missing child or children born, and registered, there too.

These children may have died in infancy (which you can check from the death registers); they may have been staying with relatives; or they may have been working away from home when the census was taken. If the birth of Alexander (aged 19 in 1871) was not found in the Old Parish Register for Galston where he was said to have been born, then try searching in Irvine, as his mother, Margaret, may have gone home to her mother to have the first baby!

You will note from the census return that Margaret Murray was born in Irvine, so their marriage may have taken place either in Kilmarnock, where her husband was born, or in Galston, where he was farming, or in Irvine, where she came from. Proclamation of banns for the marriage may have been called in both parishes, and you may find Margaret's family in a census return for Irvine.

It is possible to find a married couple recorded in a census return who had had a family, but whose children were never recorded with them. So do not forget about boarding schools, apprentices and servants. Children sometimes did, and still do, leave home from about the age of seven onwards. Children whose parents had died and who were not to be found living with grandparents or other relatives, may sometimes turn up in the census returns for a poorhouse or an orphanage, and occasionally the names of children whose mother had been convicted of some crime may appear in the census return for a prison.

Assuming that your search using records after 1854 has led you to an address or to a parish from which to order a census return, then the following are the steps you should now take.

Census Index Reference Books

There are three. One is for reference numbers concerning the 1841 and 1851 returns, one for the 1861 and 1871 returns, and one for the 1881 and 1891 returns. The 1841 and 1851 book contains an alphabetical index to parishes and districts. Each parish or district is assigned a registration number. For example, Kilmarnock, Co. Ayr, is 597. Having found your parish in the index, note its number, look up this number in the book, and you will find a page like the one illustrated here (Figure 3).

If you decide to order the 1841 census for Kilmarnock, Co. Ayr, you will need Census No. 597, and you will know from the index that there are 41 enumeration books to be read through!

Beware! If you decide to order the 1851 census return you will notice that the registration district reference number is different.

This, of course, applies to all other parishes and districts when dealing with the 1851 census return; but do check that you have been given the correct microfilm. It is confusing; so when you are ordering an 1851 census return you would be well advised to write the name of the parish beside the district or parish number, although this is not general practice for other years.

The 1861 and 1871 index book has been arranged differently. It contains no separate index but shows parishes and districts in alphabetical order. Each parish or district is assigned a registration number, and there is a column which shows how many enumeration books cover each parish. This applies also to the 1881 and 1891 index books.

Looking at the sample page from the 1861 census index (Figure 4) you will notice that the Kilmarnock census return has a street index, indicated by an asterisk (597*). At the foot of the page you will note the instruction to 'see Kilmarnock Street Index, Vol. 9'. This street index is usually to be found on the shelf near the main census index books. Look up Kilmarnock in Vol. 9 – some of these street index books contain indexes for more than one town – and there you will find listed all the streets and roads. If you want to find Dundonald Road, turn to 'D', look for Dundonald Road, and you will find:

Name of street or road	Dundonald Road
No. of Registration district	597
No. of Enumeration district	25

Make a note of this in your own notebook and complete a yellow order slip (Figure 14). Remember to write on the order slip: (1) The year for which you want the census; (2) The registration district number and the enumeration book number; (3) Your name and the number of your desk/seat.

When the microfilm is brought to your desk, check that you have, in fact, been given the microfilm number which you ordered. Mistakes are rare but the repository assistants who bring your order deal with hundreds of requests during the day and they cannot always spare the time to come back to ask what you meant if your writing is not clear. Make sure you have put your seat/desk number on the requisition slip or the assistant will not know where to bring the microfilm. If you are at all uncertain about how to use a microfilm reader, do not hesitate to ask for assistance from whoever is on duty in the room. If you do not use it correctly, and rewind it correctly, then the next user will be confronted with a film which is upside-down and back-to-front!

Once you have found the entry you want, you must take time to write out all the information clearly. Miss nothing out. Leave nothing to memory. Most of all, be sure you have made a note of where you found the entry: write down the full reference numbers and the year.

The entry in your notebook should be headed:

Census 1861/597/25/16 at 2 Dundonald Road, Kilmarnock, Co. Ayr

Now anyone else who may decide to continue the search, or you yourself, if you want to recheck the entry, will know that Dundonald Road in Kilmarnock, Co. Ayr, in the 1861 census return is to be found in Registration District number 597 (which is the number for Kilmarnock), enumeration book number 25, page number 16.

If the name of the place you want for a census return does not feature in the list of places in the index, then probably it is not a parish in its own right, in which case you will have to find a gazetteer. I recommend Groome's *Gazetteer of Scotland*, in six volumes, 1882–5, a copy of which is held in New Register House and in most main libraries in Scotland. From this you should find the information you need to lead you to a parish. For example, '*Camelon*, a village and quoad sacra parish in Falkirk parish, Stirlingshire'. Therefore, if you were hoping to find your family in Camelon, you would have to search through the Falkirk census return.

Beware! Some parishes have 'look-alike' names, such as Kilmarnock, Kilmaronock, and Kilmaronaig, and some have the same name, but are in different counties, such as Ruthven, a village in Aberdeenshire, and Ruthven, a parish in County Angus; also Liberton in Edinburgh, and Libberton in Lanarkshire. County Angus used to be known as County Forfar, or Forfarshire, and County Elgin used to be known as County Moray or Morayshire! When you order the census make quite sure that you have looked up the correct number, or you could spend several hours searching through the wrong census.

Confusion sometimes arises over which is the name of the parish, and which is the name of the county. I always write the name of the parish, then a comma, followed by the name of the county. For example, Irvine, Co. Ayr. You could, of course, form the habit of writing 'shire' (Ayrshire) in stead of 'Co.' (Co. Ayr).

Having reached the stage of searching the census returns, we may now summarise what you can expect to find in the various years.

The 1841 Census Return

Taken on the 7 June, this census return included all the people living in the parish on the previous night. It was the first full census return to be taken, but it does not contain as much information as the later years. Searching in the 1841 census you will find no kinship or marital status recorded; you must therefore be suspicious of any entry which reads, for example:

John Smith (age) 40
Mary Smith (age) 30.

John and Mary Smith may well have been brother and sister, and not husband and wife: unless, of course, there were children recorded with them, in which case it is fairly safe to assume that they *were* husband and wife, and that the children were theirs. I say 'fairly', as it is never absolutely safe to assume anything in genealogy or you may end up being guilty of 'wishful-linking'!

Beware of assuming that the ages are accurate. In 1841 it was the policy after the age of 15 to round down the age to the nearest five years; for age 20–24, you should read 20; for age 25–29, read 25; for age 30–34, read 30, and so on. This was normal practice, but in *some instances* the enumerator recorded the actual age; so you must read 'your' entry, and read the entries either side of it, to see whether you are dealing with an enumerator who was sticking to the rules or not.

Unlike the census returns for 1851, 1861, 1871, 1881 and 1891, the returns for 1841 did not record the place of birth of the subject; instead you will find 'Y' or 'N', which stands for 'Yes' or 'No', and indicates whether or not the subject was born in the county where the census was taken. If the subject was born in England or Ireland then 'E' or 'I' will be found in this column; if abroad, then 'F' for Foreign will appear.

From the 1841 census return for Kilmarnock (Figure 5), you can see how much information is available.

Heading for the 1841 census return for Kilmarnock, Co. Ayr (597)

1. Parish of Kilmarnock
2. Name of Village, Street, Square, Close etc.
3. Uninhabited building
4. Inhabited building
5. Name and surname of each person who abode in the House on the Night of 6th June

6. Age. (This column is subdivided to show Male & Female)
7. Occupation. Of what Profession, Trade, Employment or whether of Independent Means
8. Where born. This column is subdivided:
    (a) If born in Scotland, state whether in County or otherwise
    (b) Whether Foreign, or whether in England or Ireland.

From this sample page it is apparent that although the Christian name and surname were recorded, there was no kinship shown.

A double line (//) separated families or households at the same address. A single line (/) dividing the names denoted, either (1) Another member of the family living with the head of the house, who was not one of his immediate family; or (2) People living in the house who were not related to the head of the house. They may have been apprentices, lodgers, boarders, and occasionally a baby being wet-nursed. From Figure 5 you can see that a Female Servant (F.S.) was living in the household of John Walker, but divided from the names of the rest of the family by a single /.

Occupations were nearly always, in 1841, written in brief – for example, Female Servant was recorded as F.S., and Hand Loom Weaver as H.L.W. If you are in any doubt about an abbreviation, you should turn back to the introduction to the census return where you will find instructions printed for the use of the enumerator. These instructions include a list of abbreviations to be used for different occupations. In Appendix I at the end of the book I have listed some occupations, their abbreviations, and their meanings.

Beware! Widows often reverted to their maiden surnames on the deaths of their husbands, so do not dismiss such an entry as being wrong for your search. Unnamed babies were sometimes recorded as N(ot) K(nown) in the name column, but the sex may be determined by noticing in which column the age was written. There was one column for males and one for females. Some names are confusing, and it is not always possible to tell whether or not the person was male or female, again, look at the age column to establish this. These last points are, of course, applicable to the later census returns as well as to the 1841 census return.

The 1851 Census Return

Taken on 31 March, this was the first census return to show kinship, marital status and the parish or place of birth, if the birth was in Scotland. You may now check that 1841 census entry of John and Mary

Smith to see if they really were brother and sister, or if they were husband and wife.

Information from the heading for the 1851 census return for Kilmarnock, Co. Ayr (597)

Top line:

1. Parish of Kilmarnock
2. Quoad Sacra Parish of [blank]
3. Within the limits of the Parliamentary Burgh of Kilmarnock
4. Within the limits of the Royal Burgh of Town or Village of Kilmarnock.

Second line:

1. Name and Surname of each person who abode in the house on the night of 30th March 1851
2. Relation to Head of Family
3. Condition (i.e. married, single, widow or widower)
4. Age. (This column is subdivided to show Male & Female)
5. Rank, Profession or Occupation
6. Where born
7. Whether Blind, Deaf or Dumb.

Here the information was more detailed than in 1841. Kinship was now given as 'Relation to the Head of Family'. Condition (marital status) was recorded. Place of birth showed parish as well as county. Finally, 'Whether Blind, Deaf or Dumb' was also shown.

The 1861 Census Return

This return was taken on 8 April. It did away with the column relating to being 'Blind, Deaf or Dumb', but now showed the number of children in the household aged between 5 and 15 years, who were attending school, and the number of rooms in the house with one or more windows. If you are interested in parish boundaries, you will notice that the description of the parish was slightly more detailed.

Information from the heading for the 1861 census return for Kilmarnock, Co. Ayr (597)

Top line:

1. Parish of Kilmarnock
2. Quoad Sacra Parish of [blank]
3. Parish of the Parliamentary Burgh of [blank]
4. Royal Burgh of [blank]

5.   Town of Kilmarnock
6.   Village of [blank].

Second line:

1.   No. of Schedule
2.   Road, Street etc. No. or name of house
3.   Houses. (This column is subdivided to show: Inhabited, Uninhabited (U), Building (B))
4.   Name and surname of each person
5.   Relation to Head of Family
6.   Condition (i.e., married, single, widow or widower)
7.   Age (This column is subdivided to show Male & Female)
8.   Rank, Profession or Occupation
9.   Where born
10. No. of children aged 5–15 attending school (each family)
11. No. of rooms with one or more windows.

The 1871 Census Return

Taken on 3 April, this reverted to stating whether the subject was deaf, etc., and added 'Imbecile' or 'Idiot' or 'Lunatic' – a fine distinction! There was a column for the number of children at school – this time between the ages of 6 and 18 years, and it allowed for some children being educated at home.

Information from the heading for the 1871 census return for Kilmarnock, Co. Ayr (597)

Top line:

1.   Civil Parish of Kilmarnock
2.   Quoad Sacra Parish of [blank]
3.   Parliamentary Burgh of [blank]
4.   Royal Burgh of [blank]
5.   Police Burgh of Kilmarnock
6.   Town of Kilmarnock
7.   Village or Hamlet of [blank]

Second line:

1.   No. of Schedule
2.   Road, Street etc. No. or name of house
3.   Houses (This column is subdivided to show Inhabited, Uninhabited (U) Building (B))
4.   Name and surname of each person
5.   Relation to Head of Family
6.   Condition (i.e., married, single, widow or widower)

7. Age (This column is subdivided to show Male & Female)
8. Rank, Profession or Occupation
9. Where born
10. Whether 1. Deaf and Dumb; 2. Blind; 3. Imbecile or Idiot; 4. Lunatic
11. Number of children aged 6–18 attending school or being educated at home.
12. Rooms with one or more windows.

The 1881 Census Return

This was taken on 3 April. There was no longer a column for the number of scholars, although of course 'scholar' was recorded in the occupation column. However, the description of the parish was shown in much more detail. It can be seen that in 1881 Kilmarnock was a Civil Parish, with a quoad sacra Parish of High Church. It was in the School Board District of Kilmarnock; it was a Parliamentary Burgh, but not a Royal Burgh; it was in the Police Burgh of Kilmarnock; and it was in the Town of Kilmarnock!

> *Information from the heading for the 1881 census return for Kilmarnock, Co. Ayr (597)*

Top line:

1. Civil Parish of Kilmarnock
2. Quoad Sacra Parish of High Church (Q.S.)
3. School Board District of Kilmarnock
4. Parliamentary Burgh of Kilmarnock
5. Royal Burgh of [blank]
6. Police Burgh of Kilmarnock
7. Town of Kilmarnock
8. Village or Hamlet of [blank]

Second line:

1. No. of Schedule
2. Road, Street etc. No. or name of House
3. Houses: (This column is subdivided to show Inhabited, Uninhabited (U) or Building (B))
4. Name and surname of each person
5. Relation to Head of Family
6. Condition as to Marriage
7. Age (last birthday). (This column is subdivided to show Male & Female)
8. Rank, Profession or Occupation
9. Where born

10.   Whether, 1. Deaf; 2. Blind; 3. Imbecile or Idiot; 4. Lunatic
11.   Rooms with one or more windows.

The 1891 Census Return

This was the most detailed of all, taken on 5 April. As can be seen from
Figure 6, it showed all the details about the parish; it now had a column
for Gaelic, or Gaelic and English speakers, as well as a column to show
if the subject was an employer or an employee or working on his or her
own account.

When reading a census return, do not be deterred by the fact that the
ages have all been crossed out! This only shows that at one point some
work was done on the census relating to the ages of the inhabitants, and
the figures were ticked as the work progressed.

All the information and the photocopy headings are taken from the
census returns for Kilmarnock, Co. Ayr. and from these examples you
can see there is a great deal to be found out from a census return. Not
only the ages and kinship of your family, but how many of their rooms
had windows, and what kind of town or village they inhabited.

Census Returns for Shipping

As well as the census returns for Scottish Parishes, there are some
pertaining to shipping, as listed below:

1861 Census, Merchant Navy

This census contains a list of persons on board merchant vessels which
were, on the night of Sunday 7 April 1861, in Scottish ports. These
ports are named. It records (1) The name and type of ship (fishing
vessel, ketch etc.) and to which port she belonged; (2) Name and
surname of each person on board; (3) Age, marital status and place of
birth.

1871 Census, Merchant Navy

This census contains similar information. Taken on 2 April 1871 it
records a more detailed list of ports. Scottish merchant ships in English
ports are also recorded.

1881 Census, Merchant Navy

This census contains lists of Scottish shipping in English and European
ports and shipping at sea. Although these were Scottish ships, the crews
were officers and men from all over the world, including Lascar
seamen. All names, occupations, places of birth etc. were recorded.

There was one entry for the passenger ship *Manitoban* which contained a list of passengers who embarked at Glasgow, including a page listing the names of orphan boys aged between 6 and 10 years. There was no indication of the destination of this vessel.

1881 Census, Royal Navy

This census listed drill ships and cutters in Scottish ports, recording the usual information about the crews and vessels.

1891 Census, Merchant Navy

This census contained lists of ships in dock or offshore in ports all round the coast of Scotland, from Shetland to Wigtown. The usual information was recorded about the crews and vessels.

1891 Census, Royal Navy

This census listed drill ships, a cruiser and gunboats in Scottish ports, and recorded the usual information about the crews and vessels.

These shipping census returns are not listed in the index to census returns, and at the moment they do not have a reference number. therefore, if you are searching in New Register House, and you would like to see them, you will have to ask specially for them.

Census returns in Scotland have continued to be taken decennially since 1891 except for the year 1941, when the census was omitted because of World War II. However, since the latest date available to the public for searching is 1891, I have not commented on the later returns.

SEARCHING REGISTERS PRIOR TO 1855

The number of registers and records which exist prior to civil registration of births, marriages and deaths in 1855 is enormous, and it is not the purpose of this book to list them all.

I will, however, cover those which you are most likely to need in your search for information to further your quest for knowledge of your family history, such as Old Parish Registers in New Register House, and Testaments, Deeds, etc., in the Scottish Record Office.

Once you have done as much work as you can, using civil registers after 1854, and after you have found the names of family members in census returns, then you will be ready to turn to Old Parish Registers.

Old Parish Registers

Old Parish Registers (OPRs) were kept by the session clerk or the minister of the church or parish concerned. They tend to vary in content and accuracy because there was no standard form of recording information. While most parishes have records of births/baptisms and proclamations/marriages, unfortunately not many have registers of deaths or burials. Even if the session clerk or minister has kept death or burial records, they seldom give enough information for you to tie them in accurately with a family.

It is not normally possible to examine the original books, owing to the huge number of people who have become interested in looking at them over the years. However, in fairly recent times, the Mormon Church requested permission to microfilm these records for their own religious purposes, and an arrangement was made whereby the Mormons filmed the books and supplied microfilm copies to Register House. If you wish to examine the OPRs you will be provided with a microfilm, for use with a microfilm reader. Usually the entire OPR has been filmed, but occasionally a page has been omitted, or, more often, repeated several times. Watch the dates and page numbers, and if you find a page missing, report it to the searchroom supervisor who may be able to let you see the original book. The same applies if the microfilm is in bad order and too faded to read, but I must stress that the issuing of the original is entirely at the discretion of the supervisor.

If you are not using the records in New Register House for your search, you may be able to obtain the OPR microfilm of your choice from a Mormon library, or, if you intend to search in a parish known to you, then the local record office or library, or a local family history society, may have copies of the microfilm which you may be allowed to search. If you decide to work in a local library or in a Mormon library, then you should write to make prior arrangements. Ask if there is a fee involved, the times when the library is open, and if there are facilities for you to visit and do the search yourself. You should also ask whether you need to book a place or a microfilm reader in advance. In Appendix II you will find a list of Local Record Offices and Family History Societies in Scotland.

If, however, you intend to visit New Register House in Edinburgh to do your searching there, then read on!

The 1553 OPRs for Errol in the County of Perth are the earliest surviving registers. In Appendix III there is a list of OPRs giving the earliest extant date of their entries.

It should be noted that some Presbyterians, such as the Original Seceders of 1733, ceased to be members of the established Church of Scotland and did not always record their births and marriages in the parish register. However, it is worth searching the OPRs as well as the various Free Church records. (See Chapter 2 on 'Searching Records in the Scottish Record Office'.) Over the years many off-shoots have formed from the established Church of Scotland, and I have included a chart showing these (Figure 7). If you are interested in reading more I would recommend D. J. Steel's *Sources for Scottish Genealogy and Family History* (see book list).

In 1783 the Stamp Act (applicable to the whole of Great Britain) was passed, imposing a tax of 3d (three old pence) on every entry of a birth/ baptism, marriage and burial. Although this Act was repealed in 1794 it did have the effect of deterring people from registering births, marriages and deaths for about ten years. Ministers who did not agree with the tax refused to keep records and so could not be fined for not having collected the tax! Understandably, people did not always come forward to register a birth, marriage or death if there was a tax to be paid. In addition to the compulsory statutory or civil registration of births, marriages and deaths since 1855, ministers have continued to keep parish registers in respect of their own congregations.

OPRs are essentially registers of the established Church of Scotland, and only very seldom do they contain entries relating to other denominations, such as Episcopalians, Roman Catholics, Methodists, Quakers, etc. Occasionally such exceptional entries may prove useful. Episcopal, Roman Catholic, Methodist and Quaker registers, as well as the registers of the Free Churches of Scotland, are held in the Scottish Record Office. (See Chapter 2 on 'Searching Records in the Scottish Record Office'.) For Jewish Archives see Chapter 3 on 'Other Sources' and Appendix II for addresses.

Before beginning your search, you must find out what indexes exist. You should remember that approximately one-third of the OPRs in Scotland have been indexed on microfiche by the Mormons. This is not their own International Genealogical Index (IGI), but names and dates taken from the OPRs. It is a most useful index, but I would warn you that the name of the parish is in the index, and not the name of the place within that parish.

If you have access to the OPR index, then you can check under which parish your particular place-name can be found. If not, then you should refer to a gazetteer. See book list in Appendix IV.

For example, in Shetland, births and marriages in Bressay (Ref. 1/1) and Burra and Quarff (1/2) are all given as *Bressay*. Those in Dunrossness (3/1), Sandwick & Cunningsburgh (3/2) and Fair Isle (3/3) are all given as *Dunrossness*. Those in Tingwall (10/1), Whiteness & Weesdale (10/2) are all given as *Tingwall*. (Weesdale's modern spelling is Weisdale.) Those in Walls (12/1), Sandness (12/2), Papa Stour (12/3) and Foula (12/4) are all given as *Walls*. For instance, if you know your ancestor was born prior to 1855 in Burra & Quarff, you will find the microfiche index records the place of birth as Bressay. This principle applies when searching any parishes with joint names.

Since the main objective of the Mormons in recording entries is for use in their own religious observances, it is worth bearing in mind that if there are two dates shown in an OPR of births (before 1855), then the date chosen by the Mormons for their index may be that of the *baptism* and not that of the birth.

To order an OPR you have to work with registration numbers and not the name of the parish, as you discovered when ordering births, marriages, deaths and census returns from 1855 onwards. All parishes prior to 1855 have been assigned a registration number, and while most of these coincide with the numbers with which you have been working up to now, there are some which are different. It is always safer not to assume you know the reference number, but to look it up in the index and make sure. For registration purposes, parishes in Scotland have been numbered alphabetically within the county, working from north to south.

In Appendix III you will find a list of parishes, their registration numbers, and the date of the earliest register extant for that parish. This date can be misleading; although the earliest date may be, for example, 1666, there may be gaps in the registers, and after a couple of entries for that year there may be nothing else for twenty or thirty years. Most parish registers were well kept, with the entries made in chronological order. Nevertheless, some were kept in a most haphazard manner, with dates which are jumbled up and easy to miss. Some microfilm boxes are labelled 'RNE', which stands for 'Register of Neglected Entries'. These are entries, nearly always births, which were not registered at the time they occurred, but when statutory registration was introduced in Scotland in 1855 and were registered in retrospect. It is worth winding on to the end of a reel containing 1820 to 1854 births in order to see if there are any late entries, even if you have found your family in the correct time-span.

Reading Old Handwriting

Parish Registers were written in English, or at least in old Scots in the early years. They are not in Latin, nor as some people think when they see the old-style handwriting, in Gaelic. In Appendix I I have compiled a list of words and contractions which you might find useful during your search.

Despite the exceptions referred to, most OPRs are in good condition and are not difficult to read until you get back to the early 1700s; then it is useful, though not essential, to have had some experience in reading the old Scots handwriting. You will find the long 's' looking like an 'f', but without the little horizontal line; the letter 't' was not always crossed; a capital F was often written as two small 'ff's; 'z' and 'y' were interchangeable. The word 'possesses' looks like 'poffeffes'; the name 'Russell' looks like 'Ruffell'; the use of two small 'ff's for a capital transforms 'Finlay' into 'ffinlay'; and you may find the place and surname Dalziel spelled 'Dayell'. In fact, in some areas of Scotland, Dalziel is pronounced Deyell. Of course, what looks like 'ye' means 'the', as 'y' is an ancient character called a 'thorn' and is the equivalent of 'th'.

Spelling variations must be expected, such as Dumfreis for Dumfries. The prefix 'Old' translates as 'Auld', so Oldhamstocks becomes Auldhamstokkis. Ochtirgavin = Auchtergaven; St Kevokiss, or Sanct-Kevokis = St Quivox; Richardtoun = Riccarton; Lessuaid = Lasswade; Erlistoun = Earlston; Locquhunzeoch = Lochwinnoch.

Reading and understanding numbers may cause you some difficulty, as they tend to be written in roman numerals for the years and items of money. Dates can present some problems at first: when you meet 'jaj' do not despair! This is the sign for a thousand; it is a corruption of 'im' which was originally written as four strokes, the first and last were elongated while the middle one degenerated into 'a'. Four is often written as 'iiii' instead of 'iv', and the last 'i' of a sequence is usually written as 'j'. Hence, viij = 8.

In the seventeenth century and earlier, sums of money are usually expressed in Scots money. The value of Scots in relation to Sterling dwindled over the decades, and by 1600 had become one twelfth, at which figure it remained. Sums were expressed in terms of pounds (£) or in merks which were worth 13s 4d (2/3 of £1 before decimalisation). You will find amounts of money written in wills (testaments) and also in accounts in parish registers. These entries show payments made to parishioners who were listed by name, one of whom may well have been your ancestor. Some of the earlier OPRs contained detailed information on how the parish money was spent as well as entries of births, marriages and deaths. The following examples may help you to read some of these entries:

li or lib (which can look like 'liv') = £ (pound)
s = shilling (20s = £1)
d = penny (12d = 1s which was written 1/-)
ob = halfpenny (not often found)
Summa = Total (or sum)
xix li iiis. iiijd. = £19 3s. 4d.

The way handwriting has changed over the years is a fascinating study, and I would recommend Grant Simpson's book, *Scottish Handwriting 1150–1650* (see book list in Appendix IV).

If you have to search an OPR from 1854 backwards as far as it goes (say, to the early 1700s), then I would advise you always to start with the latest date, 1854, and work backwards; thereby you will get used to seeing the names, which will repeat themselves, and as the handwriting changes you will recognise a name which you might not otherwise have been able to read. I suggest you have the name or names that you want to find written on a piece of paper in front of you so that you can glance at it from time to time, or keep saying the name to yourself over and over again. It is so easy to become mesmerised by a microfilm.

Most OPRs are lists of people's names, and details of the births and/ or baptisms, proclamation of banns/marriages and occasionally deaths and/or burials. Some are mainly minutes of the kirk session and only contain births and/or baptisms, proclamations/marriages, deaths and/ or burials inasmuch as a fee was paid and this was entered in the accounts. In these instances the information is brief and although it takes a long time to read through the OPR to find the information you need, it is often most rewarding as it gives you an insight into the affairs of the parish and its people, not to mention the ways of the session clerk or of the minister.

Births in OPRs (Entries prior to 1855)

In the birth/baptismal registers of a parish you may find: (1) The date on which the entry was made in the register; (2) The date of the birth and/or the baptism, the name of the child and of its parent or parents. Not all registers record more than one date (which may be either birth or baptism), but when you are reading these dates do make sure which of the dates you have noted. Many people, when reading the entry, mistake either the date when the entry was made in the register, or the date of the baptism, for the date of birth.

This point is particularly worth remembering when you are using the Mormon microfiche index, because if the OPR shows both a birth and a baptismal date, then the baptismal date and not the birth date may be the one recorded by the Mormons.

Some OPRs give a wealth of detail, such as those for Dundee, where you will find the names and kinship of the people after whom the child was named. This is most useful when making collateral lines. In other records you may find recorded the occupation of the father, the place of birth (for example, the name of the farm), and witnesses or sponsors who were often uncles and aunts or grandparents.

At the other extreme, in some parish records the name of the mother was not recorded, nor was the name or sex of the child. Instead of 'a lawful son called Nicholas' you may read 'a lawful child called Nicholas' and as you will read in the chapter on 'Names', some names were unisex even in those days!

Once you have discovered in which parish you need to search for your family line, then you must find the index to OPR registration numbers. You will be shown where to find this index on the shelves. There are two such index books, one for parishes from 1 to 490, and one for parishes from 491 to 901. Each book is indexed and contains a list of parish names with the registration number applying to each parish.

Turn now to the index for the parish of your choice; note its number: then turn to that number in the index book, and you will find a page with the left column bearing the reference OPR and a series of parish registration numbers. Allied to each number are the dates for either births, marriages or deaths by that registration number.

More and more parishes are being indexed. Some are indexed in book form, and some in microfiche form. It goes without saying that you must look to see if your parish's entries have been indexed, as that will save you so much time and effort. Naturally, human error creeps in, and sometimes entries were omitted from the index, but not often. I must again remind you to search under 'Mc' and 'Mac' as these may have been listed on separate pages in a book index, and separately on a microfiche index.

When you are ready to order an OPR, I would also once again remind you that you must order by number and not by the name of the parish. Also you must remember to fill in your name as well as the number of your desk/seat, so that the repository assistant will know where to bring the microfilm.

If, for example, you want a birth in 1816 in Inveresk, then write on an order slip 'OPR 689/10'. As you can see from the OPR reference page, volume 10 contains birth entries from 1808–19, and these years contain the births for 1816. As the index is contained in vol. 16, you may want to order OPR 689/16 as well, but that will have to be on a separate order slip; you may not write more than one item on an order slip. A reproduction of a completed order slip for an OPR is shown in Figure 16.

When you fill in the order slip, remember to make a note of the numbers in your own notebook, so that you can check that you have received the microfilm which you ordered.

Volume 10 contains only birth/baptism entries, but for some parishes one volume will contain marriages as well as births, so you must read right across the OPR reference page very carefully. Many microfilms cover more than one parish (the numbers are written on the box which holds the film), so make sure that you have wound the film on to the parish that you want to read. Almost every film has its number at the top of every page, so you should have no difficulty. Having wound the microfilm to reach the appropriate year you must start reading the page for the name you require. This will be easier in some registers than others.

When searching for siblings and using OPRs prior to 1841 (after that date census returns are useful), and having found a birth entry, I suggest you next search for the marriage of the parents. Once this date has been established, you have a time-frame within which to work when searching for their children. Do not neglect to start the search for children in the year of the marriage, as it has been known for a couple to marry in the ninth month of pregnancy and still have another child the following year. Or it may be that the child whose birth you found was the last of a long line of children, and the parents were married up to thirty years previously, so don't give up too soon! Having reached this point in your search, it is sometimes difficult to go back much further with any certainty.

For example, when you have a couple marrying in 1816, then it would be reasonable to suppose that the bridegroom had been born between 1800 and 1776, i.e., aged between 16 and 40 at the time of marriage. If this man lived until 1855 then his death certificate should show the names of his parents, and the search for his birth entry can be undertaken in the knowledge that it could be recognised if it had been registered. If, however, this man had died prior to 1855, then the names of his parents are pure conjecture unless you can find them by some other means, such as a known sibling who did live until 1855.

In some cases a search for a birth will get back to a point where two or more possible candidates present themselves, and the parents' names are unknown. There was one such case where a search led me to two possible birth entries:

(1) 1791 William Sutherland s/o Alex. Sutherland & Katherine Ross
(2) 1794 William Sutherland s/o Robt. Sutherland & Isobel Munro.

The William Sutherland I was searching died in 1850 in Perth, and had been a sergeant in the Army. His Army records gave his place of birth as Alness, County Ross, and his age on enlistment in 1811 was 18. So he was born *circa* 1793. Unfortunately his Army records did not state parentage.

The 1841 census return for Perth showed a William Sutherland aged 46, Army P. (Pensioner); not born in county, and his wife Ann, who was born in Ireland.

I searched Monumental Inscriptions for Perth (tombstones from which genealogical information has been noted), where I found an entry which showed William and his brothers. The ages were not accurate, but this was probably due to the condition of the lettering on the tombstone:

'William Sutherland, late colour serjeant, aged 42, died 1850 w. (wife) Ann Mckeone, aged 43, died 1845. bro (brother) John late of the 42nd aged 43 died 1813 (?1833?) Spain. bro. Hector late serjeant maj. died 1840 Montreal.'

Now knowing that William Sutherland had brothers named John and Hector, I searched the birth records for County Ross, where I found John born 1791 and Hector born 1799 both sons of Robert Sutherland and Isobel Munro.

This not only proved that the 1794 birth entry of William Sutherland was correct for the search, but added colourful and interesting information about his brothers, whose deaths I would never otherwise have found.

So you see, if you dig around, it is sometimes possible to find the birth, and even more information, about a person who died prior to 1855 and whose parentage was unknown to me.

Marriages in OPRs (Entries prior to 1855)

In the marriage registers of a parish the date you find is more likely to have been the date of the Proclamation of Banns or the date when the marriage was contracted, than the date of the actual marriage, though in some registers both dates are recorded. As in birth/baptismal entries, the form varies from parish to parish, but in marriage entries you will nearly always find recorded the name of the *parish* of the *groom* and the name of the *parish* of the *bride*. This is essential to note. If, for example, an entry found in an OPR for Dunfermline read 'James Murray of this parish and Katherine Henderson of the parish of Kinghorn', it would be worthwhile examining the OPR for the parish of Kinghorn for the marriage entry. Kinghorn having been the bride's parish they may well have been married in the church there, and that record may therefore contain information in greater detail, such as the name of her father.

OPRs for larger parishes usually show marriage entries as a straightforward record of the facts. You should find the date of the Proclamation of Banns and/or of the marriage, names of the bride and groom, sometimes the name of the father of the bride, often the occupation of the groom, but seldom the name of his father. However, in smaller parishes it is common to find that the session clerk has merely kept an account of the monies paid in (as already stated for births), and so the marriage entry would consist of only the names of both parties, or in some cases, the name of the groom only, and a note of the fee paid.

When a couple gave intimation of marriage (Proclamation of

Marriage or Banns) they often had to consign a sum of money as a surety for good behaviour before the marriage and a guarantee to marry within forty days of contracting. This sum of money was called a *Pawn, Pand* or *Pledge* and most of it was retrievable on marriage, provided that the bridal couple had behaved themselves to the satisfaction of the elders of the Kirk and the minister, when a smaller amount was paid to the poor of the parish.

Where you find a couple were 'irregularly married' – an irregular marriage is one which is perfectly valid but for which no Banns were called, rendering the marriage clandestine – the couple were often severely reprimanded by the Kirk Session, who tended to fine and forgive!

The whole subject of marriage in Scotland is an interesting one and for further reading I would recommend D. J. Steel's *Sources for Scottish Genealogy and Family History* as well as *Irregular Border Marriages* by 'Claverhouse'. (See book list.) The latter is, I believe, out of print, but well worth reading from a library or searching out from a secondhand bookshop, as I did. Arthur A. Brack has undertaken a great deal of work on irregular and clandestine marriages, and has published an interesting article in the *Genealogists' Magazine* (June 1984) entitled 'The "Gretna Green" for Ireland'. This article relates to irregular marriages at Portpatrick in Wigtownshire.

Deaths in OPRs (Entries prior to 1855)

Here we come across problems, as not many parishes recorded deaths, and of those which did, only a few recorded them in enough detail to enable the entry to be verified as belonging to the search in hand. There are a few death registers which, in recording the deaths of people in the parish, give cause of death, age, and even address, as well as some degree of kinship, but as with some births and marriages, most deaths were only recorded by the session clerk if a fee was involved – for the hire of a mortcloth or pall.

Monumental Inscriptions

Luckily, over the past years people have been collecting information from tombstones all over Scotland, and now it is a race against time before the stones deteriorate. This work is of great assistance to the field of genealogy, through recording the inscriptions on tombstones which otherwise might have been lost, and collating this information with references to early testaments and hearth and poll tax lists. Printed lists of tombstone inscriptions are usually referred to as Monumental Inscriptions (MIs).

I have shown previously how it is possible to pinpoint a birth entry through a tombstone; so do not neglect this valuable source of information. These MIs are held in their entirety by the Scottish Genealogy Society, Edinburgh, and copies of most of them are in the library at New Register House, and in some local libraries. Copies of monumental inscriptions volumes are on sale from the Scottish Genealogy Society, and members may write and ask for an entry to be forwarded in a stamped addressed envelope; if you are not a member then there is a fee involved (see Appendix II for list of addresses).

2

Searching Records in the Scottish Record Office

The Scottish Record Office (SRO), or, to give it its full title, HM General Register House, Princes Street, Edinburgh, is often referred to as 'The Old House', to distinguish it from New Register House which is usually known as 'The New House'.

The building of HM General Register House was started in 1774. It was designed by Robert Adam as the repository for the principal legal registers and the older historical records which were previously kept in the Laigh Parliament House. The main holdings include state papers and administrative records prior to the Union of the Parliaments in 1707, registers of the Court of Session, High Court of Justiciary, Sheriff, Commissary and other courts, registers of Sasines and Deeds, local records, including local authority records, valuation rolls, church records, with gifts and deposits (private archives). Lists, and other guides to the records, are available for consultation in the Historical Search Room.

The Scottish Record Office is on a split site, with a branch repository, the West Register House, in Charlotte Square, Edinburgh. This is a conversion (1968–71) of the former St George's Church designed by Robert Reid and founded in 1811. It is used for modern records and series requiring specialised storage. The main holdings include records of government departments and nationalised industries in Scotland, court processes, maps and plans.

The Historical Search Room in HM General Register House, Princes Street, and the West Search Room in West Register House, Charlotte Square, are open from 9 a.m. to 4.45 p.m. from Mondays to Fridays. As with New Register House, these search rooms are closed for some local and public holidays, so you are advised to write or telephone in advance to check this.

There is no fee for searching the records held in the Historical Search Room in the SRO in Princes Street, or in the West House, for literary and historical purposes (including ancestry research), but you

42

will have to obtain a reader's ticket to enable you to have access to the records. You have to apply personally (not by post), and produce some evidence of identity. Tickets issued in the Historical Search Room are valid in the West House and *vice versa*. Access is difficult for wheelchairs, but facilities can be made available there, as in New Register House, by prior arrangement. It is about a ten to fifteen-minute walk from the SRO to the West House, and there are buses which run along George Street (see end-papers for a street plan of Central Edinburgh).

The information concerning the holdings in both buildings is contained in the SRO's leaflet No. 7. This is an impressive list of documents, but only a few of them are likely to be used by the searcher of family history.

The system in the SRO is similar to that in New Register House, except that you may choose any desk which happens to be free when you enter the search room. Each seat has a number on the back, and this number is the one you write on the order slip. Waiting time is longer than in New Register House as the building is larger, and so it takes longer to fetch some of the records; but you do have the advantage of nearly always working with an original document, and not with a microfilm. In the SRO it is even more important to use a *lead pencil* always, as most of the documents, being originals, are invaluable and irreplaceable. There are strict rules here, too, about no smoking and no eating in the search room.

There are many avenues of search available to you here, and to start with I shall deal with the **Church records** which are grouped under the reference CH. (SRO).

CH1 = Church of Scotland General Assembly Papers

These papers are very varied and deal mostly with internal matters within the Church, ministers writing about moving from one parish to another, and various complaints. For example:

> CH1/2/38/78–102. Case of John Dunlop, Minister of Mousewald, deposed by Synod of Dumfreis in 1715 for not administering Sacrament, clandestine proclamation of his daughter's marriage, travelling on Sunday, neglecting family worship, assaulting parishioners.

> CH1/2/82/289/300. Irregular marriage, John Buchanan, baker in Glasgow, and Mary Robertson, widow of Peter Barlinnie, fencing master there. 29 Sept. 1742.

This information is to be found in the index, so you need only order the volumes containing details pertaining to your search.

CH2 = Church of Scotland Synods, Presbyteries and Kirk Sessions

Of these records, the most useful to the genealogist are the Kirk Session Records. Searching through the OPRs in New Register House, you may have found birth, marriage, and death entries recorded within the Kirk Session Minutes for some parishes, but this is not so in the majority of cases. Most kirk session records are held in the SRO, and are not part of the OPRs.

The Kirk Session is composed of elders of the congregation with the minister as moderator. They are responsible for the general organisation of the affairs of the congregation, and concern themselves with discipline over members. Kirk Session Minutes give an interesting insight into the workings of a parish, and into the lives of its parishioners. There you may find details about illegitimate births, reporting the name of the alleged father. Some kirk session records contain lists of male heads of families who were communicants, which is useful pre-census information.

Sometimes parishioners were issued with certificates when they moved from one district to another. These were known as *Testificates* or *Testimonials*, and were the attestation given by the minister, or by the Kirk Session, of the moral character of a church member, who was about to leave one parish for another. Finding these Testificates for your family can often help you to follow their journeyings from place to place.

As the parish was responsible for looking after its poor people, it obviously did not want to have more of them on the books than necessary! Lists of monies paid out to the poor and needy form a large part of the accounts of any parish.

Presbyterian Churches in England

Some records are held in the SRO and they are noted in the CH2 index. Otherwise, apply to the Church of Scotland Office at 121 George Street, Edinburgh.

CH3 = Free Church Records

These include the records of the United Free, the United Presbyterian, and other smaller churches. As many United Free Churches agreed to union with the established Church of Scotland in 1929, and consequently altered their designations, it is essential that these two repertories (CH2 and CH3) should be consulted in conjunction with each other, since pre-1929 and post-1929 records of a particular church may be split. Where a direct cross-reference is possible, for example, Longforgan Free Church and Invergowrie East Church of Scotland, this is inserted in the appropriate entry in each repertory.

Records of Presbyterian churches which were not within the established Church of Scotland are also housed in the SRO, and will be found under Ref. CH3 and CH13. These records are all indexed by parish and church or chapel, and you will be shown where on the shelves to find the index books, and how to look them up and order the ones you need. CH3 contains mainly session minutes, but sometimes there are lists of members and seat rent books which can be a useful source.

CH9 = Ministers' Widows' Funds Records

These records were transmitted to the SRO by the trustees of the fund in 1968, following an agreement between the trustees and the Keeper of the Records, Scotland. They are made up of two different schemes; firstly, the records of the original Ministers' Widows' Fund of the Church of Scotland with records dating from 1743, and secondly, the records of the Free Churches' Ministers' Widows' Fund dating from 1844. The two funds were united following the union of the Churches in 1929. Some of the material is indexed. For example, CH9/14 contains an alphabetical list of widows from 1752 to 1801.

CH10 = The Religious Society of Friends (Quaker) Records

CH10/1   Relates to the South East Scotland Monthly Meeting 1569–1959;
CH10/2   Relates to the Aberdeen Two-Monthly Meeting (19 Items) 1931–65;
CH10/3   Relates to the Aberdeen Religious Society of Friends 1664–1983.

Not all this material is of genealogical interest, but there are some entries concerning births and marriages. These are indexed by subject and not by name. Quaker records are also to be found in New Register House among the Miscellaneous Records. Births, Marriages and Deaths 1622–1890 (MP5/2 NRH).

CH11 = Methodist Records

These records are arranged in alphabetical order of place, and contain lists of members and seat holders. The dates vary greatly from place to place. The records are closed for sixty years, unless written permission has been given by the Superintendent Minister of the Circuit.

CH12 = The Episcopal Church in Scotland

This series comprises records deposited by congregations, dioceses, and others of the Episcopal Church in Scotland, and records deposited in 1983 by the trustees of the Episcopal Theological College, Edinburgh (Ref. CH12/10–24, 26, 28, 29, 33–35). The arrangement of the papers in the 'Episcopal Chest' by the Rev. J. B. Craven, and others, has been retained (Ref. 12/12). The papers comprising the (Bishop) 'Jolly Kist' have been grouped as CH12/10–11, 26, 28–29, 33–35. Most of these records relate to church matters, and letters from one clergyman to another, but there are some instances where early births, marriages and deaths were recorded. A detailed list of records not deposited in the SRO has recently been produced, and may be found in the surveys of the National Register of Archives for Scotland.

CH13 = Records of the United Free Church of Scotland

These records were deposited in the SRO in 1976, under an agreement similar to that with the Church of Scotland. These records are of congregations which did not join in the Union of 1929 between the Church of Scotland and the United Free Church. They should be consulted in conjunction with the records listed, as CH3 which includes the former United Free Churches which joined in the 1929 Union.

RH21 = The Roman Catholic Church in Scotland (SRO)

This comprises a list of holdings in the SRO with an index to parishes and dioceses. The records consist of baptismal and marriage registers, together with lists of Easter communicants, which have been copied as negatives (white writing on black page), and some of them are difficult to read.

The information given in church records varies from church to church or chapel and so does the time-span covered. Many of the registers are held locally, so it would be worthwhile to visit the local parish and church or chapel should your family not be members of the established Church of Scotland.

Again, I would remind you to write in advance before you make the journey, as it is wise to establish what records are held locally. A letter addressed to 'The Minister or Session Clerk', or to 'Priest-in-Charge', or to 'The Incumbent', followed by the name of the church or chapel, and the parish, should find them if you do not have a name and address. Or you could write either to the local public library or the local Record Office and they would probably help you, although they are not obliged to do so (see Appendix II for list of addresses).

Testaments or Wills

If you are lucky and find a testament left by a member of your family, this may help a great deal and give names not otherwise known to you. In Scotland there are two kinds of testaments: (1) A *Testament Testamentar* which applies when a person dies testate, i.e., leaves a will and names the executor or executors; (2) A *Testament Dative* which applies when a person dies intestate, i.e., does not leave a will and the executor is appointed by the court. The executor so appointed was usually a near relative such as a spouse or a son. In either case (Testament Testamentar or Testament Dative) an inventory was usually made of the deceased's 'goods, gear, debts and sums of money', or, as you may see in the will, which was often written in Scots, 'guidis, geir, debtis and soumes of monie'.

Prior to 1868 testaments were only concerned with *moveable property* and not with land (which descended according to a certain law). It is therefore worthwhile to look for a testament or will of somebody of fairly humble origin. For example, a man may leave the tools of his trade to his son or son-in-law, and a woman may leave a brooch or some other favourite piece of jewellery to a daughter or a granddaughter; and of course, there was always the linen and furniture to be divided up between the remaining members of the family.

When a widow and children survived, the movable estate would be divided into three parts. One-third would go to the widow, one-third to the children (known as the 'bairns' pairts') and the remaining third would be left to whomever the deceased wished. When the husband or wife was deceased, then one half of the property would go to the children and the other half to whomever the testator wished. If there were no children, then the estate would be divided in two.

Until 1823 testaments are kept with the records of the Commissary Courts (reference in the Scottish Records Office 'CC'). These took over the jurisdiction of the Bishops' Courts after the Reformation. The commissariots correspond roughly to the old dioceses – not to the counties.

For more detailed information about testaments I would recommend the books by Gerald Hamilton-Edwards, D. J. Steel, Anthony J. Camp and J. S. W. Gibson (see book list in Appendix IV).

Testaments may be recorded in the Commissary or in the Sheriff Court of the parish where the person died, or in Edinburgh. It is particularly important to search the Edinburgh Commissary Court or Sheriff Court records in cases of persons who may have died abroad or outside Scotland. If you do not find the testament listed in the year of the death, then you should continue to search, as testaments were sometimes recorded several years later when the need to prove something arose. Or they may never have been recorded at all, as happened in the more remote parts of the country when the goods and gear were disposed of within the family without recourse to law.

Until 1800 there are printed indexes to testaments for each commissariot, and from 1801 to 1823 there is a typescript index for all

commissariots, except for those of Edinburgh, Glasgow and St
Andrews, which are covered by separate indexes. After 1823 the
boundaries of the commissariots and sheriffdoms were aligned and
testaments with indexes are kept with the records of the Sheriff Courts
(Ref. SRO 'SC'). I have included here a copy of an index to Sheriff
Court Commissary Records to be found in the SRO (Figure 8).

Index to Inventories of Personal Estates of Defuncts

This covers all commissariots from 1846 to 1867 and shows in which
Sheriff Court the inventory was recorded, the year it was recorded and
the date of the deceased's death. At the beginning of each volume there
is a key to the abbreviations used throughout. You will be able to order
the records you require by using the numbers found in the index books
marked 'CC' and 'SC', and you will be shown how to do this by a
member of the staff. In each case you will need three numbers on your
order slip, e.g., CC1/5/2 or SC5/2/3.

From 1876 all testaments are fully indexed. On the spine of the
books you will see the year and 'Calendar of Confirmations and
Inventories'. Inside, the book is arranged alphabetically by surname
followed by first name. There is an abridged extract of the contents of
the testament, so it is easy to spot the one you want. It is possible to buy
copies of any of the testaments or inventories which you may have
found, and it is advisable to do so, as you can then enjoy reading them
over again once you have arrived home, and you will not have had to
spend time writing down the contents. Inventories hold so much
information other than family names. You can often tell how your family
lived and how much money they had. Even though it seems little by our
standards they were probably more comfortably off than it appears.

In Appendix III you will find a list of parishes showing the
commissariot and date of the earliest testament for each parish.

Just occasionally you will find a splendid entry in the index to one of
the commissariots such as this one in the index to the Commissariot of
Lanark (1595–1800):

'Campbell, John, servant to John Stewart, younger, in Moat, son to the
deceased George C., in Lows, par. of New Cumnock, who was brother-
german to umquhile Euphame C., who was spouse to John Arthur of
Borland Smithy, par. of Lesmahago. 22 June 1733.'

In the Commissariot of Dumfries Index there is this entry which
takes the family back a couple of generations.

'Hay, Margaret, widow of William Carruthers, physician in Dumfries,

thereafter in Quarrellwood, and only lawful daughter to umquhile Mr
John Hay, apothecary, who was son of mr Alexander Hay, his Majesty's
apothecary, and Mary Blackburn, spouses. 11 June 1775.'

Register of Deeds

This is another valuable source for the genealogist. The Scottish
Record Office has produced a leaflet (No. 19) of indexes in the
Historical Research Room to Deeds, Sasines and Testamentary
Records. There is a Register of Deeds kept by the Court of Session,
extant from 1554 until the present time, and it is in three series:

1. The first series is 1554–1657.

2. The second series is 1661–1811. It is in three sections containing
registrations by the three principal clerks whose names were
Dalrymple, Durie and MacKenzie. The abbreviations 'Dal', 'Dur' and
'Mack' are used when ordering records for the years 1661–1811.

3. The third series is from 1812 to the present time and is growing
at a great pace each year.

Various kinds of deeds were registered, but for the purposes of
family history, some of the more useful are marriage contracts. These
marriages may not have been found in Old Parish Registers; sometimes
the record was incomplete, and sometimes pages have been damaged
or lost. You will also find wills, trust dispositions and settlements in
which mention is made of children, and people nominated as their
guardians, who also may have been relatives.

If you are working in the SRO in Edinburgh, you will find the
following references in use for the different series of deeds: Register of
Deeds: General ... RD/ ... (etc.); Sheriff Court ... SC/ ... (etc.); Burgh
... B/ ... (etc.).

D. J. Steel in his book, *Sources of Scottish Genealogy and Family History*
(1980), gives a detailed list of Registers of Deeds.

Register of Sasines

After an heir proves right to the land etc., or when it is transferred to
a grantee rather than to an heir, the act of taking possession, known as
sasine or *seisin* (pronounced 'saysin'), is recorded. A notary recorded the
action in an Instrument of Sasine, and this constituted title to the
property. *Sasine* is a mode of investiture in lands. In giving sasine of
lands, the symbols were *earth and stone of the lands;* of an annual rent out
of lands, *earth and stone, with a penny money;* of fishings, *net and coble;* of
mills, *clap and happer;* of houses within burgh, *hasp and staple;* of
patronage teinds, *a sheaf of corn,* of patronage, *a psalm-book and the keys
of the church;* of jurisdiction, *the book of court.*

Delivery is the test of the transfer of property, whether heritable or moveable. As the actual delivery of heritage is impracticable, the law of Scotland recognised a symbolical delivery which was indispensable in the transference of such property.

However, by the Infeftment Act, 1845 (8 & 9 Vict. c.35), the ceremony of giving sasine on the lands was dispensed with, and a simpler means of infeftment was provided.

A sasine can be of use to the genealogist because it often narrates earlier transactions concerning the land which may have belonged to the family for some time; it may also refer to persons who rent property, and to occasions where property was used to raise money. In all these instances mention of kinship may be found.

From 1781 onwards you have the advantage of being able to use the printed abridgements. These will probably give you all the information you require without consulting the original document, and will certainly give you the reference number to enable you to order the Register of Sasines and to read the whole document for yourself if you so wish. These abridgements are arranged by county and each county is indexed by 'Places' and 'Persons'. So first, look along the shelves until you find the county in which you are interested, then find the index marked 'Places' (that's if you know the place name of your family's residence), and the index marked 'Persons', and see if your family is there. You will find a number written against each 'Place' entry and against each 'Person' entry, and if any of these numbers coincide, then turn to the Sasine Register abridgements which contains the numbers and read the abridgement.

If you do not know the place name, but only that the family came from a certain county, then you will have to search through the 'Persons' index for that county, noting all the numbers against the name you are searching, and look them up in the abridgements.

Note: There is a gap in the index for 'Places' from 1830 to 1872.

Searching sasines prior to the indexed abridgements in 1781 is, naturally, a more difficult task. There exists: (1) The Secretary's Register, 1599 to 1609 (some indexes); (2) The General Register of Sasines, 1617 to 1868 (some indexes); (3) The Particular Register of Sasines, which run parallel with the General Register.

The Secretary's Register (a register begun in 1599 under the superintendence of the Secretary of State) was discontinued in 1609. However, in 1617, by Act of Parliament, a new register was begun consisting of *particular registers* (each for a district, which was not necessarily a county), and *a general register* for sasines of lands in more than one jurisdiction.

There was a new Land Registration Act in 1868, but it did not have any effect on burgh registers of sasines which were eventually abolished under the 1926 Burgh Registers (Scotland) Act. This laid down procedures for discontinuing the registers, which took effect at different dates for each royal burgh; the last register (Dingwall) was not discontinued until 1963.

More details about sasines are given in George J. Bell's *Dictionary and Digest of the Law of Scotland* and Robert Bell's *A Dictionary of the Law of Scotland* (see book list, Appendix II).

Service of Heirs or Retours

When lands were inherited by an heir and not given to a grantee, a brieve was issued from Chancery. This instructed the Sheriff of the county concerned to empanel a jury whose responsibility it was to discover what lands the deceased possessed at the time of his death, and to obtain proof from the heir as to his right to inherit. The jury returned or 'retoured' their verdict to Chancery who then issued the heir with his 'retour' and the heir could then take possession of his inheritance.

As with Sasines, Services of Heirs are worth searching as they give information on the kinship of the heir to the previous holder, together with places and a date of death. It is worth remembering that sometimes heirs were not served heir to the property for several years after the death of the owner, particularly if they emigrated. Do not give up the search too soon!

Services of Heirs up to 1699 have been indexed and published under the title *Inquisitionum ad Capellam Domini Regis Retornatarum Abbreviatio*, known simply as 'Retours'.

From 1700 onwards, there are decennial indexes which give kinship and most of the information in the original document, albeit in a shorthand form. These ten-yearly abridgements continued from 1700 to 1860, after which time they were produced annually. More detail about these records is contained in Gerald Hamilton-Edwards's *In Search of Scottish Ancestry* (1983), and in D. J. Steel's *Sources of Scottish Genealogy and Family History* (1980).

3
Other Sources

Details of the various taxes which have been imposed over the years may be found among the Exchequer Records (Reference E) in the Scottish Record Office.

Hearth Tax Records (Ref. E69 SRO)

In 1690 Parliament granted a tax of 14s on every hearth within the kingdom for one year, the proceeds to be applied towards paying off the sums advanced by the shires and burghs and the arrears of the army. The tax was payable by Candlemas (2 February) 1691 by the inhabitants of all houses having hearths; hospitals and poor persons living on the charity of the parish were exempted. The records, arranged by shires, comprise:

1. Lists of hearths on which tax was collected, with lists of deficients (hearth books).
2. Accounts of hearth money collected, which are in the same form but record the actual sum paid.
3. Reports of the new surveys made in 1692 (Aberdeenshire only).
4. General accounts, depositions of surveyors, and miscellaneous papers.

Poll Tax Records (Ref. E70 SRO)

Poll tax (poll money) was first imposed by Parliament in 1693, for paying debts due to the country, and the arrears of the army from 1 November 1689 to 1 February 1691. It was to be levied at the rate of 6s *per capita* and upwards according to a scale based on rank and means, poor persons living on charity and children being exempt. The Commissioners of Assessment for the shires, and the magistrates of burghs were to make up lists of pollable persons, and payment was to be made at or before Martinmas (11 November) 1694. In 1695, a second poll-tax was granted for providing ships of war and maintaining seamen. Two poll-taxes were granted in 1698 for clearing the arrears due to land and sea officers, and seamen.

These poll books and lists are arranged by shires or counties. The information they contain varies greatly from parish to parish within a county, but the best of them give a record of everybody liable to be taxed over the age of 16, and in some cases, of children under the age of 16. They do not, however, contain the names of the poor as these are shown in separate lists.

Assessed Taxes (Ref. E326 SRO)

By the Act 20 Geo. II, cap. 3 (1747) under which assessed taxes were first levied in Scotland, duplicates of all assessments (otherwise called surveys) were ordered to be transmitted to the Office of the King's Remembrancer. These duplicate schedules furnished the necessary checks and charges upon the Receivers-General of the respective duties, as well as upon the collectors in the several counties and burghs. It was also upon them that all prosecutions on account of the duties were founded. On receiving the schedules the King's Remembrancer was required to examine them to see that the assessments or charges were made in strict conformity with the Acts of Parliament imposing the duties. The extant schedules for the various taxes are arranged in the following sections:

1. Window Tax (duties on houses and windows), 1748–98
2. Commutation Tax (additional duties on houses and windows), 1784–98
3. Inhabited House Tax, 1778–98
4. Shop Tax (duties on retail shops), 1785–89
5. Servants Tax (duties on male servants), 1777–98
6. Female Servants Tax, 1785–92
7. Cart Tax (duties on carts and wagons), 1785–92
8. Wheel Carriage Tax (duties on carriages with two wheels and four wheels), 1785–98
9. Horse Tax (duties on carriage and saddle horses), 1797–98
10. Farm Horse Tax (duties on workhorses and mules), 1797–98
11. Dog Tax, 1797–98
12. Clock and Watch Tax, 1797–98
13. Aid and Contribution Tax, 1798–99
14. Income Tax, 1799–1802

Following the Consolidating Acts (38 Geo. III, cap. 40 and 41), the duties on windows, inhabited houses, male servants, carts, carriages and dogs were incorporated on comprehensive assessed taxes schedules. Income tax, and later, property tax, remained on separate schedules. No property tax schedules have been preserved, and there are comprehensive assessed taxes schedules for 1798–99 only. There are, however, assessed taxes and property tax schedules for Midlothian, 1799–1812 (E327 SRO).

The following records are to be found in the SRO in Princes Street, or in West Register House in Charlotte Square, Edinburgh:

Valuation Rolls (Ref. VR SRO)

These rolls are available for every year since 1855 to the present day, and cover every piece of property in Scotland. They show the name and the value of the property, the name of the owner and the name of the tenant and occupier. It is necessary to know the name of the county or the burgh, and, as some of the earlier rolls are not indexed, a search may take some time.

Customs and Excise (Ref. E. WRH)

The SRO holds a list of excise officers taken from the salary books, 1707–1830. These contain name, name of wife (or widow), names of children, and dates of births, marriages and deaths. This list of excise officers is a modern compilation and is available only on microfilm.

Records of the Board of Customs & Excise (Ref. CE 1–61 SRO)

Desposited in the SRO in 1958, the records contained in this inventory should be ordered by entering on a production slip the class reference and piece number only. The Class references are shown at the top left-hand corner of each page. The piece numbers are shown in the left-hand margin.

The Scottish Board of Customs Minute Books (closed for 75 years) was established following on the Act of Union of 1707. In 1722 a statute (9 Geo. 1.c.21) authorised the creation of a single Board of customs for Great Britain, and in the following year a unified board was established by patent. However, certain of the commissioners named in this unified board were deputed to reside in Edinburgh for the transaction of business. In 1742 an independent Scottish Board of Customs was again appointed in terms of a new patent and was continued until the year 1823 when a unified board for the United Kingdom was established by statute (4 Geo. IV c.23). Certain powers were delegated to a subordinate board in Scotland. This subordinate board ceased to operate with effect from 5 July 1829 and was formally abolished in 1833 (3 & 4 Will. IV. c.511). Until 1 May 1798 the Commissioners of Customs also controlled the collection of salt duties.

Muster Rolls (Ref. E100 SRO)

Before the Union of the Parliaments of Scotland and England in 1707, Scotland had only a very small standing army, and landowners were compelled to provide forces according to their financial means. The best source of information containing names is to be found in the muster rolls for 1641–1707. For more detailed information concerning Scottish army records, I suggest you read Gerald Hamilton-Edwards's book *In Search of Army Ancestry* (see book list in Appendix IV).

Burgh Records (Ref. B. SRO)

The records of the burghs and the royal burghs of Scotland are another useful source for genealogists. These include council minutes, craft records, burgess rolls, apprentice rolls and their own land registers from the seventeenth century. Extracts from the early records have been printed by the Scottish Burgh Record Society, and indexes to some of the records have been printed by the Scottish Record Society.

Copies of printed burgh records and indexes are also held by the Scottish section of the Edinburgh Central Library on George IV Bridge and the Mitchell Library in Glasgow, as well as other large libraries.

Burgess and Guild Records (NRH and SRO)

A burgess was originally an inhabitant of a burgh who held a piece of land there from the Crown, or other superior. In later years, however, a burgess was a merchant or a craftsman who was influential in burgh affairs. The Scottish Record Society has published a number of Burgess and Guild Rolls. As a man could become a burgess, or a guild brother, through marriage, or through his own family, these lists are of great value and interest.

Burgess Tickets from 1584 (Ref. RH/10 SRO)

These records are arranged alphabetically by place, and then chronologically; they contain useful genealogical material, e.g., RH10/501 'John Lamb, (in right of spouse Elspeth Thomesoune, daughter of John T. Merchant). 1 July 1646'.

Apprentice Records (SRO, PRO and Society of Genealogists)

The Scottish Record Society has published lists of apprentices, and some apprentice rolls are to be found in burgh records. Other sources are the Society of Genealogists (London) and the Public Record Office, Kew, where you will find an index of masters' names and apprentices' names. These include Scottish masters and apprentices (see Appendix II for list of addresses).

The Register of the Privy Council (SRO)

The Council was the chief administrative body of Scotland before the Union of 1707, and dealt with every topic. The Register, 1554–1691, is printed and indexed, and is on the open shelves in the Historical Search Room. The volumes are written in old Scots, and require time and study if they are to be understood. But the reward is well worth the effort to gain an interesting insight into the lives of Scots at that period. It is also a source of names and relationships. (See 'The Plantation of Ulster' in Chapter 3.)

County Records (Ref. CO.SRO)

There is a list of all the County Records in the SRO, but many of these are now held only by the local authority. The poor relief records are mainly those of parochial boards and parish councils which are classed as county records. These records contain a great deal of personal information on families applying for relief, some of it extremely lurid! The SRO now only holds parish records for East Lothian, Midlothian and Wigtownshire and these do not include many registers of the poor.

Forfeited Estates (Ref. E. SRO)

The Forfeited Estate Papers are those papers which concerned the estates forfeited by Jacobites involved in the risings of 1715 and 1745. As a class they are part of the Exchequer records, i.e., the records of financial administration, because the estates were in the charge of commissioners of the Exchequer.

Court of Session Records (Ref. CS WRH)

The records of the civil cases which have come before the Court of Session over about four hundred years are massive – both volumes of Acts and Decreets and bundles of Processes – but they are difficult of access owing to the great dearth of indexes. There is a card index to the Processes.

Justiciary Court Records (Ref. JC WRH)

Details of criminal court cases are to be found in these records, and some of them make a fascinating study.

Consistorial Processes and Decreets (SRO)

The various civil jurisdictions exercised by the Ecclesiastical Courts prior to the Reformation, included causes or actions relation to marriage, legitimacy and divorce, as well as executry. The Commissary Court of Edinburgh, instituted in 1563–4, acted as a general court for the whole country for such matters. Local commissary courts retained a more limited jurisdiction. In 1830 almost the whole of the old commissary jurisdiction was transferred to the Court of Session.

Chapter 5 of Professor Gordon Donaldson's *Scottish Church History*, published in 1985 by Scottish Academic Press, deals with Church Courts. The Scottish Record Society published a useful index to the Consistorial Processes and Decreets, 1658–1800, for the Commissariot of Edinburgh (1909). The following extracts are examples of the kind of information you could expect to find there:

> 1663. Process of Divorce – Jean Reid, now residenter in Edinburgh against William Paul, now keeper of the store in the Citydeal of Leith, her husband, married June 1650, within the Old Kirk of New Aberdeen.

> 1677. Process of Divorce – Catherine Sutherland, lawful daughter of Robert Sutherland, residing in Elgin, against Andrew Dunbar, son to Robert Dunbar, sometime in Peterhead, her spouse, married in December 1667 in the parish kirk of St Geull's Elgin.

> 1704. Process of Declarator of Illegitimacy, etc., George Dundas of that ilk, against William Dundas, merchant in Edinburgh pretending to be son to Ralph Dundas, eldest son to Walter Dundas of that ilk, and his wife Elizabeth Sharp, sister to Houston Sharp, and claiming heir-male of the family of Dundas, complainer alleging said Ralph Dundas was impotent.

> 1751. Conjoined Processes of Declaration of Marriage – Thomas Gray, merchant in Edinburgh, against Mrs Jacobina Moir, daughter and only lawful child to the deceased Mr James Moir of Earnlaw, and her tutors and curators, *et e contra* alleged marriage 3 May 1751. Defender assoilzied from declarator of marriage and decree in her favour against said Thomas Gray, 6 May 1752. On 24 July the said Thomas Gray, Christina Duncan, mantua maker in Paterson's Court, Lawnmarket, James Syme, merchant Edinburgh, and Thomas Brown, alias William Jamieson, were convicted by the High Court of Justiciary of the abduction of the said Jacobina Moir, and banished to His Majesty's plantation in America.

As you can see, the index itself gives a great deal of genealogical information.

Home and Health Records (Ref. HH WRH)

A detailed repertory (catalogue) and the HH records are held in West Register House, Charlotte Square. These records contain, among other things, prison and police registers, criminal records and hospital registers, some dating from 1794. A copy of the summary catalogue is held in the SRO in Princes Street.

General Medical Council: Scottish Branch Records (Ref. GMC WRH)

The Scottish branch office of the General Medical Council was established in 1858. It has been responsible for the registration of doctors qualifying at Scottish universities, and at the Royal Colleges of Surgeons and Physicians, and it has maintained up-to-date records of doctors registered in Scotland, whether practising or not. The branch office was closed in January 1982, and its functions were transferred to the London office of the Council. These records, which are open to public access, are held in West Register House, Charlotte Square, Edinburgh.

Maps and Plans (SRO and WRH)

The SRO holds thousands of plans and maps. Some of these relate to the colonies, and show the early divisions of the country.

Universities

Lists of graduates have been printed for the older universities. These are also available in most large libraries, in New Register House and in the Scottish Record Office.

Schools

Most schools' records or lists of pupils, if they have survived the passage of time, are to be found in local archives. However, there are printed books for many of the fee-paying schools which contain names of pupils. They are to be found in most large libraries in Scotland, as well as in New Register House and in the Scottish Record Office.

Fasti Ecclesiae Scoticanae

If you have an ancestor who was a minister in the established Church of Scotland, you will find *Fasti Ecclesiae Scoticanae* an invaluable source of information. This book is usually known simply as 'Fasti'. With additional addenda and corrigenda it gives not only the succession of ministers from the middle of the sixteenth century up until 1975, but records details of each minister's family, parentage and education. 'Fasti' is indexed by the name of the congregation as well as by the name of the minister (see book list in Appendix IV).

For Presbyterian Ministers not in the established Church of Scotland there are the following printed sources which are also found in the book list:

History of the Congregations of the United Presbyterian Church 1733–1900 is a history of the congregations. It contains a certain amount of genealogical information about ministers, but it does not give names of wives and/or parents. It is indexed by the name of the congregation and the name of the minister.

The Fasti of the United Free Church of Scotland 1900–1929 is set out in the same fashion as *Fasti Ecclesiae Scoticanae*, and contains similar information.

Jewish Records

Searching for births, marriages and deaths from 1855, of course, presents no problems. However, searching records earlier than that date may be more difficult. The early Jewish community in Scotland consisted mainly of immigrants from Eastern Europe who only came in any number in the middle 1800s; consequently, census returns are invaluable in helping to discover places of birth.

The PRO at Kew, Surrey, holds naturalisation papers and records for change of name for the whole of Great Britain, and there you may find your family. The information contained in these records should tell you the place of birth of your ancestor, and family details at the time of his or her naturalisation.

The Scottish Jewish Archives Centre in Glasgow (see Appendix II for address) has collected material of use to the genealogist. The two main newspapers are the *Jewish Echo*, which has been the paper of Scottish Jewry since 1928, and the *Jewish Chronicle*, which is the national Jewish newspaper, published in London since 1841. The *Jewish Chronicle* has always covered Scotland and is useful for providing information prior to 1928. These newspapers record events such as births, bar mitzvahs, engagements, marriages and deaths, as well as advertisements and social comment.

Gifts and Deposits (Ref. GD. SRO)

'GDs' are the deposited collections of private papers; they are mostly family muniments, but they also include papers from business firms and lawyers' offices. Where the collection belongs to an important landed family it will contain documents such as land titles, legal writs, marriage contracts and wills, correspondence and estate papers. Estate papers are of particular importance to the genealogist, for, while it may be possible to find the owner of lands in the Register of Sasines, tenants are more difficult to trace.

The two invaluable sources here are *leases and rent rolls* (tacks), whereby the owner granted certain parts of his lands for a specified rent for a certain number of years to the tenant. If you are searching here it is necessary to know in which part of the country your ancestor lived, or, at least, at county level to whom the lands belonged, and where the family papers are. To guide you through the maze of papers, the SRO has produced a list of topics, mainly for GDs, and a summary catalogue, which, in turn, will lead you to the papers concerned. I have only listed those topics which I think will be of some use to a genealogist; when you see the entire list you may find other topics of interest: Africa, South and South-East Asia, Australia, Brewing and Distilling, Business Archives, Canada, Emigration, France, Germany, Highlands and Islands, Jacobites, Mexico, Military Affairs, Naval Mercantile, Netherlands, New Zealand, Orkney and Shetland, Russia, Schools, Skye, South America, Sweden, USA, West Indies. Much of this material consists of letters which will give you background information, but of course you will find names as well. There is an index to the summary catalogue but the list is only the tip of the iceberg, so do allow yourself plenty of time to search.

For collections not held in the SRO you should refer to the surveys of muniments in private hands drawn up by the NRA(S) – the National Register of Archives (Scotland). A copy of these surveys may be seen in the SRO, Edinburgh, and in the manuscript department of the National Library of Scotland, George IV Bridge, Edinburgh, which holds many family papers.

Miscellaneous Manuscript Records

Those records are in the custody of the Registrar General for Scotland (Ref. MR in New Register House). They consist mainly of duplicate or scroll copies of Old Parochial Registers, fragments of other kirk session records and private records of births, etc. kept by individual ministers. Also included are a few registers of secession and other churches placed in the Registrar General's custody for preservation. An index of places covered is given at the end of the inventory. I have listed here a few items which would be of use to a genealogist:

'Blotter Marriages': Affidavits that parties desiring proclamation have no legal impediment to marriage. The prospective bridegroom is usually one of the signatories. ('Blotter': A term applied in counting houses to a waste-book. A rough draft of a letter. – *Oxford English Dictionary*.)

Glasgow 'Blotter' Marriage Registers (MR2/17–25 NRH): These registers cover the years 1815–54.

Barony Parish 'Blotter' Marriage Registers (MR3/1–100 NRH): These registers cover the years 1829–54.

Edinburgh 'Blotter' Notebooks of Births/Baptisms and Affidavits prior to Proclamation of marriage: The entries are transcribed into two separate series of scroll registers of baptisms and marriages.

Edinburgh Scroll Registers of Births/Baptisms (MR4/23-42 NRH): These registers cover the years 1724–1850 and include marriages for the years 1724–26.

Edinburgh 'Blotter' Marriages (MR4/43–69 NRH): This series apparently runs parallel with volumes MR4/1 to MR4/22. These registers cover the years 1780–1854.

St Cuthbert's Parish, Edinburgh (MR5/1–11 NRH): Scroll registers of births/baptisms. These registers cover the years 1743–1855, and include marriages for the years 1744–55 and 1768–72.

St Cuthbert's scroll proclamations of Marriage (MR5/12–18 NRH): These registers cover the years 1818–55.

Canongate Parish, Edinburgh (MR6/1–6 NRH): Kirk Session Treasurer's Accounts 1689–93. Including *Baptisms, Marriages and Mortcloth dues* (MR6/2 NRH): A private register of *Marriages* kept by the Rev. William Dun, minister of New Street Chapel-of-Ease, Canongate, 1814–22 (MR6/4).

Jenat Thomson's Midwife Register of Births (Ref. MT/1–4): Kilmarnock 1777–1829.

W.S. (Writers to the Signet)

Writers to the Signet are solicitors. *The Register of the Society of Writers to the Signet* (1983) has superseded previous lists and provides details of all members from the fifteenth century to the 1980s. This list is arranged alphabetically. It records the member's date of birth, the name of his father, the date of his marriage and name of his wife; also to whom the member was apprenticed. A copy of this register is available in the Historical Search Room in the SRO.

The Faculty of Advocates

In Scotland, an advocate is a barrister, and the Faculty of Advocates is the Scottish Bar. The Lord Advocate is the principal law-officer of the Crown in Scotland. A very useful book was edited by Sir Francis J. Grant which contains names from 1532 to 1943, with genealogical notes (see book list in Appendix IV).

Chartered Accountants

Dr Stephen P. Walker has recently written *The Society of Accountants in Edinburgh 1854–1914*. This book contains information of genealogical interest and the author has donated a copy to the Scottish Geneaology Society's library (see book list in Appendix IV).

Company Records

If you want to find out about business records, then a visit to Companies Registration Office, 100 George Street, Edinburgh, will be necessary. This office is open from 9.45 a.m. till 3.45 p.m. and you will be able to inspect company records in the search rooms. For £2.50 you can buy a microfiche copy of the records you need, and there you can read the records and make copies for 10p per page. Do allow time for this, as I was told by a member of the staff that there can be a wait of 45 minutes to an hour at the public counter.

Companies House holds the records of over 50,000 companies with a registered address in Scotland. The range of documents includes annual returns, accounts, memoranda of association, articles of association, charges registers, liquidators/receivers statements of accounts and appointments of liquidators. You will find that most annual returns contain a list of shareholders. Companies House also holds some dissolved companies' papers. There is a postal service available if you do not have time to visit Edinburgh (see Appendix II for address).

West Register House, Charlotte Square, Edinburgh, also holds some records of dissolved companies, and extensive shipbuilding and engineering records are held by the Strathclyde Regional Archives in Glasgow (see Appendix II for address).

Newspapers

I have never found as much information in newspapers as I had hoped for. If the person was well known in the locality, then most probably there will be an obituary, but if not, then it is unlikely that the death entry will appear in the earlier papers. However, as years went by it became the practice of families to insert death notices listing all the names of those who mourned the loss – often in verse, or worse! It may be worth searching through newspapers if you know the date and place of a death, to see if a member of the family, unknown to you, was mentioned. In local papers you may find articles about families who emigrated or, on occasion, news from such a family.

Joan P. S. Ferguson has compiled a list of newspapers with dates and places of availability (see book list in Appendix IV).

Chelsea Pensioners

You may find in a census return, in the column for occupation, the words Chelsea P. or Chelsea Out P. This stands for Chelsea pensioner or Chelsea out-pensioner. Chelsea Hospital in London was founded by King Charles II in 1682, and up to the present day it gives shelter (in-pensioners) and pensions to certain ex-servicemen. Those pensioners who continue to live at home are known as out-pensioners.

The records for Chelsea pensioners are held in the PRO at Kew, Surrey, and if a member of your family was a pensioner it is well worth a visit to search these records. If you do not know the name of the regiment, then it is a long search, but there are some short-cuts if you know where the pensioner died, and where he was likely to have been paid his pension.

For example, I was searching for a John Williamson, found in the 1851 census for Stromness, County Orkney, aged 70, a widower, 'Chelsea out P.' and born in Antrim, Ireland. He had died prior to statutory registration in 1855.

In the PRO at Kew, I searched WO 22, noted all the Pension Returns Offices in Scotland, and chose the two most likely to have handled the returns for Orkney. These were Aberdeen and Thurso. I knew John Williamson was alive in 1851, and probably deceased by 1855, so I started searching the records in 1851, and found his name in the Thurso Pension Returns for 1851.

WO 22/139. Thurso Pension Returns (including Kirkwall & Lerwick)

Returns of Charges.	Pension ceased by death.
Regt.	9th Veterans
Rate of Pension	-/9d
Date of Admission to Out-Pension	30th Aug 1814
Rank	Drumr. (Drummer)
Name	John Williamson
	Permanent Pension
Date of Decease	20th August 1851
Age at Decease	70

Knowing now that John Williamson had been a drummer in the 9th Veterans, I turned to WO97/1135: 9th Battalion, Veterans 1760–1854, Soldiers' Documents, and found out more about him. Without knowing which regiment he had served with, the search for the Soldiers' Documents would have taken days!

Pension returns included transfers from one place to another, so if a pensioner moved around it should be possible to follow his tracks. The *Payment Offices* listed for Scotland are: Aberdeen, Ayr, Dundee, Edinburgh, Glasgow, Inverness, Paisley, Perth, Stirling and Thurso.

Shipping Lists

Recently there have been several books published giving lists of names of persons who emigrated to America and Canada (see book list in

Appendix IV), though naturally they cannot contain the names of everybody who left Scotland.

One of the great drawbacks to searching in this area is the lack of shipping lists. These lists were usually kept at the port of arrival, so nothing survived in Scotland. There are no lists of emigrants or shipping lists held in the SRO; in fact, a comprehensive record of shipping lists is not extant until the very end of the nineteenth century, when the Board of Trade in London began to keep them.

However, there are other avenues of approach which can be tried. For those who wished to emigrate but did not have the means to purchase a passage, there was the *indenture*, whereby the emigrant bound himself to service in return for a passage. It is difficult to search in this area unless it is known by whom the servant was employed. These papers may be found in GDs but only if you know which ones to search! If you have the time to search diligently through the GDs, you should find enough information in the index to enable you to choose which papers to order. For example:

> *GD 170/3339. Inventory of Campbell of Barcaldine Muniments*
> *(3 vols)*

1737. Indentures between John McLeod, indweller in Edinburgh, and William Campbell, son of deceased Hugh Campbell, tenant in Argyllshire, for 4 years from said William's arrival in Carolina.

The actual document recorded that William had no parents alive and was aged 16.

EMIGRANTS

It is well known that many of the Scottish emigrants to America came by way of Ireland, which is not surprising, considering how close the south-west of Scotland and the east coast of Ireland are. However, in the late fifteenth and early sixteenth centuries, the kind of people who went to Ireland were unlikely to figure prominently in the records. In many cases they were disaffected to the central government, particularly in the Border region of Scotland; others were mercenary soldiers, also unlikely to appear in the records.

Information concerning Scots who emigrated from Ireland is often found in unexpected places, for example, in a petition to the General Assembly of the Church of Scotland (Ref. CH1) where Irish people of Scots descent living in Pennsylvania wrote to the General Assembly, in 1706, requesting a minister (Figure 9).

It is not at all easy to trace the names of people who left Scotland for Ireland; it is perhaps easier to try to trace from Irish records the names of Scots who arrived there. (See Appendix IV for book list and II for addresses.)

The Plantation of Ulster

In the introduction to Volumes VIII (pp. lxxii–xciv) and IX (p. lxxix) of the printed *Register of the Privy Council* there is a wealth of interesting information concerning King James VI's scheme for the Plantation of Ulster.

After the suppression of the O'Dogherty Rebellion in 1608 came King James's scheme in 1609. There were a great many forfeited Ulster lands at the King's disposal, so it was decided that 'there was to be no general dispossession of the native occupants of the Ulster lands; but there was to be introduced among them a sufficient number of Protestant colonists from the main island to temper and overawe the native Irish material and constitute a Protestant core of the Ulster population for the future'.

There follows a summary of the scheme, describing the location and size of the estates to be parcelled out to the first seventy-seven applicants. These are listed alphabetically with their designations, the names of their sureties and the quantities of land for which they had applied. However, too many people applied for too small parcels of land for the scheme to be workable, so proceedings were halted until the autumn of 1610, by which time the original list had been super-seded by careful selection and new competition. This left only a proportion of the seventy-seven who had first applied. A new survey of the forfeited lands was found to be necessary, and in 1610 the Scottish part of the business of the Ulster Plantation was withdrawn from the Scottish Privy Council altogether, and taken into the hands of King James himself and his English Council in London. Thereafter the allotments of Scottish shares as well as English shares and shares reserved for the native Irish, were made under the Great Seal of England.

While the 1609 probationary list consisted of 77 persons, the 1611 list consisted of only 59, in which only 18 of the original list appear. These lists, to be found in Volume IX, pp. lxxx and lxxxi, are arranged with names and designations and show to which county in Ireland each person went.

The Plantation of Ulster Papers (SRO Ref. RH 15/91/33)

These are papers relating to the Plantation of Ulster (1611 to 1617) and are listed as miscellaneous papers, but contain the names of only six people.

If you are trying to find an early ancestor who may have been part of the Plantation of Ulster, you have a great deal of research to undertake! It is important to remember that not all applicants of the first list (1609) were accepted, and that for later information (after 1610) you may have to search in England. But before you do, I suggest you read the Introduction to Volumes VIII and IX of the *Register of the Privy Council* in the SRO in Edinburgh.

The Highland Emigration Society and the Board of Relief of Highland Destitution

These are important files in connection with emigration, and are held in West Register House, Charlotte Square, Edinburgh.

Lists of Emigrants to Australia from the Highlands of Scotland

These records of persons who were assisted by the Highland and Island Emigration Society from 1852–7, are held in the SRO in Princes Street, as well as in West Register House in Charlotte Square. They give names of people, and the ships on which they sailed (Ref. HD21/53). Although this HD record is held in the SRO, all the other records with this reference, as well as HH and BT references, are held in West Register House, Charlotte Square.

The Board of Relief of Highland Destitution dealt with emigration to *America, Upper Canada and Australia* (Ref. HD WRH). Similar types of records are those of the *Board of Trade*, wherein limited companies formed to carry out mining and other activities in the colonies, are recorded (Ref. BT WRH).

American Loyalists (Ref. T50, T79, held in London)

In the PRO Treasury Papers there are documents (1780–1835) relating to American Loyalists who were eligible for pensions, and minute books of the American Loyalists' Claim Commission (1777–1812), including an index of claimants.

Among the Treasury Papers in London are four volumes (T 47/9–12) which give details of emigrants going from England, Wales and Scotland (Figure 10). Details of these sources are to be found in *Searching Your Ancestors in the PRO* (see book list Appendix IV).

Finally, one last place to try is the *Bureau of Emigration* at Merseyside Maritime Museum, Liverpool, England. So many Scots sailed from Liverpool.

4
Names

SURNAMES

If you are interested in the origin of your surname, and if it is Scottish, I suggest you consult *The Surnames of Scotland* by Dr George F. Black (see book list in Appendix IV). This is one of the 'bibles' for the genealogist; it is a most interesting, informative book, and is to be found in most large libraries. There, not only will you find the origin of the surname, but mention of some of the famous people who have borne the name. For example, the entry for *Pinkerton* starts by explaining that it originates from the name of the old barony near Dunbar, East Lothian; it refers to several people of that name who lived in the period between 1296 and 1826, and it concludes by mentioning Allan Pinkerton (1819–84), the famous American detective, who was born in Glasgow. The entry also gives the various spellings of the name Pinkerton.

There are several names which change their form, and one on which it is worth commenting is the name Dalziel. It may be found as Dayell, Deyell or even as Yell. The letters 'Z' and 'Y' are used interchangeably in some cases. (See Appendix IV for book list for Grant Simpson's book on Scottish handwriting.)

Names which are derived from occupations may be found in different versions. The name *Dyer* may be found as *Litster* and *Baker* as *Baxter*; particularly in the earlier Old Parish Registers – so, if your name is an occupational one, bear such variation in mind and do not pass them by as not being your name!

If you are searching for a name which has 'Mc' or 'Mac' at the beginning, note that these are indexed separately in the index for births, marriages and deaths after 1854; you may find the same family indexed under either spelling, so do not say that you *know* that your family was always 'Mac' and not 'Mc' or *vice versa*. You may know now, but the registrar or your ancestor may not have been so positive.

Names like McLaughlin take a long time to search, as all the variations must be examined in the index if the name is not immediately found. For example, McLauchlin, McLauchline, McLaughlin, McLaughline, McLachlan, McLachlane, McLaghlan, McLaghlane, and of course, all those variations under 'Mac' as well as 'Mc'. And I am sure that somebody reading this paragraph has heard of yet another spelling of the name!

You most probably know that 'Mac' or 'Mc' means 'son of', but you may not have come across 'Nic', which is a shortened form of 'nighean mhic', and means 'daughter of Mac'. This is not in common usage but you may meet it in Old Parish Registers in Gaelic-speaking parts of Scotland. Black's *Surnames of Scotland* gives a great deal of interesting information under 'Mac' and 'Nic'.

Irish names sometimes start with 'O', which is the Irish equivalent of 'Mac' or 'Mc', and I had one search where the family had come from Ireland to Scotland with the name *O'Fie*. This they changed to *Mac'O'Fie* which eventually became *MacFie*. And while you search Mac/McFie, do not forget all the variations of *Mac/McPhie*!

Another Irish name which changes its spelling and form is Murphy: I have found this written as *Murchie* or *Murckie* in some records.

Old handwritten registers – both the index and the actual registers – may be difficult to read, which in turn may lead to names being missed when searching the index. Here are a few names which I found only after re-searching, and which may help you to overcome the problem: Boyd/Boyce/Bryce; Stratton/Stratten/Straiton/Strachan; Stewart/Stuart; Thompson/Thomson; Robertson/Robinson/Robson, etc.; Chalmers/Chambers; Jameson/Jamieson; and Rae, which having searched under 'Rae' and 'Rea' I finally found under the spelling 'Raw'. But once I saw the death certificate, and the handwriting of the registrar, I had every sympathy with the indexer! Remember that 'Qu' = 'W', so in some Old Parish Registers you will find names such as *White* written as 'Quhytt'.

CHRISTIAN NAMES AND FORENAMES

When it comes to Christian or forenames, people in most, if not all countries tend to use names which are, or have been in the family. Scotland not only does this but has a naming pattern which is still used, although not to the same extent nowadays, since filmstars and TV programmes have left their mark. The following naming pattern is useful to know, but it is not always used: the eldest son named after the paternal grandfather; the second son named after the maternal grandfather; the third son named after the father; the eldest daughter named after the maternal grandmother; the second daughter named after the paternal grandmother; the third daughter named after the mother. There are variations on this pattern, and the late Gerald Hamilton-Edwards gives details of these in his book *In Search of Scottish Ancestry* (see book list Appendix IV).

There is a well-known story of a family where all the sons were named John through following the naming pattern, because the two grandfathers as well as the father were named John – and the mother had a brother named John too. The youngest son was always known as Baby in spite of having grown into a large and tough fisherman!

In the course of one search, I found a family where twin boys were both named William. It must have saved a lot of bother when mother wanted to call them in for tea, but it certainly made it impossible for me to be sure which man married which wife. Only local knowledge could sort out that kind of problem.

Sometimes you will find a second, or even a third child called by the same name. This was not always a case of using the grandparents' and other family names, but indicated that the previous children of the name had died.

If you find a name which does not fit in with the family list of names, there is always a chance that the child was named after the minister, particularly if the child was the first one to have been baptized by the new minister. This habit applied to girls as well as to boys. For example:

OPR Dumfries Co. Dumfries (821/3) Births and Baptisms

1806 Scot, lawful daughter to Alexander Grier, Shoemaker, born Aug 1. bapt. Aug 2.

N.B. The parents at first intended the child's name to have been Jenny but afterwards agreed to the present name because she was the first baptized by the Revd. Alexander Scot D.D. after his translation from the New to the Old or St. Michael's Church, Dumfries, and this appropriation of a name is an honour generally shown ministers.

This is all very well, but, if, when the minister was not listening, they continued to call the baby Jenny, and she grew up and married, calling herself Jenny, then her marriage and death entries will be difficult to find if anybody is researching her family line today! Such a custom of naming children still goes on.

In the north of Scotland some names which are generally thought of as male are used for girls, so if you are searching through the female index for a girl whose name is Nicholas or Bruce or John, and you do not find it there, it is always worthwhile checking the male index.

Girls' names are often made by adding 'ina' to the boys' names, e.g.,

Jamesina, Andrewina, Hughina, and are sometimes indexed under Ina (pronounced 'Eye-na').

As with male names being used for girls, there are some names which are generally thought of as feminine, but are used for boys, such as Ann and Primrose (the latter being a surname used as a Christian name). If you do not find the name in the male index, it may have been included wrongly in the female index. This also applies in cases where the subject bears a surname as a Christian name, and where consequently the sex is not obvious.

There are some Christian names which are generally considered to have a separate identity, but were, and are, used with a fine impartiality even by their owners, such as Peter for Patrick, and Donald for Daniel. While these are distinctly different to some of us, even today I know a Patrick who answers to Peter when he returns to the north of Scotland!

The Gaelic influence is still to be found. Ian/Iain is the same as John; Hamish is the same as James; and Callum is the same as Malcolm. Among girls' names, Ishbel is, of course, Isobel, but a more unusual alternative is Morag for Sarah. Ninian can be Ringan, and this is to be found in the place-name – St Ninians or St Ringans.

Diminutives, Contractions and Variations

Diminutives can cause problems. When you are searching for an Elizabeth do not forget that she may have been indexed as Eliza, Liz, Betty, Beth or Bess. A few names for which diminutives are commonplace are: Bella or Isa for Isabella/Isobel; Euphan for Euphemia; Ina for any girl's name that has been made from a boy's name (see above); Maggy/Maggie/Meg/Peggy for Margaret; Polly for Mary; Jack/Jock for John; Jamie/Jim for James; Ned/Ted for Edward; Olla for Oliver; Rob/Rab/Rabbie/Bob for Robert; Sandy/Ecky for Alexander; Tom/Tam for Thomas. The boys' names are more obvious than the girls.

As contractions are often used in an index and in the OPRs I have listed a few which you may miss, although they look obvious: Barb. = Barbara; Eliz. = Elizabeth; Isa. = Isabella; Margt. = Margaret; Alex/Axr. = Alexander; Chas. = Charles; Jas. = James; Jo(e) = Joseph (but Jo. or Jno could be John); Patk. = Patrick; Robt./Rob. = Robert (Robtson or Rtson = the surname Robertson); Rodk. = Roderick; Thos. = Thomas; Will/Wm. = William.

Several Christian names are interchangeable in Scottish registers. *Jean, Jane, Jessie* or *Janet* tend to be interchangeable and I have on rare occasions found *Janet* written as *Chunnet* or *Channet*, which, if you say it aloud to yourself, makes an odd kind of sense, particularly when you realise that in Caithness the letter J is sometimes pronounced 'Ch' as in 'chair'. Professor Donaldson tells me that this habit is also to be found in Orkney and Shetland.

Elizabeth may be spelt with an 's' as *Elisabeth*, and the name can be interchangeable with Elspet/Elspeth, although these are usually names in their own right. Elizabeth is sometimes interchangeable with Issobel/ Isabella, but not often.

Catherine may be written as *Catharine*, and both names are to be found starting with the letter K, and not C, so all spellings should be thought of when searching the index. Kathleen and Katheryn are not usual variations, but should be borne in mind.

In more modern records, and usually in Glasgow, you may find the girl's name *Senga* – if you do, then do not be surprised to find that the grandmother was *Agnes*, as Senga is Agnes written backwards! *Christina* is often *Christian*, and in some Mormon microfiche indexes it appears under 'X', as in rare cases the session clerk has written '*Xtian*' in the Old Parish Register – like writing Xmas for Christmas! *Christian* is rarely used as a boy's name in Scotland. Finally, *Grace* and *Grizel* are the same name.

Patronymics

A patronymic is a surname formed by using the father's Christian name, and this you will find mainly when searching Shetland records. For example, a *John* Donaldson's son would have *Johnson* as his surname, and if his Christian name were *Peter*, then in turn his son would have *Peterson* as his surname.

Beware! Donald and Daniel are interchangeable, so John *Donaldson* may have been the son of a *Daniel*!

Daughters' surnames tended to end with 'dr', not 'son', and were frequently contracted. For instance, you may find Ann Williams- daughter written as Ann Wmsdr or WmDr.

Working on Shetland records I once came across a family similar to the following example:

Robert Laurenceson	Widower		aged	58
Mary Laurencedr	daur	unmar	"	30
Ann "	"	"	"	28
Laurence Laurenceson	son	"	"	25

In due course the son, Laurence Laurenceson, married, and left home, after which time he was known as Laurence Robertson. His children bore the surname of Robertson until they, in turn, left home, after which time they were known as Laurenceson. His unmarried sisters kept the surname of Laurencedr, and sometimes Laurenceson, until their father died, after which time they were known as Mary and Ann Robertson. I did not find them recorded as Robertsdr.

To-Names

In the close-knit fishing communities of the north-east coast of Scotland there are not many different surnames, consequently the name of the fishing boat is tacked on to the surname and becomes an accepted part of the family's name. This is known as a to-name or a t-name. Even in the index to births, marriages and deaths well after 1855, this practice is to be found. For example, 'Bain, David, Mackenzie' is also indexed as 'Mackenzie, Bain, David'. The name of the boat will be printed in italics in the index. This usage of boats' names was to distinguish which David Bain was meant, although details on the certificates should leave the reader in no doubt. Female members of the family are also indexed under both the name of the family and the name of the boat. Once I had to write to tell a man that his name was not MacKenzie, but Smith, and that MacKenzie had been the name of his great-grandfather's fishing boat!

One last word of warning . . . some names starting with 'Mac' are not as Scottish as they may seem. Recently I was talking to an American who told me that her son had married a Vietnamese girl: understandably the couple decided to name the baby after both sets of grandparents. The two grandfathers' names were Karl and Vinh, which with a little imagination made up 'Calvin'. The two grandmothers' maiden surnames were Rea and a name which phonetically sounded like 'Mac', so they named the baby Calvin MacRea. Fortunately the grandmother is a genealogist, so I expect that not only the names, but the interesting reason for their existence will be handed down in the family history. Otherwise future genealogists might spend fruitless hours searching Scottish records in vain!

5
Heraldry

Heraldry, although allied to genealogy, is a subject in its own right, and too important to be summarily dismissed by a short paragraph. It is a fascinating study, and one which, once you have started, I am sure you will wish to continue. Just look around and you will find coats of arms on public buildings and in many other places.

In Scotland the Lord Lyon King of Arms is the final arbiter of all things heraldic, and the Court of the Lord Lyon is in New Register House, Princes Street, Edinburgh. The Court of the Lord Lyon issues a leaflet giving general information concerning armorial bearings etc., and the Lord Lyon has kindly allowed me to quote parts of it here:

> The Chief's coat of arms fulfils within the clan or family the same purpose as the Royal Arms do in a Kingdom. There is no such thing as a 'family crest' or 'family coat of arms' which anyone can assume, or a whole family can use.
>
> Armorial bearings, being for distinguishing persons of, and within, a family, cannot descend to, or be used by, persons who are not members of the family.
>
> It is not only *illegal*, but a *social crime* and error of the most grave character, to assume and purport to use your Chief's arms without due and congruent difference. Anyone who does so merely publishes their own ignorance and lapse into bad manners, and the use of such on seal or notepaper will close the doors of all the best families against the presumptious upstart.
>
> There is so such thing as a 'Clan coat of arms'. The arms are those of the Chief, and clansmen have only the privilege of wearing the strap-and-buckle crested badge to show that they are such a Chief's clansmen.
>
> You cannot have a crest without first having a shield or arms, because a crest was a later addition. Misuse of crests arises from misunderstanding of the badge rule under which junior

members of the family may *wear* in specified manner their Chief's crest as a *badge.*

The Crest of the Chief is *worn* by all members of the Clan and of approved Septs and followers of the Clan, within a strap and buckle surround bearing the Chief's motto. This is for *personal wear only,* to indicate that the wearer is a member of the Clan whose Chief's crest-badge is being worn. The badge or crest is *not* depicted on personal or business stationery, signet rings or plate, because such use would legally import that the tea-pot etc. was the Chief's property!

Those who wish to use arms in any personal sense must petition for a 'Grant of Arms' or – if they can trace their ancestry back to a direct or, in some cases, a collateral ancestor – a 'cadet-matriculation', showing their place within the family. Forms of Petition and sample proof-sheets relative to such applications can be supplied if required.

When a grant, or a matriculation of arms is successfully obtained, an illuminated parchment, narrating the pedigree as proved, is supplied to the Petitioner, and a duplicate is recorded in the *Public Register of All Arms and Bearings in Scotland.*

Application for such a Confirmation, by Letters Patent or Matriculation, from the Lord Lyon King of Arms is *the only way to obtain a genuine coat of arms,* and use of bogus heraldry only leads sooner or later to social humiliation.

British Commonwealth. Anyone domiciled in Her Majesty's overseas realms or in the Commonwealth (except those of English, Welsh or Irish ancestry, who should approach the Garter King of Arms in London or The Chief Herald of Ireland in Dublin) can apply to the Lord Lyon King of Arms, of Scotland, HM New Register House, Edinburgh EH1 3YT, for a grant or matriculation of arms.

Canada. In June 1988 a separate Heraldic Administration was set up in Canada under the control of The Chief Herald of Canada, Mr Robert D. Watt, at Rideau Hall, Ottowa, K1A OA1, Canada.

Foreign Countries. Arms are not granted to non-British citizens (though those of Scottish ancestry can apply to the Lord Lyon King of Arms for cadet-matriculation). Moreover, even if not of direct armigerous descent, foreigners of Scottish descent can often arrange for a cousin in Scotland, or in one of Her Majesty's overseas realms, to get arms established by the Lord Lyon King of

Arms, and thereafter themselves to obtain a cadet-matriculation. Each party is in such cases supplied with an illuminated parchment.

The Heraldry Society of Scotland exists for people with an interest in heraldry. You do not have to be knowledgeable to be a member – just interested! *The Double Tressure*, a journal with coloured illustrations, is issued annually (see Appendix II for the address).

6
Clans and Tartans

So much has been written about clans and tartans that I do not intend to go into detail here. I have listed some books for your pleasure and interest, where you will find names, and their clans and tartans (see Appendix IV).

Wearing of Tartan (according to the Court of the Lord Lyon)

A lady of Scottish family, married to someone not entitled to a clan, family or district tartan, shall continue to wear her own tartan in skirt, etc., but wears her sash over the right shoulder and tied in a bow over the left hip.

Unless her child or children, or one of the children, takes the mother's name, these children have no right to wear their mother's tartan at all. They are not members of their mother's clan.

Those not entitled to wear a clan, family or district tartan have no right to wear any royal tartan, and particularly not the so-called 'Royal Stuart Tartan', which is the tartan of the Royal House, and accorded to the pipers of the Sovereign's royal regiments.

Those of Scottish descent with no clan, family or district tartan wear one of the following:

1. The now so-called 'Hunting Stewart', which was originally a general Scottish hunting tartan, and only named 'Stewart' about 1888.

2. Caledonia tartan.

3. Jacobite tartan – for those with ancestors of Jacobite proclivities.

4. Black Watch or 'Government' tartan in its exact regimental form, or one of the modified forms for those of Hanoverian or whig ancestral proclivities.

There are a number of district tartans which are worn, or wearable, by persons belonging to, or descended from ancestors belonging to, these districts. The districts, however, only cover certain small areas of Scotland.

The wearing of the kilt was proscribed in Scotland from 1747 to 1783 as part of the Government campaign to break up the unity of the Highlanders, and to merge them with the Lowlanders. It was thought by some that the Highland costume enabled the wearers to endure exposure in the field, and so make them more difficult to conquer, but I doubt if that was the reason for the Government's actions!

If you are interested in finding out more about your family tartan, I suggest you write to the Scottish Tartans Museum, and/or join the Scottish Tartans Society (see Appendix II for the address). The research department of the Society answers questions on the origin of Scottish names, their connection with clans and families and their associated tartans. There is a charge for an enquiry.

7

Searching for
Present-day Relations

A great many people whose grandparents or great-grandparents left Scotland decide to try to find a present-day relation with whom they might make contact. The ease of searching depends on when your ancestor left Scotland, and if any member of the family remained behind. Assume your ancestor – let us call him Paul Barnard – left Scotland about 1865, when he was aged three, with a sister Kate (age unknown) and with his parents, whose names were James and Elizabeth Barnard. You do not know the maiden surname of Elizabeth Barnard and you do not know the names of the parents of James Barnard.

1. You would look for the birth of Paul Barnard in 1862. This would tell you the maiden surname of his mother, and the date and place of his parents' marriage.

2. You would look for the marriage of his parents, and this would tell you the names of Paul Barnard's grandparents, and possibly an address which you would use for a census search.

3. You would search the census return for 1861 or 1851 using the addresses in the birth certificate and in the marriage certificate.

4. If you have found the family, you should know the names of some brothers and sisters of Paul's parents, and the ages of his grandparents, if they were still alive.

5. If you have not found the family in the census return, then re-examine the marriage certificate, and (a) If Paul Barnard's grandparents were still alive, then search for their death entries. (Remember to search for the death of the woman first, as her married and maiden surnames should be cross-indexed.) Or (b) See if one of the witnesses at the marriage was a brother or a sister whose line could be followed.

6. From the death entries note the names of the informants.

7. If they were sons or daughters or grandchildren, then use this information to further the search.

8. Search for the deaths, and/or marriages of the informants.

9. Search for their children.

10. Use this information, i.e., the children's names, to search for a later generaton through marriages and deaths, and carry on working like this until you come to the present day, when you can look up the telephone directory or search the voters' rolls.

In some cases the names of parents are not known, but it is known where the family had lived, and it is known that the persons who left Scotland – say again Paul Barnard and his sister Kate – used to write to their cousins Alexander, William and Charles Murray. From this information it should be possible to search without knowing the names of the parents.

You would first search the index of births for the two Barnard children, Paul and Kate (this means searching all the entries for Kate, Catherine, Katherine etc.); and when you find a Barnard family with those two children, you will know the names of their parents. You would next search the index of births for the three Murray children, Alexander, William and Charles, and when you have found a Murray family with those three children, you will know the names of their parents. Now, you know they were cousins, so the kinship should be obvious from the surnames of the fathers and mothers. Once you have made this link with Scotland, you can go ahead, as suggested above, until you come down to the present day.

Once you have reached 1929, searching for a birth entry is easier. From that date, as the mother's maiden surname is shown in the index, the required entries are easily noted. Once you have reached 1929, searching for a marriage is easier. From that date the spouse's surname is shown in the index. Once you have reached 1973, searching for a death is easier. From that date the maiden surname of the mother is shown in the index.

Searching for a present-day relative without using the records held in New Register House, Edinburgh, is also possible. However, unless you have specific details it may be difficult.

1. You could visit the place where you know your ancestor originated and try to find people of the same surname still living there. As you can imagine, this approach is not very feasible if you plan to visit one of the larger cities like Edinburgh or Glasgow, and the time gap is long.

2. You could search for a will if you know when your ancestor died in Scotland. This may lead to hitherto unknown names and addresses.

3. You could search through newspapers for the district where your

ancestor died. Although it is not common to find obituaries unless the person is well known, you may find a death intimation, and this may mention members of the family.

4. Unless the surname is extremely unusual, I do not recommend trying to find somebody through calling all the names in a telephone directory!

5. In certain circumstances an address may be obtained from: Department of Social Security, Records Branch, Special Section 'A', Records 'B', Newcastle upon Tyne, NE98 1YU, England. The Department of Social Security deals with people who are drawing retirement pensions and/or any similar benefits. Naturally, addresses are not freely given; you would have to prove your kinship, and any information you received would be at the discretion of the department.

However, all this is applicable only if your ancestor left Scotland after the introduction of statutory (civil) registration in 1855. If he or she left earlier than that, particularly in the eighteenth century, then, unless you have specific information about a member of the family who remained in Scotland, it is almost impossible to bring the search down to the present day.

Perhaps in future things will be easier. I have a young friend, Ruaridh, who was born in Scotland, and his date and place of birth are reflected in his National Insurance number. The first three digits are the district number, the second two digits are the year (77) and the last three digits are the entry number in the birth book. After a certain date, provided you know somebody's National Insurance number, it should be possible to find their name and parentage!

Can you remember when . . .?

Asking questions about earlier generations in your family may not be as simple as it sounds. You may have a list of useful things you want to know, and the only reply, as I know from experience, is, 'Oh, I can't remember', or, 'What do you want to know all that rubbish for?'. Memories not only play people false, but some of them may be painful: so ca' canny along the way.

Unless you have a keen and co-operative person to ask, I suggest you try to record a conversation, having previously decided the direction which you want the conversation to take. Most people enjoy talking about themselves, and I found my mother was fascinated to hear her own voice when I played back the tape-recording. I had previously tried to elicit the information by giving her a list of questions which had only a 'yes' or 'no' answer, but she steadfastly refused to read it. So I borrowed a tape-recorder. I found the best line of approach was to ask my mother about her wedding. From what she wore, we went on to who was there. That led back to her pre-marriage days; where the family lived; where my mother, her brother and sisters went to school; and finally, if her grandparents were alive either when she was at school or when she was married. Bit by bit I winkled out enough names, and approximate dates, to enable me to make a chart. Unfortunately, my father died long before I was interested in genealogy; my mother never kept up with her own family, and knew very little about my father's relations.

Let that be a lesson to all. You are never too young to start – in fact, the younger the better. You stand a much better chance of gathering information from parents or grandparents while they are in their sixties than in their nineties!

8

Questions and Answers with Notes

Q. If I were to employ a professional genealogist or record searcher to work on my family tree, how much would it cost me?

A. Most professional genealogists or record searchers charge by the hour, and it would depend largely on the name being searched and the locality. Surnames like Lumsden or Denholm have fewer entries in the index each year than names like Wilson or Macdonald. Families who lived in rural areas or in Orkney or Shetland are easier to find in census returns than people who lived in big cities such as Glasgow or Edinburgh. For a search starting about 1870 you should allow at least six hours initially. For a search starting before 1855 you could also allow six hours initially, but you may not receive as much information, as the searching in most cases takes longer, owing to the lack of indexed material and the sparsity of information in each entry. For example, marriage entries prior to 1855 do not give the surnames of the parents or the ages of the bride and groom, and they seldom give addresses.

Note: Always stipulate for exactly how many hours you want to pay initially. Do not allow yourself to be liable for a large bill. Unless you only require a specific entry, it is not practical to stipulate less than three hours.

Q. How much information will I get for a six-hour search?

A. Depending on the surname and the area, starting around 1870 you should get back between two and three generations; remember that each generation brings in more surnames. You should stipulate which surnames you would like to take priority in the search. You may want your father's line to take priority over your mother's line, or the other way round; or you may prefer to have the stipulated time divided between them both.

Note: Make sure you have contacted an accredited genealogist or record searcher to undertake the work for you. So many people have 'jumped on the band-wagon' over the past few years, and although they advertise in reputable magazines, in some cases their work can be expensive and unreliable. You may have been recommended to a searcher by a friend who can vouch for the standard of work, but if you are in any doubt you should write to the Searchers' Committee, Scottish Genealogy Society, and they will send you a list of geneaologists and record searchers whose work is of a recognised standard (see Appendix II for the address). Read this list carefully and choose someone whose description of work undertaken agrees with what you want done. Some specialise in certain areas, and not all the people whose names are on the list undertake to carry out a full genealogical search involving wills, deeds etc. Also, you will find a variation in the fee charged, so write to more than one and find out.

Q. What is the minimum amount of information needed to start a search in Scottish records?

A. *If your ancestor left Scotland after 1854,* you must give the *full names* of your ancestor (many people write 'my father' or 'my grandmother' without supplying a name for either the father or the grand-mother!), approximately when he or she was born and some piece of information to make identification possible. For instance, John Wilson, born about 1890, in Scotland, place unknown, parents' names unknown, is an impossible search. There were ninety-nine John Wilsons born in 1890 in Scotland, and unless you know the names of his parents or of some of his brothers or sisters, it would not be possible to identify the correct entry. If, however, John Wilson married and had children before he left Scotland, then the search should be possible.

    If your ancestor left Scotland before 1855, then in addition to the above information, you need to know at least the county in Scotland from whence he or she came. As there are over 900 parishes in Scotland, it would be too time-consuming, and expensive, to search them all.

Q. Is there any way out of the difficulty if I do not even know the name of the county of origin?

A. Yes. Sometimes the subject is to be found in either David Dobson's or Donald Whyte's directories of settlers or emigrants, and sometimes in the Mormon IGI (International Genealogical Index). Any of these sources should show a place of origin (see book list).

Note: Just occasionally it is worth looking at the early names of farms and houses of your own family. People coming from 'the old country' liked to bring with them the name of their old home or farm even when they had to leave behind everything else.

Q. Can the name of the ship be found?
A. This is more easily done from your end as not many shipping lists exist in Scotland; there are a few lists to be found in the Scottish Record Office.

Note: Bear in mind that your ancestor may have disembarked at a port and travelled some distance from there before settling. The shipping list is most likely to be found at the first port of call.

Q. Can I undertake the search myself although I live overseas?
A. Yes. More and more libraries and family history societies are buying microfilm copies of the old parish registers and census returns, and the IGI is a useful tool as long as you remember that it is not a complete list of all the births, marriages and deaths recorded in the parish. Remember, the IGI is only an index; if you are in any doubt you can write to New Register House and they will send you a full official copy of the entry for a small charge.

Note on records: In English records 'B' may stand for Burial as well as Birth, and a Baptism is usually called a Christening, so when you read 'C 1890', the contraction could mean either 'C(hristened) 1890' or C(irca) 1890', whereas in Scottish records 'B' stands for Birth, Baptism is generally contracted to 'Bapt', and 'D' stands for Death. 'Burials' is usually written in full. Therefore in the Scottish records there is less chance of confusion. The Mormon microfiche index uses 'C' for Christening and not 'B' for Baptism. Of course, 'M' stands for Marriage whichever record you read!

'Stayed' in Scotland infers a permanent place of abode, whereas in England this suggests a temporary place of abode and 'lived' infers a permanency. To a Scot, 'I stayed in Brunstane Road, in Edinburgh' means that that was his permanent address, but to an English person this means that he was merely there with friends or as a lodger.

Q. What if I cannot find the Christian name or names I need in the index?
A. Read Chapter 4 on 'Names' and see if the Christian name you want may have a shortened form or a diminutive which was used in the index, such as Elizabeth being indexed as Eliz, Liz, Lizzie, Beth, or Betty.

Q. I know my grandfather was George William King, because he signed his name when he was married, but I cannot find his birth in the General Register of Births Index *circa* 1858.

A. Often the order of Christian names became changed, or a name was added in later life. Search under William George, George William, or just William or just George, and do not forget that William may be entered as Wm. – so look for that too.

Q. I have searched for a birth using every possible spelling variation and over a wide time-span after 1855, but cannot find it at all. It is a Scottish birth.

A. The child may have been born before the parents married, in which case it may have been registered under the mother's surname. An illegitimate child is registered under both surnames only if paternity is admitted. Even if the parents were married in Scotland and all the siblings were born in Scotland, there is just the chance that one child was born in England, Wales or Ireland. Try to find a census entry for the family.

Q. I have found an entry in an OPR of an illegitimate child; is there any chance of finding the name of the father?

A. Yes, search the Kirk Session Records for this parish, because the father may have appeared before the kirk session. (See 'Kirk Session Records' in Chapter 2.)

Q. The census return states that my great-grandfather was born in a certain parish, but I can find no trace of him there, although I did find entries for his siblings.

A. Try searching the surrounding parishes, or the parish where the mother was born, or where the parents were married. Census returns are sometimes inaccurate. Your great-grandfather may have wrongly supposed he was born in the same place as his brothers and sisters, or his birth may not have been registered; it was not compulsory before 1855.

Q. I found a great-*grandfather* whose Christian names were Ann Primrose. Was this a mistake made by the registrar or session clerk?

A. No. There are some Christian names which, although we attribute them to girls, are sometimes given to boys. Ann is one of these, and Primrose is a surname used as a Christian name. (See Chapter 4.)

Q. Are there any boys' names given to girls?

A. Yes, most common are Nicholas, Bruce and John. (See Chapter 4.)

Q. In an OPR I found a birth entry in which the child's Christian
    names were Gibson Kennedy, and the entry only stated 'lawful
    child', not 'lawful son' or 'lawful daughter'. How can I tell whether
    this child was a boy or a girl?
A. In Scotland, surnames, usually the name of a grandmother, were,
    and still are, often used as Christian names. Unless this child grew
    up and married, or died in Scotland after 1855, or was found in a
    census return, I am afraid you may never know!

Q. My grandmother's name is sometimes Jean, sometimes, Janet, or
    Jessie. Which is the correct form?
A. The name used in the birth (after 1854) or birth/baptism (prior to
    1855) register is the correct form, but these names tend to be
    interchangeable. (See chapter 4.)

Q. When my grandfather died the name of hs mother given on the
    death certificate was not the same as that given when my
    grandfather was married.
A. There are several possible explanations: (1) Are you sure you
    found the correct death entry? For instance, was the spouse's name
    correct? Were the age, address and/or informant's name known to
    be correct? (2) Who was the informant? A son-in-law, daughter-in-
    law, grandchild or neighbour may not have known the Christian
    name and/or the maiden surname of your great-grandmother,
    especially if your grandfather was an old man when he died. (3)
    Did the informant sign his or her name or was it 'His/Her X Mark'?
    On a death certificate the subject is hardly in a position to rectify
    any wrong information! The information on the marriage
    certificate is therefore more likely to be correct.

Q. What do 'Her X Mark' and 'His X Mark' mean?
A. This means that the person testifying to the information, as an
    informant or as a witness, could not write, so the name was written
    by somebody else, and the informant wrote 'X' in the presence of a
    witness. If a person could not write then it was more than likely that
    he or she could not read either; any information from such a
    source may therefore be inaccurate, and is at least suspect.

Q. When I searched in England I found the information on a death cer-
    tificate to be rather scant. Is it worth searching for deaths in Scotland?
A. Yes. In Scotland death records after 1854 are of great importance
    and a great deal of information is to be gained from them. (See
    Chapter 1.)

Q. I found my family in a census return, and I know the village where they were born, but I cannot find it in the list of parishes for Old Parish Registers.

A. This is probably because it is not a parish in its own right, but a village or a hamlet within a parish of another name. Consult a gazetteer; look up the name of the place you know and this should tell you the name of the parish you need. (See Chapter 1.)

Q. I was told that our family came from 'the Mearns'. What or where is that?

A. The Mearns is another name for Kincardineshire. It is not to be confused with Mearns, which is the name of parish in Renfrewshire.

Note: Other such places are (1) Badenoch, a district in south-eastern Inverness-shire, which comprises the parishes of Alvie and Rothiemurchus; (2) Cunninghame, a district in Ayrshire, which comprises the parishes of Ardrossan, Beith, Dalry, Dreghorn, Dundonald, Dunlop, Galston, Irvine, Kilbirnie, W. Kilbride, Kilmarnock, Kilwinning, Loudon, Stevenston, Stewarton and Symington.

Q. My ancestor was a minister in the Church of Scotland; are there any printed records I could search?

A. Yes. Look at *Fasti Ecclesiae Scoticanae*, which is a list of biographies of all the ministers in the Church of Scotland since the Reformation. It is usually known as 'Fasti' and is found in most libraries. (See Chapter 3 and book list in Appendix IV.)

Note: For ministers of other – Free, etc. – churches in Scotland, see Chapter 3 and book list in Appendix IV.

Q. I found a marriage in 1820 where the groom was of the parish of Edinburgh and the bride was of the parish of Bathgate. I found birth entries of their children in Edinburgh from 1825 onwards, but none for the years 1820–24 in Edinburgh. Where else should I search?

A. Remember that Edinburgh is in three different districts for OPRs: Edinburgh (685^1), St Cuthbert's (685^2) and Canongate (685^3). If you have searched all these Edinburgh parishes, I suggest you try Bathgate, where the mother came from. She may have gone home to her mother to have the first child. Check that there is no gap in the records. Lastly, if you do not find any other children, unless you know something to the contrary, perhaps there was none born alive any earlier than the one you found.

Q. What is the difference between the IGI and the OPR microfiche index?

A. The Mormons (The Church of Jesus Christ of Latter-day Saints) have produced three sets of microfiche indexes – in 1981, 1984 and 1988. These are known as the IGI (International Genealogical Index) and contain baptism and marriage information submitted to them by their members. Names and dates from family bibles as well as family histories are included, up to 1875. As this information was not collected only from original sources (e.g. from OPRs), there is some hearsay to be found, and I would strongly advise you to use the IGI only as a useful guide. Bear in mind, too, that the main reason for collecting these records was for the Mormons' own religious purposes and rites. Consequently, the date recorded was usually that of a baptism, and not that of a birth, and death entries were not recorded.

The Registrar General arranged to allow the Mormons to index the Old Parish Registers (OPRs), and this index is to be found on microfiche. This OPR index contains birth/baptism and marriage information taken from original sources. At the time of going to print (1990) work has been halted on this project, and only the OPRs for Glasgow and Dundee and for the following counties have been indexed: Aberdeen, Angus, Banff, Bute, Caithness, Clackmannan, Dumbarton, Inverness, Kincardine, Kinross, Moray, Nairn, Orkney, Ross and Cromarty, Shetland, Sutherland.

The Dundee index includes not only all the parishes of Dundee (Ref. 282) but also the parishes of Liff and Benvie (Ref. 301), Mains and Strathmartine (Ref. 307) and Monifieth (Ref. 310). *The Glasgow index* includes all four parishes of Glasgow, i.e., Glasgow (Ref. 644[1]), Gorbals (Ref. 644[2]), Barony (Ref. 622) and Govan (Ref. 646).

There is also a microfiche index to births and marriages under Christian names, which may help when searching for a patronymic. The following counties, in addition to Glasgow (incomplete) and Dundee, are so indexed: Aberdeen, Banff, Caithness, Inverness, Kincardine, Moray, Nairn, Orkney, Ross and Cromarty, Shetland, Sutherland.

Note: Many entries in the OPRs were not recorded in chronological order. You may find an entry in a given year in the index, but the entry is not recorded in that year in the OPR. To help you to find such entries note the frame number written in the miscellaneous column on the microfiche index, e.g., FR246. This number will be found at the top of each page/frame of the microfiche. Although in some cases it is almost illegible, it should help you to find the entry if you persevere.

Q. I should like to visit the church where my great-grandparents were married in 1890. How can I find it?

A. If your great-grandparents were married in Scotland and you have a copy of the marriage certificate, this should give you the name of the church and the name of the minister or priest. In a country area there will not be many churches, so you should find it easily. In a city or a town it may be more difficult, but from reference books held in the library of the parish you should be able to find out where that church was. Unfortunately, owing to building developments in cities or towns, there is always the chance that the church is no longer there.

Note: Not all Scottish marriages took place in church. It was not uncommon for the ceremony to have been held in a hotel, in a house, or in the manse.

Q. On a marriage certificate I found the words 'cousin german'. What does that mean?

A. The word 'german' placed after brother, sister or cousin means that they are in the fullest sense of relationship. Cousins german are first cousins. A brother or a sister german have the same parents. German is pronounced 'germane'.

Q. What is a second cousin, and what is a second cousin once removed?

A. *A first cousin* (or german) is the child of one's uncle or aunt; *a second cousin* is the child of one's parent's first cousin; *a first cousin once,* or *twice,* etc. *removed* is (1) The child of one's first cousin (grandchild etc.); (2) The cousin of one's parents, grandparents, etc.

Q. Why do some OPR birth/baptism indexes record only the names of sons, and not of daughters?

A. When you come across such an index, showing only male names, these will be the names of the fathers, and not the names of the children.

Q. What does 'H.E.I.C.S.' after a name mean?

A. This means that the person was in the Honourable East India Company Service.

Q. I found the words 'Baptized Do.' in an OPR birth entry. What does 'Do.' mean?
A. 'Do.' stands for 'Ditto' meaning 'the same as before'. So if a child was born on 18 January and baptized '24th Do.' that means that the child was baptized on 24 January.

Note: 'inst.' stands for instant, and means this month; 'ult.' stands for ultimo, and means last month.

Q. What does 'RCE' at the side of an entry mean?
A. This means 'Register of Corrected Entries': for a birth or a marriage entry, generally recording an alteration of name or date, or a subsequent marriage making a child legitimate. For a death entry, generally recording the result of a precognition if the death was sudden, or the result of an accident. It is possible to view the register and copy down the information.

Note: One final thought. When you are noting the father's occupation from a birth certificate, do not confuse this with the name of the father. I overheard the following conversation between a searcher and Mr Alex Cunningham, Senior Repository Assistant:

Searcher: 'Why has this child got two fathers?'
A.C.:   'The entry states "Father: James Brown, Bill Poster". There is only one father.'
Searcher: 'Then who was Bill Poster?'

Illustrations

Extract of an entry in a register of MARRIAGES

Registration of Births, Deaths and Marriages (Scotland) Act 1965

District No	742	Year	1979		Entry No	56

Marriage registered in the district of Canongate and Portobello

1. When and where married	19 79 **March Twentyfourth** St Mark's Episcopal Church, Edinburgh

2. Surname	**Bridegroom** Kozowyk	**Bride** Cory
Name(s)	Ned John	Alison Catherine Barnard
	Signed Ned John Kozowyk	*Signed* Alison Catherine Barnard Cory

3. Occupation	Professional Engineer	————

4. Marital Status	Single	5. Date of birth	Year 1947	Month 5	Day 4	4. Single	5. Year 1955	Month 10	Day 26

6. Birthplace	Canada	Bermuda

7. Usual residence	6 Weybridge Court Islington, Ontario, Canada	4 Brunstane Road Edinburgh

8. Father's name(s) surname and occupation	Alex Kozowyk Sprinkler Fitter (retired)	Paul Alexander Barnard Cory Clerk in Holy Orders (deceased)
Mother's name(s) surname(s) and maiden surname	Betty Kozowyk m.s. Panagapko	Kathleen Beatrice Cory m.s. Reed

9. Person solemnizing the marriage	*Signed* Kenneth Riches	*Designation* Bishop of
	Lincoln (retired)	
Witnesses with addresses	*Signed* Vern Lennox	Witness
	Rural Route No 1, Mar, Ontario, Canada	
	Signed Eleanor A Logan	Witness
	16 Lorne Crescent, Monifieth, Dundee	

10. When registered	Year 19 79	Month 3	Day 26	11. *Signed* .... Gwyneth C Forbes .... Asst. Registrar

12.	

The above particulars are extracted from the register of marriages for the district of ...Canongate and Portobello...........
on 26th March, 1979

Gwyneth C. Forbes Asst. Registrar

The above particulars incorporate any subsequent corrections or amendments to the original entry made with the authority of the Registrar General.

It is an offence under section 53(3) of the Registration of Births, Deaths and Marriages (Scotland) Act 1965 for any person to pass as genuine any copy or reproduction of this extract which has not been made by a district registrar or assistant registrar and authenticated by his signature.

Any person who falsifies or forges any of the particulars on this extract or knowingly uses, gives or sends as genuine any false or forged extract is liable to prosecution under section 53(1) of the said Act.

XM4(R)
Jun 75

Dd. 402977 900 Pads 6/76 C.L. Co.

Fig. 1 1979 Marriage Certificate

1861 – 1965

Extract of an entry in a REGISTER of DEATHS

Registration of Births, Deaths and Marriages (Scotland) Act 1965

No.	1 Name and surname, rank or profession and whether single, married or widowed	2 When and where died	3 Sex	4 Age	5 Name, surname, and rank or profession of father; Name and maiden surname of mother	6 Cause of death, duration of disease, and medical attendant by whom certified	7 Signature and qualification of informant, and residence, if out of the house in which the death occurred	8 When and where registered and signature of registrar
338	Charles Hubert REED Captain, General List Married to Beatrice King	1947 May Twelfth 5h. Om. A.M. 25 Belgrave Crescent, Edinburgh (Usual residence: 20-22 Torphichen Street, Edinburgh)	M	54 years	William Reed Naval Officer (deceased) Alice Reed m.s. Cooke (deceased)	Cardio vascular degeneration Bronchitis As Cert. by J. L. Carmichael M.B.	Beatrice Reed Widow Crown Hotel 20-22 Torphichen Street, Edinburgh Present *Signed*	1947 May 12th At Edinburgh *Signed* Geo. B. Houston *Registrar*

The above particulars are extracted from a Register of Deaths for the .... District .... of .... St. Andrew

in the .... City .... of .... Edinburgh

Given under the Seal of the General Register Office, New Register House, Edinburgh, on 25th November 1976

RXD3
March

Fig. 2 1947 Death Certificate

NO	PARISHES	1841 CENSUS		1851 CENSUS	
		Reference	Remarks	Reference	Remarks
		CEN 1841	Enumeration Books	CEN 1851	
	AYR - contd.				
587	Dalry	587	15　　"	529-530	
588	Dalrymple	588	4　　"	489	
589	Dreghorn	589	5　　"	510	
590	Dundonald	590	12　　"	509, 522	
591	Dunlop	591	6　　"	450, 526	
592	Fenwick	592	11　　"	519	
593	Galston	593	10　　"	507	
594	Girvan	594	18　　"	480-482	
595	Irvine	595	7 for Irvine Harbour see Dundonald Book 12	521-2	
596	Kilbirnie	596	11　　"	533	
597	Kilmarnock	597	41　　"	512-517	
598	Kilmaurs	598	7　　"	511	
599	Kilwinning	599	11　　"	525-6	
600	Kirkmichael	600	8　　"	485	
601	Kirkoswald	601	18　　"	486	
602	Largs	602	7　　"	532	
603	Loudoun	603	12　　"	518	
604	Mauchline	604	11　　"	504	
605	Maybole	605	19　　"	487-8	

Fig. 3 Census Index Page

REGISTRATION DISTRICT	1861 CENSUS			1871 CENSUS		
	Reference	No of Enum. Books	No of Vols containing foregoing Enum. Books	Reference	No of Enum. Books	No of Vols containing foregoing Enum. Books
	CEN 1861			CEN 1871		
Kilbirnie	596	8	2	596	8	1
Kilbrandon and Kilchattan	515	6	1	515	6	1
Kilbride	553	9	1	553[2]	6	1
Kilbucho	763	1	1			
Kilbucho, Broughton and Glenholm				763	5	1
Kilcamonell	516[1]	2	1	516[1]	2	1
Kilchoman	540	7	1	540	7	1
Kilchrenan	517[1]	3	1	517[1]	3	1
Kilconquhar	436	9	1	436	8	1
Kildalton	541	7	1	541	7	1
Kildonan	52	8	1	52	8	1
Kildrummy	208	4	1	208	4	1
Kilfinan	518	4	1	518	4	1
Kilfinichen and Kilvickeon	542	7	1	542	7	1
Killean and Kilchenzie	519	5	1	519	5	1
Killearn	482	5	1	482	5	1
Killearnan	68	4	1	68	4	1
Killin	361	9	1	361	9	1
Kilmacolm	569	6	1	569	6	1
Kilmadock	362	8	1	362	8	1
Kilmallie	520	16	2	520	16	2
Kilmany (Fife)	437	2	1	437	2	1
Kilmarnock	597*	30	6	597*	33	5
Kilmaronock	497	4	1	497	4	1

*See Kilmarnock Street Index (Vol 9)   *See Kilmarnock Street Index (Vol 14)

Fig. 4 1861 Census Heading

Parish of _Kilmarnock_

5

1			2			3		4	
PLACE	HOUSES		NAME and SURNAME, SEX and AGE of each Person who abode in each House on the Night of 6th June.			OCCUPATION		WHERE BORN	
Here insert Name of Village, Street, Square, Close, Court, &c.	Uninhabited or Building	Inhabited	NAME and SURNAME	AGE		Of what Profession, Trade, Employment, or whether of Independent Means.		Whether born in Scotland, England, or otherwise.	Whether Foreigner, or whether Born in England or Ireland.
				Male	Female				
Portland Street			James D°	2				y	
			Thomas D°	3 months				y	
			Sarah Waugh		65				E
			Margret Williamson		15	F. S.		y	
		1	James Gilmour	45		H. L. W.		y	
			Janet D°		15	Straw Hat M		n	
			Jean D°		15			n	
		1	Elizabeth Mile		25			y	
		1	John Wood	30		Cabinet M		y	
			Elizabeth D°		25			y	
			Archabald D°	10				y	
			John D°	8				y	
			Ann D°		4			y	
			David D°	2				y	
		1	Peter Clark	20		Journeyman Slater		y	
			Mary D°		20			y	
		1	Elizabeth D°		5 months			y	
		1	Robert Roxburgh	20		H. L. W.		y	
			Elizabeth D°		20			y	
		1	James Mair	75		Shoe maker		y	
			James D°	6				y	
		1	John Walkei	40		Shoe		y	I
			Mary D°		25				I
			Robert D°	7				n	
			Cathart Hutton		15	F. S.		y	
TOTAL in				13	12	50			

Fig. 5 1841 Census Heading

1891 Census Kilmarnock (597/0/6)

Page 6)

The undermentioned Houses are situate within the Boundaries of the

Civil Parish of	Quoad Sacra Parish of	School Board District of	Parliamentary Burgh of	Parliamentary Division of	Royal Burgh of
Kilmarnock	Kilchrist	Kilm k	Kilm k	Kilm t district of Burgh	
Municipal Burgh of Kilm t	Police Burgh of Kilm k	Burgh Ward of Kil.. k	Town of Kilm k	Village or Hamlet of	Island of

No. of Schedule	ROAD, STREET, &c., and No. or NAME of HOUSE	HOUSES Inhabited	Unin-habited (U.) or Building (B.)	NAME and Surname of each Person.	RELATION to Head of Family.	CONDITION as to Marriage.	AGE last Birthday Males | Females	PROFESSION or OCCUPATION.	Employer.	Employed.	Neither Employer nor Employed, but working on own account.	WHERE BORN.	Gaelic, or G. & E.	Whether 1. Deaf and Dumb 2. Blind 3. Lunatic, Imbecile, or Idiot	Rooms with One or more Windows

Fig. 6 1891 Census Heading

CHURCHES IN SCOTLAND

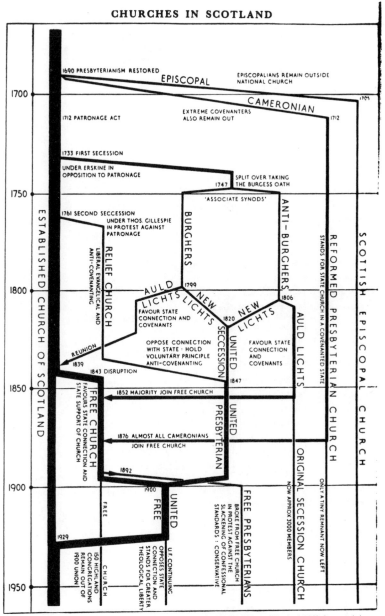

Churches in Scotland (reproduced from J. H. S. Burleigh *A Church History of Scotland*, 1960, by permission of J. K. Burleigh, Mrs Anne Macrae and the Hope Trust)

Fig. 7 Burleigh's Chart of Scottish Churches

INDEX TO SHERIFF COURT COMMISSARY RECORDS (arranged by counties)

Aberdeenshire	1824-1900	SC.1	Aberdeen	
Angus	1824-1900	SC.47	Forfar	County of Angus (Forfarshire)
	1832-1900	SC.45	Dundee	Dundee only
Argyllshire	1815-1900	SC.51	Dunoon	(typed index 1815-1900)
Ayrshire	1824-1900	SC.6	Ayr	
Banffshire	1824-1900	SC.2	Banff	
Berwickshire	1823-1900	SC.60	Duns	
Buteshire	1824-1900	SC.8	Rothesay	
Caithness	1824-1900	SC.14	Wick	
Clackmannan	1824-1900	SC.64	Alloa	Includes Kinross-shire 1824-46
Cromarty	1824-1900	SC.25	Dingwall	(typed index 1824-1900)
Dumbartonshire	1824-1900	SC.65	Dunbarton	
Dumfriesshire	1806-1900	SC.15	Dumfries	See also CC.5 Dumfries up to 1827
East Lothian	1830-1900	SC.40	Haddington	Prior to 1830 included with Midlothian
Fife	1824-1900	SC.20	Cupar	(typed index 1823-92)
Inverness	1823-1900	SC.29	Inverness	
Kincardineshire	1824-1900	SC.5	Stonehaven	
Kinross-shire	1847-1900	SC.22	Kinross	Prior to 1847 included with Clackmannan
Kirkcudbright	1824-1900	SC.16	Kirkcudbright	
Lanarkshire	1824-1900	SC.36	Glasgow	
	1888-1900	SC.37	Hamilton	(typed index 1888-99)
	1888-1900	SC.38	Lanark	
Midlothian	1808-1900	SC.70	Edinburgh	Includes East & West Lothian up to 1830 Printed indexes 1824-67
Morayshire	1823-1900	SC.26	Elgin	Includes Nairnshire 1824-39 and 1861-76
Nairnshire	1839-1900	SC.31	Nairn	1824-39,1861-76 included with Morayshire
Orkney	1824-1900	SC.11	Kirkwall	Records held at Orkney Library, Kirkwall
Peebleshire	1814-1900	SC.42	Peebles	
Perthshire	1824-1900	SC.49	Perth	(typed index 1824-1900)
	1824-1900	SC.44	Dunblane	(typed index 1824-1900)
Renfrewshire	1824-1900	SC.58	Paisley	(typed index 1824-99)
Ross & Cromarty	1824-1900	SC.25	Dingwall	(typed index 1824-1900)
	1826-1840	SC.33	Stornoway	Isle of Lewis only (index with SC.25)
Roxburghshire	1827-1900	SC.62	Jedburgh	Prior to 1827 see CC.18 Peebles
Selkirkshire	1824-1900	SC.63	Selkirk	
Stirlingshire	1809-1900	SC.67	Stirling	(typed index 1809-1900)
Shetland	1827-1900	SC.12	Lerwick	Records held at Shetland Archives, Lerwick
Sutherland	1799-1900	SC.9	Dornoch	Not indexed prior to 1851
West Lothian	1831-1900	SC.41	Linlithgow	Prior to 1831 included with Midlothian (typed index 1831-97)
Wigtownshire	1826-1900	SC.19	Wigtown	Prior to 1826 see CC.22 Wigtown

Note: For persons dying outside Scotland, or with no fixed residence within Scotland check indexes for SC.70 Edinburgh.

FOR 1846-67 THERE ARE PRINTED INDEXES COVERING ALL COURTS:- These should be used in conjunction with the photocopied indexes.

Fig. 8 Index to Sheriff Court Commissary Records

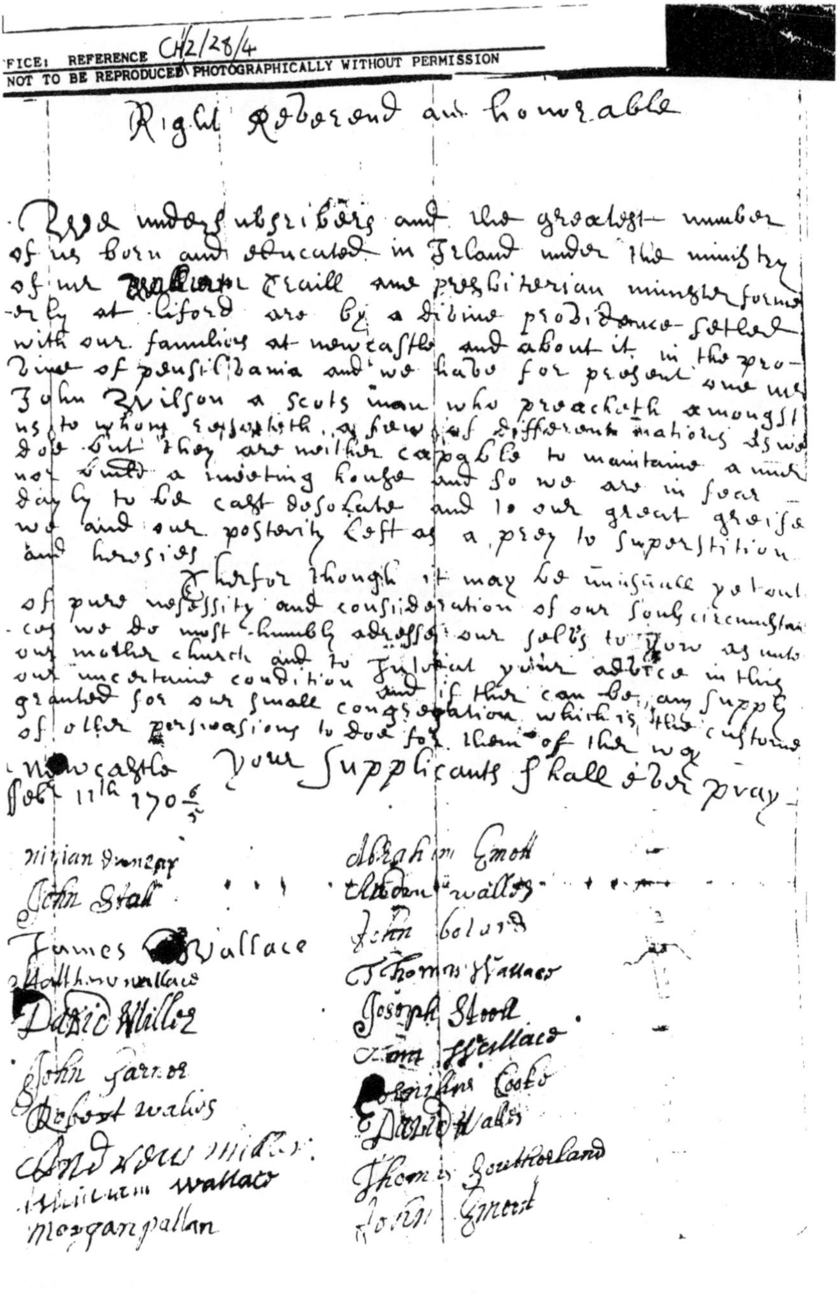

Right Reverend and honorable

Wee undersubscribers and the greatest number of us born and educated in Ireland under the ministry of mr William Traill one presbiterian minister formerly at Liford are by a divine providence settled with our families at newcastle and about it in the province of pensilvania and we have for present one mr John Wilson a scots man who preacheth amongst us to whom resorteth a few of different nations as we doe but they are neither capable to maintaine a mr nor build a meeting house and so we are in fear daily to be cast desolate and to our great greiffe we and our posterity left as a prey to superstition and heresies

Therefor though it may be unusuall yet out of pure necessity and consideration of our soul circumstances we do most humbly address our selfs to you as unto our mother church and to Judicial your advice in this our uncertaine condition and if there can be any supply granted for our small congregation which is the custome of other perswasions to doe for them of the way

newcastle   your Supplicants shall ever pray
febr 11th 170 6/5

nician Dunepy   Abigham Emott
John Stall   Thomas wallos
James Wallace   John bolord
Matthew wallace   Thomas Wallaer
Davie Miller   Joseph Stool
John garnor   Tom Wallace
Robort wahes   Leigine Cooke
Andrew Miller   David Wallis
william wallace   Thomas Southerland
morgan pallon   John Emott

Fig. 9 Letter to General Assembly from Pennsylvania

NEW SOUTH WALES.

GOVERNMENT EMIGRATION OFFICE,
PARK STREET, WESTMINSTER.

REGULATIONS
FOR THE SELECTION OF EMIGRANTS, AND CONDITIONS ON WHICH PASSAGES ARE GRANTED

QUALIFICATIONS OF EMIGRANTS.

1. The Emigrants must be of those callings which, from time to time, are most in demand in the Colony. They must be sober, industrious, and of general good moral character :—of all of which decisive certificates will be required. They must also be in good health, free from all bodily or mental defects; and the Adults must, in all respects, be capable of labour, and going out to work for wages. The Candidates most acceptable are young Married Couples without Children.

2. The separation of husbands and wives, and of parents from children under 18 will in no case be allowed.

3. Single women cannot be taken without their parents, unless they go under the immediate care of some near relatives.

4. Single men cannot be taken except in a number not exceeding that of the Single women by the same ship.

5. Persons who intend to buy land, or to invest capital, in trade ;—or who are in the habitual receipt of parish relief ;—or who have not been vaccinated, or had the small-pox ;—or whose families comprise many young Children, cannot be accepted.

APPLICATION AND APPROVAL.

6. Applications must be made to the Commissioners in the Form annexed. The filling up of the Form, however, confers no claim to a passage ; and implies no pledge that the Candidates, though apparently within the Regulations, will be accepted.

7. If approved of, the Applicants will receive a printed "Approval Circular," calling for the Contribution required by Article 8, and pointing out how it is to be paid. After it is paid, they will, as soon as practicable, receive an Embarkation Order (*which is not transferrable*), naming the Ship in which they are to embark, and the time and place of joining her.

PAYMENTS TOWARDS PASSAGES.

8. The Contributions above-mentioned, out of which the Commissioners will provide Bedding and Mess Utensils, &c., for the Voyage, will be as follows :—

CLASSES	Age		
	Under 40	40 and under 50	50 and upwards
	£	£	£
I. Married Agricultural Labourers, Shepherds, Herdsmen, and their Wives; also Female Domestic and Farm Servants—per Head...	2	6	11
II. Married Country Mechanics, such as Blacksmiths, Bricklayers, Carpenters, Masons, Sawyers, Wheelwrights, and Gardeners, and their Wives also Females of the Working Class, not being Domestic or Farm Servants—(when they can be taken) per Head	5	8	15
III. Children under 14—per Head	2		
But if there be more than two Children under 14 in any Family, at the time of Embarkation, for each additional Child there must be paid, instead of £2	5		

IV. Single Men of 18 years and upwards, of any of the above callings and whether part of a family or not, £1 additional.

The expense of reaching the Port of embarkation must also be paid by the Emigrants *from which place they are forwarded free.*

CAUTIONS TO APPLICANTS

9. *No preparations must on any account be made by the Applicants, either by withdrawing from employment or otherwise, until they receive the "Approval Circular."* Applicants who fail to attend to this warning will do so at their own risk, and will have no claim whatever on the Commissioners.

10. The Selecting Agents of the Board have no authority to promise passages in any case, nor to receive money. If, therefore, Applicants *wish to make their payments through the Agents, instead of in the manner pointed out in the "Approval Circular," they must understand that they do so at their own risk, and that the Commissioners will be in no way responsible.*

11. Should any Signatures attached to an Applicant's paper prove to be not genuine, or should any false representations be made in the papers, not only will the application be rejected, but the offenders will be liable, under the Passengers' Act, 12 & 13 Vic. cap. 38, to a PENALTY NOT EXCEEDING £50.

12. Should any Applicants be found on personal examination at the Depôt, or on Board, to have made any mis-statement in their papers, or to have any infectious disorder, or otherwise not to be in a fit state of health to embark, or to have any mental or bodily defect likely to impair their usefulness as labourers, or to have left any of their young Children behind, or to have brought with them more Children than are mentioned in their Application Form, or expressly sanctioned by the Commissioners, or to have attempted any deception whatever, or evasion of these Rules, they will be refused admission on board the Ship, or if embarked, will be landed, without having any claim on the Commissioners.

13. If Applicants fail to attend at the appointed time and place for embarkation, without having previously given to the Commissioners timely notice, and a satisfactory reason,—or if they fail to proceed in the Ship,—or are rejected for any of the reasons specified in the preceding article, they will forfeit out of their contributions the Sum of £2 for each person, and will have no claim to a passage at any future time.

OUTFIT, &c.

14. The Commissioners supply Provisions, Medical Attendance, and Cooking Utensils at their Depôt and on board the Ship. Also, new Mattresses, Bolsters, Blankets, and Counterpanes, Canvas Bags to contain Linen, &c., Knives and Forks, Spoons, Metal Plates, and Drinking Mugs, which articles will be given after arrival in the Colony to the Emigrants who have behaved well on the voyage.

15. The Emigrants must bring their own Clothing, which will be inspected at the Port by an Officer of the Commissioners ; and they will not be allowed to embark unless they have a sufficient stock for the voyage, not less, for each Person, than—

FOR MALES.	FOR FEMALES.
Six Shirts	Six Shifts
Six pairs Stockings	Two Flannel Petticoats
Two ditto Shoes	Six pairs Stockings
Two complete suits of exterior Clothing.	Two ditto Shoes
	Two Gowns.

With Sheets, Towels, and Soap. But the larger the stock of Clothing the better for health and comfort during the voyage, which usually lasts about four months, and as the Emigrants have always to pass through very hot and very cold weather, they should be prepared for both ; 2 or 3 Serge Shirts for Men, and Flannel for Women and Children, are strongly recommended.

16. The Emigrants should take out with them the necessary tools of their Trades that are not bulky. But the whole quantity of baggage for each Adult must not measure more than 20 cubic or solid feet, nor exceed half a ton in weight. It must be closely packed in one or more boxes ; but no box must exceed in size 10 cubic feet. Large packages and extra baggage, if it can be taken at all, must be paid for. Mattresses and feather beds will in no case be taken.

17. On arrival in the Colony the Emigrants will be at perfect liberty to engage themselves to any one willing to employ them, and to make their own bargain for wages ; but if they quit the Colony within 4 years *after landing, they must repay to the Colonial Government a proportionate part of their Passage-money, at the rate of £3 per Adult, for each year wanting to complete four years' residence.*

18. All Applications should be addressed, Post-paid, to S. Walcott, Require, No. 9, Park Street, Westminster.

By Order of the Board,

STEPHEN WALCOTT,
Secretary.

Fig. 10 Details of Emigrants from England Wales and Scotland

007400

1922–1965
Extract of an entry in a REGISTER of MARRIAGES
Registration of Births, Deaths and Marriages (Scotland) Act 1965

No	1 When, where and how married	2 Names in full of parties with signature Rank or profession and whether bachelor, spinster, widower, widow or divorced	3 Age	4 Usual Residence	5 Name, surname and rank or profession of father Name and maiden surname of mother	6 If a regular marriage signature and designation of minister or registrar and signatures and addresses of witnesses If an irregular marriage, date of decree of declarator or of Sheriff's warrant	7 When and where registered and signature of registrar
	1922 on the Nineteenth day of July at 11 Wildale Crescent Edinburgh	Archibald Young Archibald Young Ironmonger Bachelor	53	18 Dudley Terrace Leith	Thomas Young Ordained Minister Margaret Young M.S. Wedgrove	Signed J.F. Taylor 15 Vilta Place Ensol Church Edinburgh Wm Scott	1922 July 20th at Edinburgh
196	Allen Hanna according to the forms of the Congregational Church	Barbara Wilkinson Henderson Barbara W. Henderson Spinster	31	31 Chatlewode Street Edinburgh	James Grant Henderson (deceased) Margaret Craig Henderson M.S. Wilkinson	8 Arden Street Edinburgh Wynne Evelyn Loch 3 Lansdale Terrace Edinburgh Witness	M Campbell Registrar.

The above particulars are extracted from a Register of Marriages for the .... District .... of ...... Edinburgh, Canongate ....
in the .... Lock .... of ....
Given under the Seal of the General Register Office, New Register House, Edinburgh, on 12ᵈ September 1985.

The above particulars incorporate any subsequent corrections or amendments to the original entry made with the authority of the Registrar General.

This extract is valid only if it has been authenticated by the seal of the General Register Office. If the particulars in the relevant entry in the statutory register have been reproduced by photography, xerography or some other similar process the seal must have been impressed after the reproduction has been made. The General Register Office will authenticate only those reproductions which have been produced by that office.

Warning

It is an offence under section 53(3) of the Registration of Births, Deaths and Marriages (Scotland) Act 1965 for any person to pass as genuine any copy or reproduction of this extract which has not been made by the General Register Office and authenticated by the Seal of that Office.

Any person who falsifies or forges any of the particulars on this extract or knowingly uses, gives or sends as genuine any false or forged extract is liable to prosecution under section 53(1) of the said Act.

RXM6(CI) 976

Fig. 11 1922 Marriage Certificate

ORDER SLIP STATUTORY REGISTER	**A separate slip** must be completed for **each** item required. Please write in pencil.				FOR OFFICIAL USE
	EVENT	YEAR	REGISTRATION DISTRICT No.	ENTRY No.	
	Birth	1869	685²	326	
	Death				
	Marriage				
	Other (please specify)				

If using an index book (not computer terminal), change registration district name to a
number using wall chart or booklet "Guide for researchers: No. 2". Entry number is given
in end column of index book.

Reader's name (BLOCK CAPITALS) YOUR NAME	Date	Seat No	SU 12A 289

Fig. 12 Order Slip for Statutory Register

ORDER SLIP CENSUS	A separate slip must be completed for each item required. Please write in pencil.		FOR OFFICIAL USE
	YEAR	DISTRICT No	ENUMERATION BOOK No. *	
	1841	689		

* Please quote this number only if a street index is available. Where the list of census
records indicates that a street index exists the index should be consulted for the precise
reference number of the enumeration book required.

Reader's name (BLOCK CAPITALS) YOUR NAME	Date	Seat No	SU 12C 289

Fig. 14 Census Order Form

ORDER SLIP OLD PARISH REGISTER (OPR)	A separate slip must be completed for each item required. Please write in pencil.	FOR OFFICIAL USE
Reference		
689 / 13		

Please find reference number in "List of OPRs".

Reader's name (BLOCK CAPITALS) YOUR NAME	Date	Seat No	SU 12B 289

Fig. 16 Old Parish Register Order Form

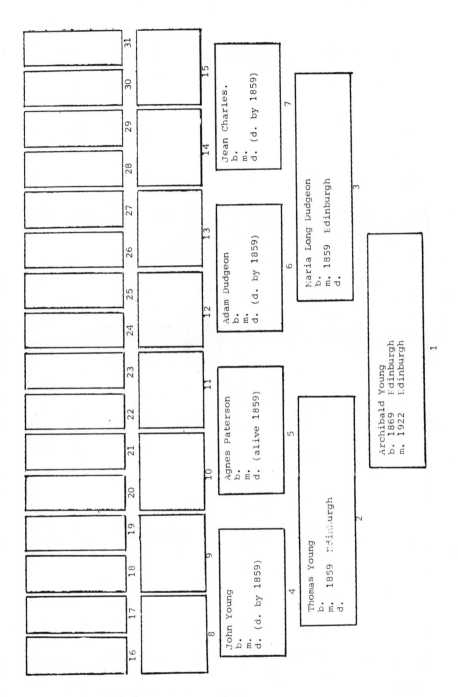

Fig. 13 Family Tree Chart (Squares)

Parish of *Inveresk*

1		2			3	4	
PLA...	HOUSES	NAME and SURNAME, SEX and AGE, of each Person who abode in each House on the Night of 6th June.			OCCUPATION	WHERE BORN	
Her ...sert Name of Village, Street, Square, Close, Coun. &c.	... or ...	NAME and SURNAME	AGE		Of what Profession, Trade, Employment, or whether of Independent Means.	If Born in Scotland, state whether in County or otherwise.	Whether Foreigner, or whether Born in England or Ireland.
			Male	Female			
Smart's Wynd		William Currie	70		Lab.	Y	
do.		Helen Scott		60	Ind.	Y	
do.	1	John Finlie	50		Mill Wright	Y	
		Jane do.		55		Y	
		Robert do. Jun	40		...wher		J
do.	—	Robert Northwick	45		Potter J.	Y	
do.	—	William Sinclair	60		Tailor		E
		Elizabeth do.		50		R	
		Thomas do.	15		Shoe M. ap	Y	
do.	1	Rebecca Raver		65			J
		Catharine do.		20	Flax Spinner		J
		Rebecca do.		18	do.		J
		Samuel Kinley	60		Potter J.	R	
		James do.	18		do. J.	R	
do.	—	Adam Dadgeon	20		Flesher	Y	
		Jane do.		20		Y	
		Maria L. do.		1		Y	
		William R. Hayart	6 months			Y	
do.		Alexander Cameron	20		Natter J.	Y	
		Jane do.		20		Y	
		Jane do.		1 month		Y	
		John McGregor	60		do.	R	
do.	1	Janet Clark		88	Ind.	Y	
		Adam do.	30		Tailor	Y	
		Mary do.		28		Y	
TOTAL Page 29	3		13	12			

Fig. 15 1841 Census for Inveresk

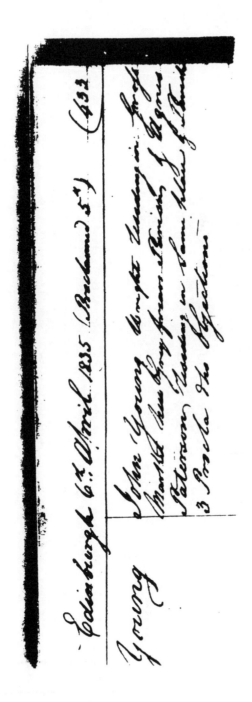

Fig. 17 1835 Marriage Entry

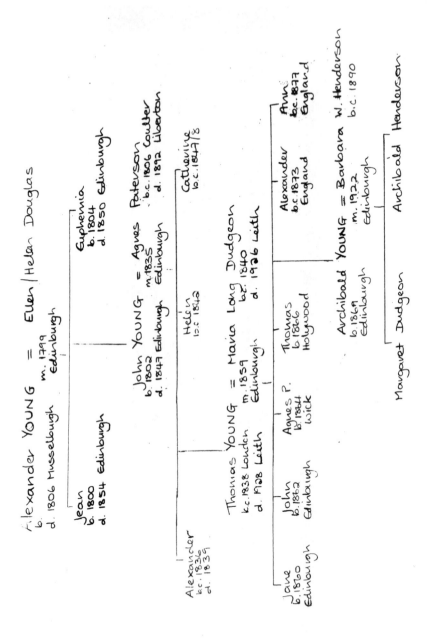

Fig. 18 Family Tree Chart (Drop-line)

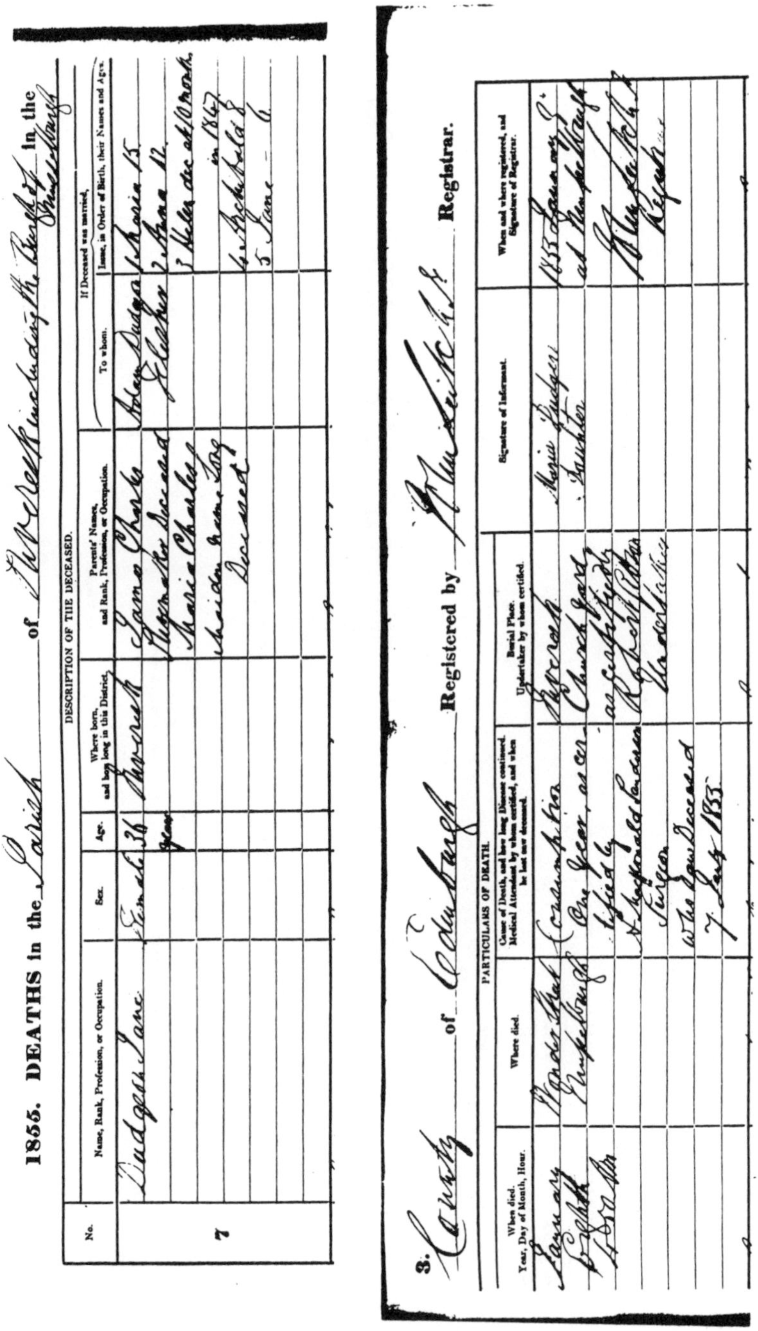

1855. DEATHS in the Parish of Inveresk including the Burgh of Musselburgh in the County of Edinburgh Registered by [illegible] Registrar.

No.	Name, Rank, Profession, or Occupation.	Sex.	Age.	Where born, and how long in this District.	Parents' Names, and Rank, Profession, or Occupation.	If Deceased was married, To whom.	Issue, in Order of Birth, their Names and Ages.
7	Dudgeon Jane	Female	36 year	Inveresk	James Clark Shipmaster Deceased; Maria Charles maiden name [illegible] Deceased	Adam Dudgeon Flesher	1 Maria 15; 2 Anna 12; 3 Helen dec at 10 month in 1847; 4 Archibald 8; 5 Jane 6

PARTICULARS OF DEATH.

When died. Year, Day of Month, Hour.	Where died.	Cause of Death, and how long Disease continued. Medical Attendant by whom certified, and when he last saw deceased.	Burial Place. Undertaker by whom certified.	Signature of Informant.	When and where registered, and Signature of Registrar.
January Eighth 4 PM	Wonderhall Musselburgh	Consumption One year as cer[illegible] [illegible] Surgeon Who saw Deceased 7 Jan 1855	Inveresk Churchyard as certified by [illegible] Undertaker	Maria Dudgeon Daughter	1855 January 8th at Musselburgh [illegible] Registrar

Fig. 19 1855 Death Certificate

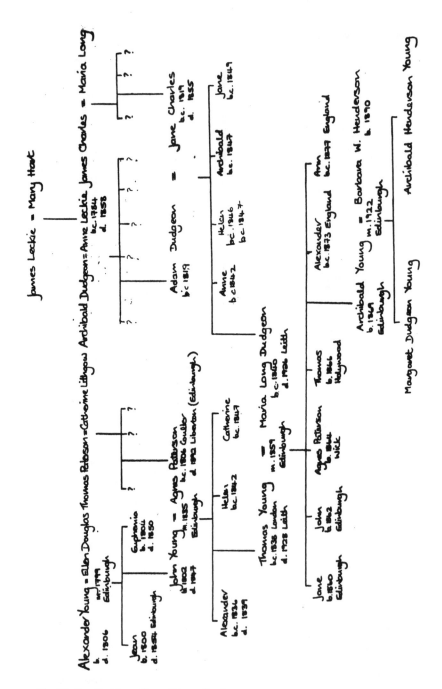

Fig. 20 Family Tree Chart (Drop-line)

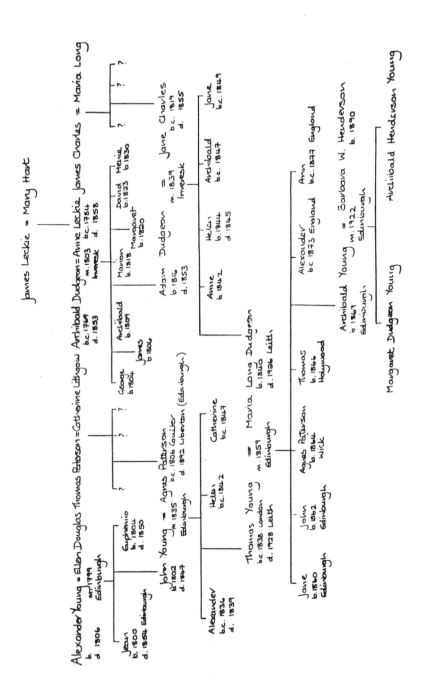

Fig. 21 Family Tree Chart (Drop-line)

Appendix I

Glossary of occupations, terms and contractions found in Scottish records and census returns

ag. lab.	agricultural labourer
agnate	agnates are persons related through the father
allenarly	only (when associated with a life-rent, prevents this from being construed as a fee)
annual rent	interest on money which has been lent
annuit.	annuitant (has yearly fixed sum)
app.	apprentice
B. or Bach.	bachelor
bailie	magistrate in a Scottish burgh
bairn	child
bairn's part of gear	the part of a parent's moveables to which children are entitled on parent's death: one-third when the other parent survives; one-half otherwise
barony	the right of a baron or person holding land directly from the Crown or the land itself
baxter	baker
bigging	building
bond	written obligation to do some act or pay some money
Books of Adjounal	books or records of the Justiciary Court
Books of Council & Session	registers of deeds and probative writs
boll	measure of grain (six bushels)
bro.	brother
burgh	town
c.	*circa* (about); c. 1800 = about 1800
Candlemas	a term-day (2 February)
cautioner	surety; sponsor
cen.	census
cess	land tax
Chelsea P.	Chelsea pensioner (sometimes Chelsea out pensioner)
close	street; alley
cognate	cognates are persons related through the mother
commissariot	court mainly concerned with wills

compear (of a defender)	appear in an action, to appear before the kirtk session for censure
compt.	account
consanguine	a brother or sister is consanguine with another where they have a common father but different mother
cordiner/ cordwainer	shoemaker
courtesy	the life-rent enjoyed by a widower of the heritage of his late wife
croft	smallholding
cur. or curr.	current; now
curator	person appointed to administer the estate of another as in the case of a minor
D. or dau. or daur.	daughter
dead's part of gear	the part of his moveable estate that a man can leave in his will
dispone	to assign, make over or grant
dissenter	non-conformist
Ditto, Do.	a repeat of what was previously written
dom.	domicile
dom. servt.	domestic servant
Edin.	Edinburgh
eik	an addition
emp.	employing; employed
eodem die	same day
F.	father
factor	strictly speaking, someone appointed to act for a person in a particular capacity, but more usually an estate manager
factory	a deed where A allows B to act for him as his factor, particularly in the management of an estate
Fasti	*Fasti Ecclesiae Scoticanae*: Brief biographies of ministers in the Church of Scotland from the Reformation
fee	full right of property in heritage; wage-agreement for employment on farm
feu duty	a perpetual lease; annual payment for use of ground; abolished 1974 by land tenure reform
fiar	owner of a fee
fiars	prices of grain
filiation	determination of the paternity of a child, usually illegitimate
flesher	butcher
flitting	moving house
F.S.	female servant
General Assembly	the highest court in the Church of Scotland or the Free Church of Scotland
grieve	farm overseer
guid	good

guidsire or gudesir	grandfather
gutcher or gowcher etc.	grandfather, a relation, cousin
H.	head of household
haill	all, the whole of
heirs portion-ers	women succeeding to heritage jointly where there are no male heirs
H.L.W.	hand loom weaver
horning	the charging of a debtor to pay
Ilk	same (name, place or landed estate, particularly in 'of that Ilk' used after a surname; e.g., 'Dalziel of that Ilk' means that his name and his lands were both Dalziel)
illeg.	illegitimate
ind.	independent (of independent means)
indweller	inhabitant; resident
inf.	infant; informant
infeftment	a man was infeft when put into possession of heritable property
inst.	instant; this month or week
interregnum	time between; between reigns of kings and queens, but mainly found as time between departure of one minister and the appointment of the next
inventory	list of deceased's moveable goods
J./Jour.	journeyman; the stage between being apprentice and a master of a trade
Justiciary, High Court of	the supreme criminal court of Scotland
kin/kindred	relations
kye	cattle, cows
L.	lawful; e.g., l.s. or l.d. = lawful son or lawful daughter
lab.	labourer
Lady Day	a term-day (25 March) when contracts were made and terminated
laigh	low
lair	a grave; a burial plot in a graveyard
laird	a landowner
Lammas	a term-day (1 August)
litster	a dyer
Lord Lyon King of Arms	the principal administrative officer (also a judge), in Scottish heraldic matters
M. or mar.	married
m. or min.	a miner; a minister
mail	rent
major	a person of full legal age

Mark or Merk	an old Scottish coin
Martinmas	a term-day (11 November)
Michaelmas	a term-day (29 September)
minor	a young person between the ages of 12 and 21 if a girl, or between 14 and 21 if a boy
monie	many
mort-cloth	the pall carried over the coffin at a funeral
mortification	a bequest of property, usually for charitable purposes
moveable estate	property which is not heritable, and which passes to the next-of-kin
mournings	mourning clothes to which a widow has legal rights out of her husband's estate
moyr	mother
M.S.	maiden surname; Merchant Service (merchant navy); male servant
nat.	natural, i.e., illegitimate; a natural son or daughter is an illegitimate son or daughter
nevoy	nephew
o/oe/oi/oy/ oye/oey	grandson or nephew
outwith	outside; beyond
P.	pensioner (usually Army or Navy)
pand or pawn	pledge (usually a sum of money, found in an OPR marriage entry)
panel or pannel	prisoner at the bar
pendicler	an inferior tenant
penny wedding	a wedding at which guests gave money towards the food and drink, any balance being given to the bride and groom
penult.	penultimate, last but one
policies	grounds of a house
portioner	proprietor of a small feu
precept of sasine	a written order for the delivery of land or property
procurator fiscal	public prosecutor in the Sheriff Court
pupil	a child up to the age of 12 for a girl and 14 for a boy
qu-, or quh	wh-
quha	who
quhilk	which
quhytt	white
quoad sacra	as far as concerns sacred matters (of a parish disjoined for ecclesiastical purposes only)
relict	widow
RCE	Register of Corrected Entries

RNE	Register of Neglected Entries
roup	auction
sasine/seisin	a method of investiture in lands, originally involving the
pronounced	giving of earth and/or other symbols, now by registration of
'saysin'	the conveyance itself
Session,	supreme civil court in Scotland
Court of	
sic	reported exactly as found written
sickerly	surely, certainly
sister-bairn	the child of a sister or the child of an aunt; a cousin
steading or	ground on which a house stands
stedding	
superior	a grantor of land to a person who became a vassal in return for perpetual payment of feu-duty
tack	lease
tacksman	holder of a lease; in the Highlands tends to be a tenant of higher class
teind	tithe
tenantry	tenants or land occupied by tenants
testament	will
tutor	guardian of children in pupillarity (see pupil)
ult.	ultimate; last month, week, etc.
umquhile	former, late or deceased
uterine	born of the same mother but of different fathers
vassal	tenant holding land under a lord
wadset	pledge of land with right of recovery by the debtor on payment
Whitsunday	a term-day; 15 May from *c.* 1696
writer	a solicitor
W.S.	Writer to the Signet; a solicitor
yett	gate
yor or yr.	younger
Zetland	Shetland

Appendix II

List of useful addresses

These addresses are arranged under counties, although the counties were superseded by regions in 1975. In most instances you will have been searching in parishes in counties which existed prior to 1975.

Archives, Libraries and Record Offices

Co. Aberdeen

Aberdeen City Archives,
Town House,
Aberdeen AB9 1AQ.

Grampian Regional Archives,
West Aberdeen House,
Dunbar Street,
Aberdeen AB2 1UE.

Co. Argyll

Argyll & Bute District Council Archives,
Kilmory,
Lochgilphead,
Argyll PA31 8RT.

Co. Ayr

Cunninghame District Library,
39-41 Princes Street,
Ardrossan,
Ayrshire KA22 8BT.

Cumnock & Doon Valley District Library,
Bank Glen,
Cumnock KA18 1PH.

Kilmarnock & Loudon District Libraries,
Dick Institute,
14 Elmbank Avenue,
Kilmarnock KA1 3BL.

Kyle and Carrick Council District Library,
12 Main Street,
Ayr KA8 8ED.

Co. Banff

Peterhead Public Library and Museum,
Apply to North East Scotland Library Service,
14 Crown Terrace,
Aberdeen AB9 2BH.

Co. Berwick

Duns Area Library,
Apply to Borders District Library,
St Mary's Mill,
Selkirk, TD7 3EU.

Co. Dunbarton

Dumbarton Branch Library,
Levenford House,
Strathleven Place,
Dumbarton G82 1BD.

Strathkelvin District Libraries,
Reference Department,
William Patrick Memorial Library,
Camphill Avenue,
Kirkintilloch G66 1DW.

Co, Dumfries

Dumfries & Galloway Regional Council Library,
Service (Archives),
Ewart Library,
Catherine Street,
Dumfries DG1 1JB.

Co. Elgin (see Co. Moray)

Co. Fife

Dunfermline District Libraries,
1 Abbot Street,
Dunfermline KY12 7NL.

Kirkcaldy Central Library,
War Memorial Grounds,
Kirkcaldy KY1 1YG.

Methil Public Library,
Wellesley Road,
Methil KY8 3PA.

North East Fife District Library,
County Buildings,
St Catherine's Street,
Cupar KY15 4TM.

Co. Forfar

Angus Libraries and Museums,
County Buildings,
Forfar DD8 3LG.

Arbroath Library,
Hill Terrace,
Arbroath DD11 1AJ.

William Coull Anderson Library of Geneaology,
Dewar House,
Hill Terrace,
Arbroath DD11 1AJ.

Dundee City Central Library,
The Wellgate,
Dundee DD1 1DB.

Dundee City Archives & Records Centre, (for Tayside Region),
14 City Square,
Dundee DD1 3BY.

Co. Inverness

The Library,
Farraline Park,
Inverness IV1 1LS.

Co. Kinross (see Co. Perth)

Co. Lanark

Glasgow District Libraries,
Glasgow Room,
Mitchell Library,
North Street,
Glasgow G3 7DN.

Glasgow City Archives,
Mitchell Library,
North Street,
Glasgow G3 7DN.

Strathclyde Regional Archives,
Mitchell Library,
North Street,
Glasgow G3 7DN.

Hamilton District Libraries,
98 Cadzow Street,
Hamilton ML3 6HQ.

Bearsden & Milngavie District Libraries,
Brookwood,
166 Drymen Road,
Bearsden,
Glasgow G61 3RJ.

Clydesdale District Libraries,
Lindsay Institute,
Hope Street,
Lanark ML11 7NH.

Coatbridge Library,
Academy Street,
Coatbridge, ML5 3AT.

Monklands District Library,
Wellwynd,
Airdrie ML20 A6.

Motherwell District Libraries,
Hamilton Road,
Motherwell ML1 3BZ.

Scottish Jewish Archives Centre,
Garnethill Synagogue,
125–127 Hill Street,
Glasgow.

Co. Linlithgow (see Co. West Lothian)

Co. Midlothian

Scottish Record Office,
Princes Street,
Edinburgh EH1 3YJ.

West Register House,
Charlotte Square,
Edinburgh EH2 4DP.

General Register House (New Register House),
Princes Street,
Edinburgh EH1 3YT.

The Court of the Lord Lyon,
General Register House,
Princes Street,
Edinburgh EH1 3YT.

National Library of Scotland,
George IV Bridge,
Edinburgh EH1 1EW.

National Library of Scotland Map Room,
137 Causewayside,
Edinburgh EH9 1PH.

Edinburgh City Archives,
Department of Administration,
City Chambers,
Edinburgh EH1 1YJ.

Church of Scotland Offices,
121 George Street,
Edinburgh EH2 4JN.

Free Church of Scotland,
Free Church College,
15 North Bank Street,
Edinburgh EH1 2LS.

Episcopal Church in Scotland,
Apply to West Register House,
Charlotte Square,
Edinburgh EH2 4DF.

Scottish Roman Catholic Archives,
Columba House,
16 Drummond Place,
Edinburgh EH3 6PL.

The Royal College of Physicians of Edinburgh,
9 Queen Street,
Edinburgh EH2 1JQ.

The Royal College of Surgeons,
18 Nicolson Street,
Edinburgh EH8 9DW.

Companies House,
Postal Search Section,
100–102 George Street,
Edinburgh EH2 3DJ.

The Scottish Genealogy Society Library,
15 Victoria Terrace,
Edinburgh EH1 2JL.

The Heraldry Society of Scotland,
c/o Stuart G. Emerson (Membership Secretary),
25 Craigentinny Crescent,
Edinburgh EH7 6QA.

Co. Moray

Moray District Record Office,
The Tolbooth,
High Street,
Forres IV36 0AB.

Co. Orkney

Orkney Archive Office,
Orkney Library,
Laing Street,
Kirkwall KW15 1NW.

Co. Peebles

Peebles Area Library,
Apply to Borders Regional Library,
St Mary's Mill,
Selkirk TD7 3EV.

Co. Perth

Perth & Kinross District Council Archives,
Sandeman District Library,
16 Kinnoul Street,
Perth PH1 5ET.

Co. Renfrew

Eastwood District Libraries,
Council Offices,
Eastwood Park,
Rouken Glen Road,
Giffnock,
Glasgow G46 6UG.

Inverclyde District Libraries,
Watt Memorial Library,
9 Union Street,
Greenock PA16 17JH.

Renfrew District Council Library & Archive Service,
High Street,
Paisley PA1 2BB.

Co. Ross & Cromarty

Western Isles Library,
2 Keith Street,
Stornoway,
Isle of Lewis PA87 2QG.

Co. Roxburgh

Hawick Library,
Apply to Borders Regional Library,
St Mary's Mill,
Selkirk TD7 3EV.

Kelso Branch Library,
Apply to Borders Regional Library,
St Mary's Mill,
Selkirk TD7 3EV.

Co. Selkirk

Galashiels Area Library,
Apply to Borders Regional Library,
St Mary's Mill,
Selkirk TD7 3EV.

Co. Shetland

Shetland Archives,
44 King Harald Street,
Lerwick ZE1 0EQ,
Shetland.

Co. West Lothian

West Lothian District Libraries,
Wellpark,
66 Marjoriebanks Street,
Bathgate EH48 1AN.

Co. Wigtown

Stranraer Branch Library,
London Road,
Stranraer DG9 8ES.

University Archives

Aberdeen University Library,
Manuscript and Archive Section,
King's College,
Aberdeen AB9 2UB.

Dundee University Library,
Archives and Manuscript Department,
Dundee DD1 4HN.

Edinburgh University Library,
Department of Manuscripts,
30 George Square,
Edinburgh EH8 9LJ.

Glasgow University Archives,
The University,
Glasgow G12 8QQ.

St Andrews University Archives,
North Street,
St Andrews KY16 9TR.

Strathclyde University Archives,
Livingstone Tower,
26 Richmond Street,
Glasgow G1 1HX.

The Scottish Federation of Family History Societies

The Scottish Association of Family History Societies was formed in October 1986 to co-ordinate the promotion of family history in Scotland.

The Secretary of the Scottish Association of Family History Societies is:

Miss Lillian Malcolm,
4 Loftus Road,
Downfield,
Dundee DD1 9TE

Addresses of societies:

Aberdeen & N.E. Scotland FHS
General Secretary,
Family History Shop,
152 King Street,
Aberdeen AB2 3BD.

Anglo-Scottish FHS
Miss P. Connor,
Honorary Secretary,
2 Beech Street,
Salford M6 5FT.

Borders FHS
Mr P. Ruthven-Murray,
Honorary Secretary,
Springhill,
Broadmeadows,
Yarrowford,
Nr. Selkirk TD7 5LZ.

Dumfries & Galloway FHS
Mrs B. Watson,
Honorary Secretary,
Kylelea,
Corsock,
Castle Douglas,
Kirkcudbright DG7 3DN.

Fife FHS
Mr D. Reid,
Chairman,
Forbes House,
Causeway,
Kennoway,
Fife KY8 5JU.

Glasgow & West of Scotland FHS
Mr J. P. Patrick,
Honorary Secretary,
11 Gartcows Crescent,
Falkirk FK1 5QH.

Guild of One-Name Studies
Box G,
14 Charterhouse Buildings,
Goswell Road,
London EC1M 7BA.

Highland FHS
Honorary Secretary,
c/o Reference Room,
Public Library,
Farraline,
Inverness IV1 1LS.

Largs & District FHS Group
Mrs M. Alexander,
Honorary Secretary,
3 Hawkshill Drive,
Largs KA30 9PD.

Scottish Genealogy Society
Miss J. P. S. Ferguson,
Honorary Secretary,
21 Howard Place,
Edinburgh EH3 5JY.

Tay Valley FHS
Mrs A. Lawson,
Honorary Secretary,
5 McDonald Street,
Dundee DD3 7BD.

Troon & District FHS
Miss P. McCaig,
Honorary Secretary,
37 South Beach,
Troon,
Ayrshire KA10 6EF.

Addresses in Northern Ireland

North of Ireland FHS
Queen's University,
Teachers' Centre,
Upper Crescent,
Belfast BT7 1NT.

Ulster Genealogy & History Guild
Honorary Secretary,
Mrs S. Clarke,
66 Balmoral Avenue,
Belfast BT9 6NT.

Addresses in England

Department of Social Security,
Records Branch,
Special Section 'A',
Records 'B',
Newcastle upon Tyne NE98 1YU.

The Public Record Office,
Ruskin Avenue,
Kew,
Richmond,
Surrey TW9 4DU.

The Society of Genealogists,
14 Charterhouse Buildings,
Goswell Road,
London EC1M 7BA.

Appendix III

List of Parishes, Counties and Commissariots

This list is arranged in alphabetical order showing the district number and the date of the earliest birth or marriage record extant for that parish to be found in an Old Parish Register. In some instances the place listed has no OPR, being a District under the Registration Act. Where these places are incorporated in a parish, the number of the parish is shown, otherwise the numbers shown are those of parishes which would be worth searching. In some parishes the records for the early years are sparse.

This list also shows the county and the commissariot as an aid to finding testaments or inventories. Where possible, the earliest date of the testament or inventory is listed. In some cases the places mentioned were not found in a gazetteer and so it was not possible to assign them to any particular parish. From 1823, testaments and inventories are to be found in Sheriff Court Records. These have not been consulted for this list.

The Scottish Record Society has produced indexes to testaments and inventories arranged by commissariot and person's name. Some parishes may be found in more than one commissariot.

N.B. County Forfar = County Angus;
County Moray = County Elgin.

Parish	District number	County	Commissariot	OPR	Testament or inventory
Abbey (*or Abbey Paisley*)	559	Renfrew	Glasgow	1676	1552
Abbey St Bathans	726	Berwick	Lauder	1715	1709
Abbotrule (*also Southdean 806*)	806	Roxburgh	Peebles Dumfries	1755	1682 1736
Abbotshall (*incl. Kirkcaldy in 1876*)	399	Fife	St Andrews	1650	1615
Abdie	400	Fife	St Andrews Edinburgh	1620	1549 1597
Abercorn	661	Linlithgow W. Lothian	Dunkeld Edinburgh	1585	1735 1576
Abercrombie (*see St Monance 454*)	454	Fife	St Andrews Edinburgh		1551 1585
Aberdalgie	323	Perth	Dunkeld Dunblane Edinburgh St Andrews	1615	1688 1654 1575 1662
Aberdeen	168a	Aberdeen	Aberdeen Edinburgh	1563	1715 1600
Aberdour	169	Aberdeen	Aberdeen Edinburgh	1698	1722 1564
Aberdour	401	Fife	Dunkeld St Andrews Edinburgh	1663	1682 1656 1564
Aberfeldy (*see Dull, 346 & Logierait, 376*)	324	Perth	Dunkeld		1697
Aberfoyle	325	Perth	Dunblane	1692	1661
Aberlady	702	Haddington E. Lothian	Dunkeld Edinburgh	1632	1570
Aberlemno	269	Forfar	St Andrews Edinburgh	1706	1606 1598
Aberlour (*also Glenrinnes 155b*)	145	Banff	Moray Edinburgh	1708	1685 1599
Aberluthnot (*see Marykirk 265*)	265	Kincardine	St Andrews Edinburgh		1597 1577
Abernethy	326	Perth	Dunblane Edinburgh St Andrews	1690	1539 1584 1607
Abernethy & Kincardine	90a	Inverness	Inverness Moray	1730	1631 1699
Abernyte	327	Perth	Dunkeld Dunblane	1667	1701 1655
Abertarff or Fort Augustus (*also Boleskine 92/1*)	92/2	Inverness	Inverness	1737	1630
Aboyne	170	Aberdeen	Aberdeen Moray	1752	1743 1738
Acharacle (*also Arisaig, Sunart/Strontian & W. Ardnamurchan 505*)	505/1	Argyll	Argyll	1829	
Advie (*see Cromdale, Inverallan & Advie 128b*)	128b	Moray	Moray Edinburgh		1594

Parish	District number	County	Commissariot	OPR	Testament or inventory
Airlie	270	Forfar	St Andrews	1682	1598
			Edinburgh		1576
Airth	469	Stirling	Stirling	1660	1608
			Edinburgh		1585
Aithsting	9	Shetland	Orkney &		1613
(see Sandsting & Aithsting 9)			Shetland		
Alford	171	Aberdeen	Aberdeen	1717	1742
			Moray		1747
Alloa	465	Clackmannan	Stirling	1609	1615
			Glasgow		1604
			Dunblane		1547
			Edinburgh		1586
Alness	57	Ross & Cromarty	Ross	1783	1803
Alva	470	Stirling	Stirling	1655	1665
		c. 1600–1832	Edinburgh		1593
		otherwise Co. Clackmannan			
Alvah	146	Banff	Aberdeen	1718	
Alves	125	Moray	Moray	1648	1688
			Ross		1803
			Edinburgh		1586
Alvie	90b	Inverness	Inverness	1713	1820
Alyth	328	Perth	Dunkeld	1623	1688
			Dunblane		1653
			Edinburgh		1583
			Stirling		1608
Ancrum	780	Roxburgh	Peebles	1703	1682
			Edinburgh		1574
Annan	812	Dumfries	Dumfries	1703	1638
Anstruther-Easter	402	Fife	St Andrews	1641	1550
			Edinburgh		1575
Anstruther-Wester	403	Fife	St Andrews	1577	1550
			Edinburgh		1567
Anwoth	855	Kirkcudbright	Kirkcudbright	1727	1667
			Edinburgh		1600
Appin	525/2	Argyll	Argyll	1751	1677
(also Lismore 525/1, Glencoe & Ballachulish 525/3, Duror 525/4)					
Applecross	58	(see Shieldaig & Kishorn 58)			
Applegarth & Sibbaldie	813a	Dumfries	Dumfries	1749	1639
Arbirlot	271	Forfar	St Andrews	1632	1583
			Edinburgh		1595
Arbroath	272	Forfar	St Andrews	1653	1591
(anciently Aberbrothock)			Brechin		1657
			Edinburgh		1592
Arbuthnot	250	Kincardine	St Andrews	1631	1605
			Brechin		1657
			Edinburgh		1582
Ardchattan	504	Argyll	Argyll	1758	1677
Ardclach	120	Nairn	Moray	1652	1688
Ardersier	91	Inverness	Inverness	1719	

Parish	District number	County	Commissariot	OPR	Testament or inventory
Ardgour, Corran of & Ballachulish *(also Kilmalie 520)*	506	Argyll	Argyll	1835	
Ardnamurchan *(also Aharacle, Arisaig, Sunart/Strontian 505)*	505/4	Argyll	Argyll	1777	1686
Ardrossan	576	Ayr	Glasgow	1734	1603
Arisaig *(as above)*	505/2	Argyll	Argyll		
Arngask	404	Fife	Dunkeld	1688	1728
	part	Kinross	Edinburgh		1595
	part	Perth	St Andrews		1551
Arrochar	492	Dunbarton	Glasgow	1759	1720
Ashkirk	781	Roxburgh	Peebles	1630	1823
Assynt *(also known as Inchnadamff)*	44	Sutherland	Caithness	1798	
Athelstaneford	703	Haddington E. Lothian	Edinburgh	1664	1581
Auchindoir & Kearn *(prior to 1811 Kearn was united with Forbes: see Tullynessle & Forbes 246)*	172	Aberdeen	Aberdeen	1694	
Auchinleck	577	Ayr	Glasgow	1693	1571
			Brechin		1671
			Hamilton & Campsie		1574
			Dumfries		1626
			Edinburgh		1577
Auchterarder	329	Perth	Dunblane	1661	1602
			Dunkeld		1714
			Edinburgh		1589
Auchterderran	405	Fife	St Andrews	1664	1613
			Edinburgh		1594
Auchtergaven	330	Perth	Dunkeld	1741	1688
			Edinburgh		1570
			Dunblane		1658
Auchterhouse	273	Forfar	Dunkeld	1645	1695
			Brechin		1657
Auchterless	173	Aberdeen	Aberdeen	1680	1723
Auchtermuchty	406	Fife	St Andrews	1649	1550
			Edinburgh		1577
Auchtertool	407	Fife	St Andrews	1708	1656
			Edinburgh		1568
Auldearn	121	Nairn	Moray	1687	1695
			Edinburgh		1583
Avoch	59	Ross & Cromarty	Ross	1727	1804
			Edinburgh		1596
Avondale	621	Lanark	Glasgow	1698	1603
			Edinburgh		1576
Ayr	578	Ayr	Glasgow	1664	1547
			Edinburgh		1569
Ayton	727	Berwick	Lauder	1743	1564
			Edinburgh		1582
Baldernock	471	Stirling	Hamilton & Campsie also Glasgow	1624	1612
			Stirling (1649–1660)		1656
			Edinburgh		1582

Parish	District number	County	Commissariot	OPR	Testament or inventory
Balfron	472	Stirling	Glasgow	1687	1617
			Stirling		1654
Ballachulish &	506	Argyll	Argyll	1830	
Corran of Ardgour *(also Kilmallie 520)*					
Ballachulish	525/3	*(see Glencoe & Ballachulish 525/3)*			
Ballantrae	579	Ayr	Glasgow	1731	1617
Ballingry	408	Fife	St Andrews	1670	1597
			Edinburgh		1597
Balmaclellan	856	Kirkcudbright	Kirkcudbright	1747	1675
			Edinburgh		1583
Balmaghie	857a	Kirkcudbright	Kirkcudbright	1768	1707
			Edinburgh		1575
Balmerino	409	Fife	St Andrews	1632	1587
			Edinburgh		1573
Balquhidder	331	Perth	Dunblane	1696	1622
Banchory-	251	Kincardine	Aberdeen	1713	1727
Devenick			Edinburgh		1588
Banchory-	252	Kincardine	Aberdeen	1670	1728
Ternan			Edinburgh		1588
Banff	147	Banff	Aberdeen	1620	1722
Bannockburn	488	Stirling	Stirling		1607
(see St Ninians & Bannockburn 488)			Edinburgh		1589
Bargrennan	857b	Wigtown	Wigtown		
(see Minnigaff 876 & Penninghame 895)					
Barony	622	Lanark	Glasgow	1672	1603
(also Glasgow 644[1], Gorbals 644[2] & Govan 646)			Hamilton & Campsie		1676
Barr	580	Ayr	Glasgow	1689	1661
Barra	108	Inverness	The Isles	1836	
			Aberdeen		1816
Barry	274	Forfar	St Andrews	1704	1591
			Edinburgh		1583
Barvas (Lewis)	86a	Ross & Cromarty	The Isles	1810	
Bathgate	662	Linlithgow W. Lothian	Edinburgh	1672	1568
Beath	410	Fife	St Andrews	1643	1650
Bedrule	782	Roxburgh	Peebles	1690	1682
Beith	581	Ayr	Glasgow	1661	1605
			Edinburgh		1582
Belhelvie	174	Aberdeen	Aberdeen	1624	1727
Bellie	126	Moray	Moray	1709	1687
Benbecula	118	Inverness	The Isles	1848	1815
(also S. Uist 118)					
Bendochy	332	Perth	St Andrews	1642	
			Dunkeld		1766
			Dunblane		1653
			Edinburgh		1587
Benholm	253	Kincardine	St Andrews	1684	1614
			Edinburgh		1565

Parish	District number	County	Commissariot	OPR	Testament or inventory
Benvie	301	Forfar	St Andrews	1655	
			Edinburgh		1579
Bervie	254	Kincardine	St Andrews	1698	1681
(or Inverbervie)			Brechin		1657
			Edinburgh		1585
Berwick North					
(see North Berwick 713)					
Biggar	623	Lanark	Lanark	1730	1621
			Edinburgh		1577
Birnie	127	Moray	Moray	1712	1688
Birsay	13	Orkney	Orkney & Shetland	1645	1612
Birse	175	Aberdeen	Aberdeen	1758	1726
Blackford	333	Perth	Dunblane	1738	1612
Blair Atholl	334	Perth	Dunkeld	1718	1688
& Strowan (also Tenandry 394c)			Dunblane		1654
Blairgowrie	335	Perth	St Andrews	1647	1591
(also Persie 386b)			Dunblane		1653
			Edinburgh		1583
Blantyre	624	Lanark	Glasgow	1677	1618
			Edinburgh		1586
Boharm	128a	Banff	Moray	1634	1686
Boleskine	92/1	Inverness	Inverness	1777	1630
(also Abertarff or Fort Augustus 92/2)					
Bolton	704	Haddington E. Lothian	Edinburgh	1686	1584
Bonhill	493	Dunbarton	Glasgow	1676	1606
			Edinburgh		1594
Borgue	858	Kirkcudbright	Kirkcudbright	1742	1682
			Edinburgh		1587
Bo'ness	663	Linlithgow W. Lothian	Edinburgh	1656	1575
(Borrowstounness)					
Borthwick	674	Edinburgh Midlothian	Edinburgh	1706	1583
(also Stobhill 689b)					
Bothkennar	473	Stirling	Stirling	1723	1608
			Edinburgh		1569
Bothwell	625	Lanark	Glasgow	1671	1547
			Edinburgh		1578
Botriphnie	148	Banff	Moray	1683	1686
Bourtie	176	Aberdeen	Aberdeen	1709	1728
			Edinburgh		1594
Bowden	783	Roxburgh	Peebles	1697	1693
Bower	34	Caithness	Caithness	1740	1663
Bowmore	536	Argyll	The Isles	1763	1726
(or Kilarrow)					
Boyndie	149	Banff	Aberdeen	1700	1741
Bracadale (Skye)	109	Inverness	The Isles	1802	1785
Braemar & Crathie	183	Aberdeen	Aberdeen	1771	1783
Brechin	275	Forfar	Brechin	1612	1578
			Edinburgh		1569

Parish	District number	County	Commissariot	OPR	Testament or inventory
Bressay *(also Burra & Quarff 1/2)*	1/1	Shetland	Orkney & Shetland	1737	1613
Bridekirk *(see Brydekirk 813b)*					
Broughton *(also Kilbucho 763 & Glenholm 761)*	758	Peebles	Peebles Edinburgh	1697	1584
Brydekirk *(also Annan 812, Cummertrees 817 & Hoddam 829)*	813b	Dumfries	Dumfries	1836	
Buchanan	474	Stirling	Glasgow	1646	1614
Buittle	859	Kirkcudbright	Kirkcudbright Edinburgh	1736	1710 1572
Bunkle & Preston	728	Berwick	Lauder Edinburgh	1704	1655 1578
Burness & Lady *(also Sanday 26)*	26	Orkney	Orkney & Shetland	1758	1615
Burntisland	411	Fife	St Andrews Edinburgh	1672	1589 1575
Burra & Quarff *(also Bressay 1/1)*	1/2	Shetland	Orkney & Shetland	1755	
Burray *(also S. Ronaldsay 29)*	29	Orkney	Orkney & Shetland	1657	1624
Cabrach	177	Aberdeen	Aberdeen	1711	1812
Cadder	626	Lanark	Hamilton & Campsie also Glasgow Edinburgh	1662	1564 1587
Caddonfoot *(see Stow 699 & Galashiels 775)*					
Caerlaverock	815	Dumfries	Dumfries	1749	1638
Cairney	178	Aberdeen	Aberdeen Moray	1738	1717
Calder, East *(also Kirknewton & East Calder 690)*	690	Edinburgh Midlothian	Edinburgh	1642	1567
Calder, Mid *(see Mid Calder 694)*	694				
Calder, West *(see West Calder 701)*	701				
Callander	336	Perth	Dunblane Dunkeld	1710	1543 1706
Cambuslang	627	Lanark	Glasgow Edinburgh	1657	1604 1582
Cambusnethan	628	Lanark	Glasgow Lanark Edinburgh	1634	1552 1626 1578
Cameron *(disjoined from St Andrews 1645)*	412	Fife	St Andrews	1695	1649
Campbeltown	507	Argyll	Argyll Kincardine Glasgow	1659	1676 1722 1608

Parish	District number	County	Commissariot	OPR	Testament or inventory
Campsie	475	Stirling	Hamilton & Campsie	1646	1564
			Dunkeld		1769
			Dunblane		1653
			Stirling (1649–1660)		1653
			Edinburgh		1581
			Glasgow		1625
Canisbay	35	Caithness	Caithness	1652	1664
Canonbie	814	Dumfries	Dumfries	1693	1676
Canongate	685³	Edinburgh Midlothian	Edinburgh	1564	1568
(also Edinburgh 685¹ and St Cuthbert's 685²)					
Canna	116	Inverness	Small Isles	1855	1717
(also Small Isles 116)					
Caputh	337	Perth	Dunkeld	1670	1688
			Dunblane		1653
			Edinburgh		1581
Cardross	494	Dunbarton	Hamilton & Campsie	1681	1564
			Dunblane		1617
			Glasgow		1655
			Edinburgh		1592
Careston	277	Forfar	Brechin	1714	1600
Cargill	338	Perth	Dunkeld	1652	1690
			Dunblane		1652
			Edinburgh		1582
Carlaverock	815				
(see Caerlaverock 815)					
Carloway	86b				
(see Barvas 86a & Lochs 87)					
Carluke	629	Lanark	Lanark	1690	1620
			Edinburgh		1586
Carmichael	630	Lanark	Lanark	1695	1599
Carmunnock	631	Lanark	Glasgow	1654	1607
Carmyllie	276	Forfar	Brechin	1684	1610
			St Andrews		1615
Carnbee	413	Fife	St Andrews	1646	1550
			Edinburgh		1565
Carnock	414	Fife	Stirling	1652	1641
			St Andrews		1591
			Edinburgh		1599
Carnwath	632	Lanark	Lanark	1709	1601
			Edinburgh		1577
Carriden	664	Linlithgow W. Lothian	Edinburgh	1687	1583
			St Andrews		1617
Carrington or Primrose	675	Edinburgh Midlothian	Edinburgh	1653	1596
Carsphairn	860	Kirkcudbright	Kirkcudbright	1758	1674
Carstairs	633	Lanark	Lanark	1672	1596
			Hamilton & Campsie		1564
			Edinburgh		1584

Parish	District number	County	Commissariot	OPR	Testament or inventory
Castleton	784	Roxburgh	Peebles	1749	1770
			Kirkcudbright		1680
Cathcart	560 part	Renfrew Lanark	Hamilton & Campsie	1701	1620
			Glasgow		1550
			Edinburgh		1572
Catterline	262	Kincardine	St Andrews		1605
(see Kinneff & Catterline 262)			Brechin		1623
			Edinburgh		1597
Cavers	785	Roxburgh	Peebles	1694	1685
Cawdor	122	Nairn	Moray	1716	1791
Ceres	415	Fife	St Andrews	1620	1550
			Edinburgh		1580
Channelkirk	729	Berwick	Lauder	1651	1561
			Edinburgh		1575
Chapel of Garioch	179	Aberdeen	Aberdeen	1763	1823
Chirnside	730	Berwick	Lauder	1660	1636
			Edinburgh		1583
Clackmannan	466	Clackmannan	Stirling	1595	1610
			Edinburgh		1577
Clatt	180	Aberdeen	Aberdeen	1680	1739
Cleish	460	Kinross	St Andrews	1700	1597
			Edinburgh		1597
Closeburn	816	Dumfries	Dumfries	1765	1642
Clova	278	Forfar	Brechin	1697	1681
(also Cortachy 278)			St Andrews		1595
Clunie	339	Perth	Dunkeld	1702	1688
			Dunblane		1653
			Edinburgh		1583
Cluny	181	Aberdeen	Aberdeen	1751	1729
Clyne	45	Sutherland	Caithness	1782	
			Inverness		1784
Cockburnspath	731	Berwick	Lauder	1642	1641
			Edinburgh		1580
Cockpen	676	Edinburgh	Edinburgh	1690	
(also Stobhill 698b)		Midlothian			
Coldingham	732	Berwick	Lauder	1690	1628
			Lanark		1683
			Edinburgh		1578
Coldstream	733	Berwick	Lauder	1690	1653
(formerly Lennel)			Edinburgh		1573
Colinton	677	Edinburgh	Edinburgh	1654	1578
or Hailes		Midlothian			
Coll	551/2	Argyll	The Isles	1776	1772
(also Tyree 551/1)					
Collace	340	Perth	St Andrews	1713	1584
			Dunkeld		1781
			Edinburgh		1597
Collessie	416	Fife	St Andrews	1696	1550
			Edinburgh		1583

Parish	District number	County	Commissariot	OPR	Testament or inventory
Colmonell	582	Ayr	Glasgow	1759	1607
			Edinburgh		1677
Colonsay (*also Jura 539/1*)	539/2	Argyll	The Isles	1796	1776
Colvend (*incl. Southwick*)	861	Kirkcudbright	Dumfries	1781	1639
			Edinburgh		1582
Comrie	341	Perth	Dunblane	1693	1543
			Edinburgh		1569
Contin	60	Ross & Cromarty	Ross	1778	
Conveth (*see Laurencekirk 263*)	263	Kincardine	St Andrews		1606
			Edinburgh		1580
			Inverness		1632
Corgarff (*see Strathdon 240*)	240				
Corran of Ardgour (*also Ballachulish 506*)	506	Argyll	Argyll	1835	
Corrie (*see Hutton & Corrie 831*)	831	Dumfries	Dumfries		1661
Corsock-Bridge (*see Parton 878*)	862	Kirkcudbright	Kirkcudbright		1679
Corstorphine	678	Edinburgh Midlothian	Edinburgh	1634	1564
Cortachy (*also Clova 278*)	278	Forfar	Brechin	1662	1610
Coull	182	Aberdeen	Aberdeen	1752	
Coupar-Angus	279 part	Perth Forfar	Dunkeld Dunblane Edinburgh	1683	1696 1653 1588
Covington & Thankerton	634	Lanark	Lanark	1772	1621
Coylton	583	Ayr	Glasgow	1723	1759
Craig (*anciently Inchbrayock*)	280	Forfar	St Andrews Edinburgh	1657	1615 1591
Craigie	584	Ayr	Glasgow Brechin Edinburgh	1679	1606 1583 1571
Craignish	508	Argyll	Argyll	1755	1676
Crail	417	Fife	St Andrews Edinburgh	1684	1549 1565
Crailing	786	Roxburgh	Peebles	1708	1681
Cramond	679	Edinburgh	Edinburgh	1651	1574
Cranshaws (*also Longformacus 750*)	734	Berwick	Lauder	1731	1636
Cranston	680	Edinburgh Midlothian	Edinburgh Lauder	1682	1578 1679
Crathie & Braemar	183	Aberdeen	Aberdeen	1717	1751
Crawford (*incl. Leadhills*)	635	Lanark	Lanark	1741	1626
Crawfordjohn	636	Lanark	Lanark Edinburgh Glasgow	1694	1601 1583 1550

Parish	District number	County	Commissariot	OPR	Testament or inventory
Creich	46	Sutherland	Caithness Sutherland	1785	1821
Creich	418	Fife	St Andrews Edinburgh	1695	1550 1578
Crichton	681	Edinburgh Midlothian	Edinburgh	1682	1580
Crieff	342	Perth	Dunkeld Dunblane Edinburgh	1692	1695 1653 1586
Crimond	184	Aberdeen	Aberdeen	1743	1754
Cromarty	61	Ross & Cromarty	Ross Edinburgh	1675	1803 1594
Cromdale, Inverallan & Advie	128b	Moray	Moray Edinburgh	1702	1712 1590
Cross, Burness & Lady (*also Sanday 26*)	26	Orkney	Orkney & Shetland	1758	1615
Crossmichael	863	Kirkcudbright	Kirkcudbright Edinburgh	1751	1679 1576
Croy & Dalcross	94	Inverness	Inverness	1719	1630
Cruden	185	Aberdeen	Aberdeen	1707	1723
Cullen	150	Banff	Aberdeen	1668	1722
Cullicudden (*also Resolis 79*)	79				
Culross	343	Perth	Dunblane Edinburgh	1641	1543 1569
Culsamond	186	Aberdeen	Aberdeen	1735	1733
Culter	637	Lanark	Lanark Edinburgh	1700	1621 1597
Cults	419	Fife	St Andrews Edinburgh	1693	1550 1586
Cumbernauld	495	Dunbarton	Glasgow	1688	1765
Cumbraes	552	Bute	The Isles	1730	
Cumlodden (*see Glassary 511 & Inveraray 513*)	509				
Cummertrees	817	Dumfries	Dumfries	1753	1624
Cumnock, New (*see New Cumnock 608*)	608				
Cumnock, Old (*see Old Cumnock 610*)	610				
Cunningsburgh (*also Dunrossness 3/1, Sandwick 3/2 & Fair Isle 3/4*)	3/2	Shetland	Orkney & Shetland	1746	
Cupar	420	Fife	St Andrews Edinburgh	1654	1549 1567
Currie	682	Edinburgh Midlothian	Edinburgh	1638	1576
Dailly	585	Ayr	Glasgow Edinburgh	1691	1607 1582
Dairsie	421	Fife	St Andrews Edinburgh	1645	1550 1581

Parish	District number	County	Commissariot	OPR	Testament or inventory
Dalarossie *(see Moy & Dalarossie 105)*	105	Inverness	Inverness		1633
Dalavich *(see Kilcrechan & Dalavich 517)*	517	Argyll	Argyll		1676
Dalbeattie *(see Urr 884)*	864	Kirkcudbright	Kirkcudbright Dumfries		1685
Dalcross *(also Croy & Dalcross 94)*	94	Inverness	Inverness	1747	1666
Dalgain *(see Sorn 613)*	613	Ayr	Glasgow		1668
Dalgety	422	Fife	St Andrews Edinburgh	1644	1655 1570
Dalkeith	683	Edinburgh Midlothian	Edinburgh	1609	1564
Dallas	129	Moray	Moray	1742	1684
Dalmellington	586	Ayr	Glasgow Edinburgh	1641	1609 1578
Dalmeny *(pre 1636 Queensferry)*	665	Linlithgow W. Lothian	Edinburgh	1679	1568
Dalry	587	Ayr	Glasgow Edinburgh	1680	1605 1584
Dalry	865	Kirkcudbright	Kirkcudbright Edinburgh	1691	1677 1575
Dalrymple	588	Ayr	Glasgow	1699	1610
Dalserf	638	Lanark	Hamilton & Campsie Edinburgh Glasgow	1738	1564 1589 1654
Dalton	810	Dumfries	Dumfries Edinburgh Glasgow	1723	1581 1795
Dalziel	639	Lanark	Glasgow Hamilton & Campsie Edinburgh	1648	1612 1578
Daviot	187	Aberdeen	Aberdeen	1723	1630
Daviot & Dunlichty	95	Inverness	Inverness	1774	1630
Deerness	14	Orkney	Orkney & Shetland	1754	1612
Delting	2	Shetland	Orkney & Shetland	1751	1613
Denny	476	Stirling	Stirling	1679	1612
Deskford	151	Banff	Aberdeen	1660	1730
Dingwall	62	Ross & Cromarty	Ross Edinburgh	1662	1805 1591
Dipple *(see Speymouth 143)*	143	Moray	Moray Edinburgh		1592
Dirleton	705	Haddington E. Lothian	Edinburgh	1664	1575

Parish	District number	County	Commissariot	OPR	Testament or inventory
Dollar	467	Clackmannan	Stirling	1701	1610
			Edinburgh		1581
Dolphinton	640	Lanark	Lanark	1717	1624
Dores	96a	Inverness	Inverness	1734	1723
Dornoch	47	Sutherland	Caithness	1730	1817
			Edinburgh		1599
Dornock	819	Dumfries	Dumfries	1773	1658
Douglas	641	Lanark	Lanark	1691	1597
			Glasgow		1608
			Edinburgh		1583
Dowally	344	Perth	Dunkeld	1705	1690
			Dunblane		1653
			Edinburgh		1590
Down	155a	Banff	Aberdeen		1769
(see Gamrie 155a)					
Drainie	130	Moray	Moray	1631	1789
(formerly Kineddar 130)					
Dreghorn	589	Ayr	Glasgow	1749	1603
			Edinburgh		1577
Dron	345	Perth	Dunblane	1682	1616
			Edinburgh		1589
			St Andrews		1641
Drumblade	188	Aberdeen	Aberdeen	1702	1740
Drumelzier	759	Peebles	Peebles	1649	1823
			Edinburgh		1573
Drumoak	189	Aberdeen	Aberdeen	1692	1724
Dryfesdale	820	Dumfries	Dumfries	1732	1630
Drymen	477	Stirling	Glasgow	1672	1610
			Stirling		1654
			Dunblane		1621
			Edinburgh		1589
Duddingston	684	Edinburgh Midlothian	Edinburgh	1631	1575
Duffus	131	Moray	Moray	1629	1684
Duirinish	110	Inverness	The Isles	1817	1715
Dull	346	Perth	Dunkeld	1703	1688
(also Foss 355b & Tenandry 394c)			Dunblane		1656
			Edinburgh		1592
Dumbarton	496	Dunbarton	Glasgow	1666	1603
			Edinburgh		1594
Dumbennan	202	Aberdeen	Aberdeen		1680
(see Huntly 202)			Edinburgh		1588
Dumfries	821	Dumfries	Dumfries	1605	1625
			Edinburgh		1568
Dun	281	Forfar	St Andrews	1642	1587
			Edinburgh		1579
Dunbar	706	Haddington E. Lothian	Edinburgh	1672	1564
Dunbarney	347	Perth	St Andrews	1594	1593
			Dunblane		1655
			Edinburgh		1586

Parish	District number	County	Commissariot	OPR	Testament or inventory
Dunblane	348	Perth	Dunblane	1658	1539
			Edinburgh		1574
Dunbog	423	Fife	St Andrews	1695	1549
			Edinburgh		1596
Dundee	282	Forfar	Brechin	1645	1578
			Edinburgh		1567
			St Andrews		1584
Dundonald	590	Ayr	Glasgow	1673	1603
			Edinburgh		1576
Dundurcas	141	Moray	Moray	1698	1696
(also Rothes 141)					
Dunfermline	424	Fife	St Andrews	1561	1613
			Edinburgh		1574
Dunino	425	Fife	St Andrews	1643	1596
			Edinburgh		1580
Dunipace	478	Stirling	Stirling	1594	1619
			Edinburgh		1581
Dunkeld	349	Perth	Dunkeld	1672	1688
			Dunblane		1653
			Edinburgh		1578
Dunlichty	95	Inverness	Inverness		1631
(see Daviot & Dunlichty 95)					
Dunlop	591	Ayr	Glasgow	1701	1606
			Edinburgh		1592
Dunnet	36	Caithness	Caithness	1751	1819
Dunnichen	283	Forfar	Brechin	1683	1576
			St Andrews		1600
Dunning	350	Perth	Dunblane	1708	1598
			Edinburgh		1586
Dunnottar	255	Kincardine	St Andrews	1672	1606
			Brechin		1656
			Edinburgh		1576
Dunoon & Kilmun	510	Argyll	Argyll	1744	1675
			Edinburgh		1584
Dunrossness	3/1	Shetland	Orkney & Shetland	1753	1612
(incl. Sandwick & Cunningsburgh 3/2 & Fair Isle 3/4)					
Dunscore	822	Dumfries	Dumfries	1777	1638
			Edinburgh		1577
Dunse (or Duns)	735	Berwick	Lauder	1615	1627
			Edinburgh		1574
Dunsyre	642	Lanark	Lanark	1687	1621
			Edinburgh		1576
Durness	48	Sutherland	Caithness	1764	
Duror	525/4	Argyll	Argyll	1833	1738
(also Lismore 525/1, Appin 525/2, Glencoe & Ballachulish 525/3)					
Durris	256	Kincardine	St Andrews	1716	1613
			Inverness		1630
Durrisdeer	823	Dumfries	Dumfries	1758	1624
			Edinburgh		1582

Parish	District number	County	Commissariot	OPR	Testament or inventory
Duthil	96b[1]	Inverness	Inverness	1766	1632
(*also Rothiemurchus 96b[2]*)			Moray		1710
			Edinburgh		1588
Dyce	190	Aberdeen	Aberdeen	1646	1737
Dyke	133	Moray	Moray	1635	1710
			Edinburgh		1590
Dysart	426	Fife	St Andrews	1582	1549
			Dunkeld		1695
			Edinburgh		1565
Eaglesham	561	Renfrew	Glasgow	1659	1602
			Edinburgh		1592
Earlston	736	Berwick	Lauder	1694	1628
			Kirkcudbright		1665
			Edinburgh		1565
Eassie & Nevay	284	Forfar	St Andrews	1728	1597
East Calder	690				
(*see Kirknewton & East Calder 690*)					
East Kilbride	643	Lanark	Hamilton & Campsie	1688	
East Kilpatrick	500				
(*see New or East Kilpatrick 500*)					
Eastwood	562	Renfrew	Glasgow	1674	1604
			Edinburgh		1592
Eccles	737	Berwick	Lauder	1699	1635
			Edinburgh		1578
Ecclesgreig	267	Kincardine	St Andrews		1595
(*see St Cyrus 267*)			Edinburgh		1576
Ecclesmachen	666	Linlithgow W. Lothian	Edinburgh	1717	1582
Echt	191	Aberdeen	Aberdeen	1678	1722
Eckford	787a	Roxburgh	Peebles	1694	1682
Eday & Pharay	15	Orkney	Orkney & Shetland	1789	
Edderton	63	Ross & Cromarty	Ross	1799	1821
Eddleston	760	Peebles	Peebles	1713	1823
			Edinburgh		1586
Eddrachillis	49	Sutherland	Caithness	1808	
Edgerston	787b	Roxburgh	Peebles		1682
(*see Jedburgh 792, Oxnam 802 & Southdean 806*)					
Edinburgh	685[1]	Edinburgh	Edinburgh	1595	1528
(*also Canongate 685[3] & St Cuthbert's 685[2]*)			Glasgow		1611
			St Andrews		1648
			Peebles		1821
Edinkillie	134	Moray	Moray	1702	1700
Ednam	788	Roxburgh	Peebles	1666	1683
			Edinburgh		1573
Edrom	738	Berwick	Lauder	1721	1628
			Edinburgh		1578
Edzell	285	Forfar	St Andrews	1684	1606
			Edinburgh		1571

Parish	District number	County	Commissariot	OPR	Testament or inventory
Egilshay (see Rousay & Egilshay 24)	24	Orkney	Orkney & Shetland		1612
Eigg (see Small Isles 116)	116				
Elgin	135	Moray	Moray Edinburgh	1609	1684 1573
Elie	427	Fife	St Andrews Edinburgh	1639	1584 1597
Ellon	192	Aberdeen	Aberdeen	1640	1732
Enzie	152	Banff	Moray	1835	1764
Errol	351	Perth	St Andrews Dunblane Edinburgh	1553	1594 1653 1577
Erskine	563	Renfrew	Glasgow Edinburgh	1705	1605 1572
Eskdalemuir	824	Dumfries	Dumfries	1724	1681
Essie (see Rhynie & Essie 237a)	237a	Aberdeen	Aberdeen Edinburgh		1577
Essil (also Speymouth 143)	143	Moray	Moray	1654	
Ettrick (also Kirkhope 776 & Yarrow 779)	774b	Selkirk	Peebles	1693	1819
Evie & Rendall	16	Orkney	Orkney & Shetland	1725	1612
Ewes	825	Dumfries	Dumfries	1700	1661
Eyemouth	739	Berwick	Lauder Edinburgh	1710	1628 1574
Fair Isle	3/3	Shetland	Orkney & Shetland	1767	
(also Dunrossness 3/1, Sandwick & Cunningsburgh 3/2)					
Fala & Soutra	686	Edinburgh Midlothian	Edinburgh Peebles	1673	1586 1691
Falkirk	479	Stirling	Stirling Dunblane Edinburgh Glasgow	1611	1610 1619 1576 1799
Falkland	428	Fife	St Andrews Brechin Edinburgh	1669	1550 1595 1577
Farnell	286	Forfar	Brechin Edinburgh	1699	1602 1594
Farr	50	Sutherland	Caithness	1790	
Fearn	287	Forfar	Dunkeld Brechin Edinburgh	1762	1688 1578 1586
Fearn	64	Ross & Cromarty	Ross	1749	
Fenwick	592	Ayr	Glasgow	1644	1605
Ferry-Port-on-Craig (Leuchars pre 1606)	429	Fife	St Andrews	1634	1591
Fetlar (also North Yell 4/2)	4/1	Shetland	Orkney & Shetland	1754	1613

Parish	District number	County	Commissariot	OPR	Testament or inventory
Fettercairn	257	Kincardine	St Andrews	1720	1605
			Brechin		1657
			Edinburgh		1576
Fetteresso	258	Kincardine	St Andrews	1620	1597
			Brechin		1656
			Edinburgh		1578
Findo-Gask	352	Perth	Dunblane	1669	1604
			Edinburgh		1564
Fintray	193	Aberdeen	Aberdeen	1728	1723
Fintry	480	Stirling	Glasgow	1659	1617
			Stirling		1607
			Edinburgh		1586
Firth & Stennes *(also Stennes 17)*	17	Orkney	Orkney & Shetland	1732	1612
Flisk	430	Fife	St Andrews	1697	1550
			Edinburgh		1594
Flotta *(also Walls 32/1)*	32/2	Orkney	Orkney & Shetland	1708	1619
Fodderty	65	Ross & Cromarty	Ross	1735	1815
Fogo	740	Berwick	Lauder	1660	1653
			Edinburgh		1582
Forbes & Kearn *(also Tullynessle 246)*	246	Aberdeen	Aberdeen	1718	1791
Fordoun	259	Kincardine	St Andrews	1693	1605
			Brechin		1657
			Edinburgh		1576
Fordyce	153	Banff	Aberdeen	1665	1732
			Brechin		1680
			Edinburgh		1582
Forfar	288	Forfar	St Andrews	1633	1587
			Brechin		1658
			Edinburgh		1576
Forgan *(also Wormit 431 & Newport-on-Tay 431)*	431	Fife	St Andrews	1695	1549
			Dunkeld		1688
			Edinburgh		1587
Forgandenny	353	Perth	Dunkeld	1695	1684
			Dunblane		1656
			Edinburgh		1582
			St Andrews		1591
Forglen	154	Banff	Aberdeen	1647	1738
Forgue	194	Aberdeen	Aberdeen	1684	1738
Forres	137	Moray	Moray	1675	1696
			Edinburgh		1697
Fort Augustus or Abertarff *(also Boleskine 92/1)*	92/2	Inverness	Inverness	1737	1737
Forteviot	354	Perth	St Andrews	1710	1599
			Dunblane		1653
			Edinburgh		1592
Fortingall *(also Kinloch-Rannoch 367)*	355a	Perth	Dunkeld	1748	1688
			Dunblane		1656

Parish	District number	County	Commissariot	OPR	Testament or inventory
Foss *(see Dull 346)*	355b				
Fossoway & Tullibole *(united in 1614)*	461	Kinross	St Andrews Dunblane Edinburgh	1609	1655 1547 1588
Foula *(also Walls 12/1)*	12/4	Shetland	Orkney & Shetland	1783	1631
Foulden	741	Berwick	Lauder	1682	1653
Foveran	195	Aberdeen	Aberdeen	1658	1733
Fowlis *(see Lundie & Fowlis 306)*	306	Forfar	St Andrews Edinburgh		1596 1565
Fowlis-Easter	356	Perth	St Andrews Edinburgh	1701	1690 1565
Fowlis-Wester	357	Perth	Dunblane Edinburgh	1674	1553 1565
Fraserburgh	196	Aberdeen	Aberdeen	1733	1727
Fyvie	197	Aberdeen	Aberdeen	1685	1724
Gairloch *(also Poolewe 66)*	66	Ross & Cromarty	Ross	1781	
Galashiels *(also Caddonfoot 774a)*	775	Selkirk	Peebles Edinburgh	1714	1698 1588
Galston	593	Ayr	Glasgow Edinburgh	1670	1604 1576
Gamrie *(incl. Macduff & Down 155a)*	155a	Banff	Aberdeen	1704	1819
Gargunnock	481	Stirling	Stirling	1615	1616
Gartly	198	Aberdeen	Moray	1709	1688
Garvald	707	Haddington E. Lothian	Edinburgh	1694	1582
Garvock	260	Kincardine	St Andrews Dunblane Brechin Edinburgh	1703	1606 1622 1657 1582
Gifford *(see Yester 725)*	725				
Gigha	537	Argyll	The Isles	1792	1787
Girthon	866	Kirkcudbright	Kirkcudbright	1699	1718
Girvan	594	Ayr	Glasgow Edinburgh	1733	1605 1577
Gladsmuir	708	Haddington E. Lothian	Edinburgh	1688	
Glamis	289	Forfar	St Andrews Brechin Edinburgh	1677	1600 1659 1565
Glasgow *(also Gorbals 644², Govan 646 & Barony 622)*	644[1]	Lanark	Glasgow Hamilton & Campsie Edinburgh	1609	1547 1609 1564
Glass	199	Aberdeen	Moray	1736	1684

Parish	District number	County	Commissariot	OPR	Testament or inventory
Glassary *(also Cumlodden 509 & Lochgilphead 526)*	511	Argyll	Argyll	1750	1674
Glasserton	885	Wigtown	Wigtown	1700	1710
Glassford	645	Lanark	Glasgow Edinburgh	1692	1605 1586
Glenaray *(see Inveraray & Glenaray 513)*	513	Argyll	Argyll		1705
Glenbervie	261	Kincardine	Brechin Edinburgh	1721	1582 1581
Glenbucket *(or Glenbuchat)*	200	Aberdeen	Aberdeen Moray	1719	1747 1754
Glencairn	826	Dumfries	Dumfries Edinburgh	1693	1624 1577
Glencoe & Ballachulish *(see Lismore 525/1, Appin 525/2, Duror 525/4)*	525/3	Argyll	Argyll		1686
Glencorse *(formerly Woodhouselee 687)*	687	Edinburgh	Edinburgh	1672	1570
Glendevon	358	Perth	Dunblane Edinburgh St Andrews	1710	1611 1583 1729
Glenelg	97	Inverness	Argyll	1792	1749
Glengairn *(see Glenmuick, Tullich & Glengairn 201)*	201				
Glenholm *(see Kilbucho 753 & Broughton 758)*	761	Peebles	Peebles		1823
Glenisla	290	Forfar	Brechin	1719	1579
Glenluce *(see Old Luce 894)*	894	Wigtown	Wigtown		1713
Glenmoriston *(also Urquhart & Glenmoriston 107)*	107	Inverness	Inverness	1785	
Glenmuick, Tullich & Glengairn	201	Aberdeen	Aberdeen	1744	1751
Glenorchy & Inishail	512	Argyll	Argyll	1753	
Glenrinnes *(see Mortlach 162 & Aberlour 145)*	155b				
Glenshiel	67	Ross & Cromarty	Ross	1785	
Golspie	51	Sutherland	Caithness	1739	
Gorbals *(also Glasgow 644[1], Govan 646 & Barony 622)*	644[2]	Lanark	Hamilton & Campsie Glasgow	1771	1612 1657
Gordon	742	Berwick	Lauder Edinburgh	1652	1561 1598
Govan *(also Glasgow 644[1], Gorbals 644[2] & Barony 622)*	646	Lanark	Hamilton & Campsie Glasgow	1690	1564 1615
Graemsay *(also Hoy & Graemsay 20)*	20	Orkney	Orkney & Shetland	1777	1614
Graitney/Gretna	827	Dumfries	Dumfries	1730	1662
Grange	156	Banff	Moray	1684	1693

Parish	District number	County	Commissariot	OPR	Testament or inventory
Greenlaw	743	Berwick	Lauder	1699	1630
			Kirkcudbright		1687
			Edinburgh		1583
Greenock	564	Renfrew	Glasgow		1607
			Dunblane		1618
Greenock, Middle or New	564[1]			1741	
Greenock, East	564[2]			1809	
Greenock, Old or West	564[3]			1698	
Gretna *(see Graitney)*					
Guthrie	291	Forfar	Brechin	1664	1583
			St Andrews		1618
Haddington	709	Haddington E. Lothian	Edinburgh	1619	1564
Hailes *(see Colinton 677)*	677				
Halfmorton	828	Dumfries	Dumfries	1787	
Halkirk	37	Caithness	Caithness	1772	1819
Hamilton	647	Lanark	Hamilton & Campsie	1645	1564
			Edinburgh		1564
			Glasgow		1652
Harray	18	Orkney	Orkney & Shetland	1784	1612
Harris *(also St Kilda 111)*	111	Inverness	The Isles	1823	1810
Hawick	789	Roxburgh	Peebles	1634	1682
			Edinburgh		1583
Heriot	688	Edinburgh Midlothian	Edinburgh	1685	1569
Hilton *(see Whitsome & Hilton 757)*	757				
Hobkirk	790	Roxburgh	Peebles	1726	1818
Hoddam	829	Dumfries	Dumfries	1746	1625
			Kirkcudbright		1687
Holm & Paplay	19	Orkney	Orkney & Shetland	1654	1611
Holywood	830	Dumfries	Dumfries	1687	1638
			Edinburgh		1576
			Glasgow		1549
Houston & Killellan	565	Renfrew	Glasgow	1720	1606
			Peebles		1686
			Edinburgh		1591
Hownam	791	Roxburgh	Peebles	1689	1685
			Edinburgh		1596
Hoy & Graemsay (combined 1651)	20	Orkney	Orkney & Shetland	1776	1612
Humbie	710	Haddington E. Lothian	Edinburgh	1648	1577

Parish	District number	County	Commissariot	OPR	Testament or inventory
Hume	744	Roxburgh	Peebles		
(see Stitchell 808)			Lauder		1564
			Edinburgh		1600
Huntly	202	Aberdeen	Aberdeen	1680	
(formerly Dumbennan & Kinnoir)			Moray		1693
Hutton	745	Berwick	Lauder	1700	1637
			Edinburgh		1600
Hutton & Corrie	831	Dumfries	Dumfries	1745	1775
Hyskier	116				
(see Small Isles 116)					
Inch	886	Wigtown	Wigtown	1729	1700
			Edinburgh		1581
Inchbrayock	280	Forfar	St Andrews		1613
(see Craig 280)					
Inchinnan	566	Renfrew	Glasgow	1722	1603
			Edinburgh		1589
Inchnadamff	44				
(see Assynt 44)					
Inchture	359	Perth	St Andrews	1619	1615
			Edinburgh		1583
Inishail	512	Argyll	Argyll		1677
(see Glenorchy & Inishail 512)					
Innerkip or	567	Renfrew	Glasgow	1694	1602
Inverkip			Edinburgh		1583
Innerleithen or	762	Peebles	Peebles	1643	1798
Inverleithen			Edinburgh		1579
Innerwick	711	Haddington E. Lothian	Edinburgh	1614	1576
Insch	203	Aberdeen	Aberdeen	1683	1734
Insh	102	Inverness	Inverness		1808
(see Kingussie & Insh 102)					
Inverallan	128b	Moray	Moray		
(see Cromdale etc. 128b)			Inverness		1631
Inveraray &	513	Argyll	Argyll	1653	1677
Glenaray (also Cumlodden 509)			Glasgow		1781
Inverarity &	292	Forfar	St Andrews	1710	1596
Methy			Brechin		1657
			Edinburgh		1577
Inveravon	157	Banff	Moray	1630	1772
Inverchaolin	514	Argyll	Argyll	1737	1675
Inveresk	689	Edinburgh Midlothian	Edinburgh	1607	1567
Invergowrie	301	Forfar	St Andrews		1598
(see Liff, Benvie & Invergowrie 301)			Edinburgh		1596
Inverkeillor	293	Angus	St Andrews	1717	1599
			Edinburgh		1575
Inverkeithing	432	Fife	St Andrews	1676	1587
			Edinburgh		1577
Inverkeithny	158	Banff	Moray	1721	
			Edinburgh		1597

Parish	District number	County	Commissariot	OPR	Testament or inventory
Inverness	98	Inverness	Inverness	1604	1630
			Moray		1798
			Edinburgh		1587
Invernochtie (see Strathdon 240)	240				
Inverurie	204	Aberdeen	Aberdeen	1611	1736
Iona (Mull)	538	Argyll	The Isles	1829	
Irongray (Kirkpatrick-Irongray)	867	Kirkcudbright	Dumfries	1757	1624
			Edinburgh		1580
Irvine	595	Ayr	Glasgow	1645	1602
			Edinburgh		1576
Jedburgh (also Edgerston 787b)	792	Roxburgh	Peebles	1639	1681
			Lauder		1763
			Edinburgh		1582
Johnstone	832	Dumfries	Dumfries	1734	1680
Jura (also Colonsay 539/2)	539/1	Argyll	The Isles	1704	1728
Kearn (see Forbes & Kearn 246, Auchindoir 172)	246				
Keig	205	Aberdeen	Aberdeen	1750	1751
Keir	833	Dumfries	Dumfries	1722	1639
Keith	159	Banff	Moray	1686	1688
			Edinburgh		1600
Keithhall & Kinkell	206	Aberdeen	Aberdeen	1678	1723
Kells	868	Kirkcudbright	Kirkcudbright	1698	1663
			Dumfries		1638
			Wigtown		1736
			Edinburgh		1582
Kelso	793	Roxburgh	Peebles	1598	1682
			Lauder		1653
			Edinburgh		1574
Kelton	869	Kirkcudbright	Kirkcudbright	1717	1668
			Edinburgh		1582
Kemback	433	Fife	St Andrews	1649	1591
Kemnay	207	Aberdeen	Aberdeen	1660	1726
Kenmore	360	Perth	Dunkeld	1636	1698
			Dunblane		1656
Kennoway	434	Fife	St Andrews	1638	1550
			Edinburgh		1576
Kettins (previously Lathrisk)	294	Forfar	St Andrews	1650	1588
			Edinburgh		1580
Kettle (also Kingskettle 435)	435	Fife	St Andrews	1633	1590
Kilarrow or Bowmore	536	Argyll	The Isles	1763	1726
Kilbarchan	568	Renfrew	Glasgow	1651	1602
			Edinburgh		1579
Kilberry (see Kilcalmonell & Kilberry 516)	516	Argyll	Argyll		1676

Parish	District number	County	Commissariot	OPR	Testament or inventory
Kilbirnie	596	Ayr	Glasgow	1688	1607
			Edinburgh		1590
Kilblane with		Argyll	Argyll		1676
Kilcolmkill *(see Southend 532)*					
Kilbrandon &	515	Argyll	Argyll	1733	1674
Kilchattan					
Kilbride (Arran)	553	Bute	The Isles	1723	1662
Kilbride	523	Argyll	Argyll		1676
(see Kilmore & Kilbride 523)			Glasgow		1608
Kilbucho	763	Peebles	Peebles	1749	1823
(also Broughton 758 & Glenholm 761)			Edinburgh		1587
Kilcalmonell &	516	Argyll	Argyll	1777	1676
Kilberry *(also Tarbert 535)*					
Kilchattan	515				
(see Kilbrandon & Kilchattan 515)					
Kilchenzie	519	Argyll	Argyll		1684
(see Killean & Kilchenzie 519)					
Kilchoman	540	Argyll	The Isles	1821	1727
Kilchrenan &	517	Argyll	Argyll	1751	1676
Dalavich			The Isles		1795
Kilcolmkill		Argyll	Argyll		1694
(united with Kilblane to form Southend 532)					
Kilconquhar	436	Fife	St Andrews	1637	1549
			Edinburgh		1580
Kildalton	541	Argyll	The Isles	1723	1738
(Islay)			Argyll		1700
Kildonan	52	Sutherland	Caithness	1791	
			Edinburgh		1579
Kildrummy	208	Aberdeen	Aberdeen	1681	1723
Kilfinan	518	Argyll	Argyll	1728	1674
Kilfinichen &	542	Argyll	The Isles	1804	1711
Kilvickeon (Mull)					
Kilgour *(see Falkland 428)*			St Andrews		1549
Killean &	519	Argyll	Argyll	1762	1676
Kilchenzie			The Isles		1723
Killearn	482	Stirling	Glasgow	1694	1611
			Stirling		1658
Killearnan	68	Ross & Cromarty	Ross	1744	1803
Killellan	565	Renfrew	Glasgow		1602
(see Houston & Killellan 565)					
Killin	361	Perth	Dunkeld	1689	1712
Kilmacolm	569	Renfrew	Glasgow	1710	1647
			Edinburgh		1586
Kilmadock	362	Perth	Dunblane	1623	1603
			Edinburgh		1587
Kilmallie	520	Argyll	Argyll	1773	1676
(also Ballachulish & Corran of Ardgour 506)					
Kilmany	437	Fife	St Andrews	1706	1549
			Edinburgh		1575

Parish	District number	County	Commissariot	OPR	Testament or inventory
Kilmarnock	597	Ayr	Glasgow	1640	1602
			Edinburgh		1575
Kilmaronock	497	Dunbarton	Glasgow	1686	1607
			Edinburgh		1596
Kilmartin	521	Argyll	Argyll	1747	1674
Kilmaurs	598	Ayr	Glasgow	1688	1603
			Edinburgh		1583
Kilmelford *(see Kilninver & Kilmelford 524)*	524	Argyll	Argyll		1676
Kilmeny	543	Argyll	The Isles	1802	1709
Kilmodan	522	Argyll	Argyll	1737	1675
Kilmonivaig	99	Inverness	Argyll	1730	1678
Kilmorack	100	Inverness	Inverness	1674	1802
Kilmore & Kilbride *(incl. Oban 523)*	523	Argyll	Argyll	1782	1676
Kilmore & Kilninian	544	Argyll	The Isles	1766	1709
Kilmorich *(also Lochgoilhead 527/1)*	527/2	Argyll	Argyll	1750	1676
Kilmory (Arran) *(see Shisken 554 and Lochranza 554)*	554	Bute	The Isles Argyll		1763 1675
Kilmuir (Skye)	112	Inverness	The Isles	1823	1729
			Edinburgh		1592
Kilmuir-Easter	69	Ross & Cromarty	Ross	1738	1814
Kilmuir-Wester *(see Knockbain 73)*	73	Ross & Cromarty	Ross Moray		1753
Kilmun *(see Dunoon & Kilmun 510)*	510	Argyll	Argyll		1675
Kilninian & Kilmore (Mull) *(also Ulva 544)*	544	Argyll	The Isles	1766	1707
Kilninver & Kilmelford	524	Argyll	Argyll	1758	1676
Kilpatrick, New or East, *(see New or East Kilpatrick 500)*					
Kilpatrick, Old or West, *(see Old or West Kilpatrick 501)*					
Kilrenny	438	Fife	St Andrews	1647	1550
			Edinburgh		1577
Kilspindie	363	Perth	St Andrews	1656	1598
			Dunblane		1652
			Edinburgh		1577
Kilsyth *(formerly Monyabroch 483)*	483	Stirling	Stirling also Glasgow	1619	1671
Kiltarlity	101	Inverness	Inverness	1714	1630
Kiltearn	70	Ross & Cromarty	Ross	1702	1813
			Edinburgh		1597
Kilwinning	599	Ayr	Glasgow	1699	1603
			Edinburgh		1581
Kilvickeon *(see Kilfinichen & Kilvickeon 542)*	542	Argyll	The Isles		1712

Parish	District number	County	Commissariot	OPR	Testament or inventory
Kincardine	364	Perth	Dunblane	1691	1604
			Brechin		1593
			Edinburgh		1597
			St Andrews		1635
Kincardine	71	Ross & Cromarty	Ross	1804	1821
Kincardine *(see Abernethy 90a)*	90a	Inverness	Inverness		1669
Kincardine O'Neil	209	Aberdeen	Aberdeen	1706	1734
			Edinburgh		1578
Kinclaven	365	Perth	Dunkeld	1726	1680
			Edinburgh		1581
Kineddar *(see Drainie 130)*	130		Moray		1789
Kinfauns	366	Perth	St Andrews	1624	1605
			Edinburgh		1577
Kingarth	555	Bute	The Isles	1727	1661
King-Edward	210	Aberdeen	Aberdeen	1701	1821
Kinghorn	439	Fife	St Andrews	1576	1549
			Edinburgh		1568
Kinglassie	440	Fife	St Andrews	1627	1550
			Edinburgh		1588
Kingoldrum	295	Forfar	Brechin	1700	1581
			Edinburgh		1591
			St Andrews		1776
Kingsbarns	441	Fife	St Andrews	1642	1592
Kingskettle *(see Kettle 435)*	435				
Kingussie & Insh	102	Inverness	Inverness	1724	1630
Kinkell *(see Keithhall & Kinkell 206)*	206	Aberdeen	Aberdeen		1633
			Dunblane		1553
			St Andrews		1740
Kinloch *(see Lethendy & Kinloch 372)*	372	Perth	Dunkeld		1685
			St Andrews		1593
Kinloch-Rannoch *(see Fortingall 355a)*	367		Dunkeld		1693
Kinlochspelvie (Mull) *(also Toronsay 549)*	545	Argyll	The Isles	1842	
Kinloss	138	Moray	Moray	1699	1751
			Edinburgh		1591
Kinnaird	368	Perth	St Andrews	1632	1598
			Brechin		1601
			Edinburgh		1581
Kinneff & Catterline	262	Kincardine	St Andrews	1616	
			Edinburgh		1582
Kinnell	296	Forfar	St Andrews	1657	1605
			Brechin		1582
			Edinburgh		1594
Kinnellar	211	Aberdeen	Aberdeen	1697	1725
Kinnethmont	212	Aberdeen	Aberdeen	1728	1728
			Edinburgh		1575
Kinnettles	297	Forfar	St Andrews	1696	1595

Parish	District number	County	Commissariot	OPR	Testament or inventory
Kinnoir (see Huntly 202)	202		Moray		1685
Kinnoull	369	Perth	St Andrews	1618	1584
			Dunblane		1657
			Edinburgh		1573
Kinross	462	Kinross	St Andrews	1676	1614
			Edinburgh		1573
Kintail	72	Ross & Cromarty	Ross	1776	
Kintore	213	Aberdeen	Aberdeen	1717	1736
			Moray		1685
Kippen	484	Stirling	Dunblane	1700	1600
	part	Perth	Stirling		1607
			Edinburgh		1588
Kirkbean	870	Kirkcudbright	Dumfries	1714	1638
			Edinburgh		1584
Kirkcaldy	442	Fife	St Andrews	1614	1549
			Edinburgh		1570
Kirkcolm	887	Wigtown	Wigtown	1779	1758
			Edinburgh		1584
Kirkconnel	834	Dumfries	Dumfries	1742	1638
			Krikcudbright		1725
			Edinburgh		1567
			Glasgow		1617
			St Andrews		1551
Kirkcowan	888	Wigtown	Wigtown	1788	1736
Kirkcudbright	871	Kirkcudbright	Kirkcudbright	1743	1667
			Dumfries		1643
			Edinburgh		1564
Kirkden	298	Forfar	St Andrews	1650	1600
			Brechin		1652
Kirkgunzeon	872	Kirkcudbright	Kirkcudbright	1702	
			Dumfries		1657
			Edinburgh		1590
Kirkhill	103	Inverness	Inverness	1726	1814
Kirkhope (also Ettrick 774b & Yarrow 779)	776	Selkirk	Peebles	1852	1691
Kirkinner	889	Wigtown	Wigtown	1694	1709
			Edinburgh		1576
Kirkintilloch (formerly Lenzie)	498	Dunbarton	Glasgow	1656	1605
Kirkliston	667	Linlithgow	Edinburgh	1675	1581
		W. Lothian	St Andrews		1711
Kirkmabreck	873	Kirkcudbright	Kirkcudbright	1703	1674
			Wigtown		1769
			Edinburgh		1581
Kirkmahoe	835	Dumfries	Dumfries	1720	1625
			Edinburgh		1586
Kirkmaiden	890	Wigtown	Wigtown	1716	1718
			Edinburgh		1594
Kirkmichael (see Resolis 79)	79	Ross & Cromarty	Ross		1823

Parish	District number	County	Commissariot	OPR	Testament or inventory
Kirkmichael	370	Perth	Dunkeld	1650	
			Dunblane		1652
Kirkmichael	600	Ayr	Glasgow	1638	1605
			Edinburgh		1581
Kirkmichael	160	Banff	Moray	1725	1594
Kirkmichael	836	Dumfries	Dumfries	1727	1658
Kirknewton & East Calder	690	Edinburgh	Edinburgh	1642	1587
Kirkoswald	601	Ayr	Glasgow	1694	1604
			Edinburgh		1581
Kirkpatrick-Durham	874	Kirkcudbright	Dumfries	1693	1638
			Edinburgh		1587
Kirkpatrick-Fleming	837	Dumfries	Dumfries	1748	1657
Kirkpatrick-Irongray *(see Irongray 867)*	867	Kirkcudbright	Dumfries		
			Edinburgh		1580
			Glasgow		1548
Kirkpatrick-Juxta	838	Dumfries	Dumfries	1694	1661
Kirktown	794	Roxburgh	Peebles	1707	1682
Kirkurd	764	Peebles	Peebles	1705	1823
			Edinburgh		1576
Kirkwall & St Ola	21	Orkney	Orkney & Shetland	1657	1611
			Edinburgh		1574
Kirriemuir	299	Forfar	St Andrews	1716	1589
			Brechin		1658
			Edinburgh		1576
Kishorn *(also Applecross & Shieldaig 58)*	58	Ross & Cromarty	Ross	1808	
Knapdale North, *(see North Knapdale 530)*					
Knapdale South, *(see South Knapdale 533)*					
Knockando	139	Moray	Moray	1757	1701
Knockbain *(formerly Kilmuir Wester & Suddy 73)*	73	Ross & Cromarty	Ross	1749	1823
Lady *(or Cross Burness & Lady, see Sanday 26)*	26				
Ladykirk	746	Berwick	Lauder	1697	1631
			Edinburgh		1582
Laggan	104	Inverness	Inverness	1775	1633
Lairg	53	Sutherland	Caithness	1768	1677
Lamington & Wandell *(see Wandell & Lamington 659)*	659	Lanark	Lanark		1622
			Edinburgh		1594
			Glasgow		1548
Lanark	648	Lanark	Lanark	1647	1596
			Glasgow		1550
			Edinburgh		1582
Langholm *(formerly Staplegortoun 839)*	839	Dumfries	Dumfries	1668	1656

Parish	District number	County	Commissariot	OPR	Testament or inventory
Langton	747	Berwick	Lauder	1728	1628
			Peebles		1686
			Edinburgh		1568
Larbert	485	Stirling	Stirling	1663	1614
			Edinburgh		1582
			St Andrews		1743
Largo	443	Fife	St Andrews	1636	1550
			Edinburgh		1576
Largs	602	Ayr	Glasgow	1723	1603
			Edinburgh		1590
Lasswade	691	Edinburgh Midlothian	Edinburgh	1617	1569
Latheron	38	Caithness	Caithness	1740	1663
Lathrisk *(see Kettins 294)*	294	Forfar	St Andrews		1549
			Edinburgh		1594
Lauder	748	Berwick	Lauder	1680	1561
			Edinburgh		1568
Laurencekirk *(formerly Conveth)*	263	Kincardine	St Andrews	1702	1715
			Brechin		1657
Leadhills *(also Crawford 635)*	635	Lanark	Lanark	1698	1629
Lecropt	371	Perth	Dunblane	1720	1601
	part	Stirling	Stirling		1607
			Edinburgh		1599
Legerwood	749	Berwick	Lauder	1689	1564
Leith (North)	692[1]	Edinburgh	Edinburgh	1615	1564
Leith (South)	692[2]	Edinburgh	Edinburgh	1599	1564
Lennel *(see Coldstream 733)*	733	Berwick	Lauder		1635
			Edinburgh		1598
Lenzie *(see Kirkintilloch 498)*	498	Dumbarton	Glasgow		1666
			Edinburgh		1587
Leochel-Cushnie	214	Aberdeen	Aberdeen	1669	
Lerwick	5	Shetland	Orkney & Shetland	1728	1648
Leslie	215	Aberdeen	Aberdeen	1699	1739
Leslie	444	Fife	Dunkeld	1673	1684
			Edinburgh		1576
			St Andrews		1650
Lesmahagow	649	Lanark	Lanark	1692	1620
			Edinburgh		1576
Lessudden *(see St Boswells 804)*	804	Roxburgh	Peebles		
			Lauder		1562
Leswalt	891	Wigtown	Wigtown	1729	1715
			Edinburgh		1598
Lethendy & Kinloch	372	Perth	Dunkeld	1698	1689
			Dunblane		1655
			Moray		1796
			Edinburgh		1589
			Inverness		1666
			St Andrews		1725

Parish	District number	County	Commissariot	OPR	Testament or inventory
Lethnott & Nevar	300	Forfar	Brechin St Andrews	1728	1597 1620
Leuchars	445	Fife	St Andrews Edinburgh	1665	1550 1576
Lhanbryde (also St Andrews Lhanbryde 142)	142	Moray	Moray	1723	
Libberton	650	Lanark	Lanark Edinburgh	1717	1597 1581
Liberton	693	Edinburgh Midlothian	Edinburgh	1624	1578
Liff, Benvie & Invergowrie	301	Angus	St Andrews Brechin	1651	1598 1640
Lilliesleaf	795	Roxburgh	Peebles	1737	1811
Linlithgow	668	Linlithgow W. Lothian	Edinburgh	1613	1564
Linton	796	Roxburgh	Peebles Lauder Edinburgh	1732	1683 1668 1575
Lintrathen	302	Forfar	St Andrews	1717	1613
Lismore (also Appin 525/2, Duror 525/4, Glencoe & Ballachulish 525/3)	525	Argyll	Argyll	1758	1679
Little Dunkeld	373	Perth	Dunkeld Dunblane	1759	1688 1653
Livingston	669	Linlithgow W. Lothian	Edinburgh	1639	1578
Lochalsh	74	Ross & Cromarty	Ross	1755	1802
Lochbroom	75	Ross & Cromarty	Ross	1798	1817
Lochcarron	76	Ross & Cromarty	Ross	1819	1821
Lochgilphead (see Glassary 511)	526	Argyll	Argyll		1675
Lochgoilhead (also Kilmorich 527/2)	527/1	Argyll	Argyll	1692	1675
Lochlee	303	Forfar	Brechin	1731	1626
Lochmaben	840	Dumfries	Dumfries	1741	1629
Lochranza (also Kilmory 554)	556	Bute	The Isles	1732	
Lochrutton	875	Kirkcudbright	Dumfries Edinburgh	1698	1678 1590
Lochs (also Carloway 86b)	87	Ross & Cromarty	The Isles	1831	
Lochwinnoch	570	Renfrew	Glasgow Edinburgh	1718	1602 1597
Logie	446	Fife	St Andrews Edinburgh	1660	1597 1587
Logie	374 part part part	Perth Stirling Clackmannan Clackmannan	Dunblane also Stirling Dunkeld Brechin Edinburgh	1688	1617 1742 1597 1596

Parish	District number	County	Commissariot	OPR	Testament or inventory
Logiealmond	375				
(see Monzie 382, Fowlis-Wester 357, Methven 380 & Redgorton 390)					
Logie-Buchan	216	Aberdeen	Aberdeen	1698	
Logie-Coldstone	217	Aberdeen	Aberdeen	1716	1731
Logie-Easter	77	Ross & Cromarty	Ross	1665	
Logie-Wester	84				
(see Urquhart & Logie-Wester 84)					
Logie-Pert	304	Forfar	St Andrews	1717	1773
			Edinburgh		1598
Logierait	376	Perth	Dunkeld	1673	1683
(also Aberfeldy 324)			Dunblane		1685
			Edinburgh		1584
Longforgan	377	Perth	St Andrews	1634	1588
			Dunblane		1656
			Edinburgh		1573
Longformacus	750	Berwick	Lauder	1654	1636
(also Cranshaws 734)					
Longside	218	Aberdeen	Aberdeen	1621	
(disjoined from Peterhead in 1640)					
Lonmay	219	Aberdeen	Aberdeen	1687	1730
Loth	54	Sutherland	Caithness	1795	1822
Loudoun	603	Ayr	Glasgow	1673	1551
			Edinburgh		1579
Lumphannan	220	Aberdeen	Aberdeen	1740	1722
Lunan	305	Forfar	St Andrews	1654	1614
Lundie &	306	Forfar	St Andrews	1667	1588
Fowlis			Brechin		1622
Lunnasting	7/2	Shetland	Orkney &	1781	1613
(also Nesting 7/1, Whalsay & Skerries 7/3)			Shetland		
Luss	499	Dunbarton	Glasgow	1698	1549
			Edinburgh		1565
Lyne & Megget	765	Peebles	Peebles	1649	1823
			Edinburgh		1588
Macduff	155a	Banff	Aberdeen	1786	1798
(also Gamrie & Down 155a)					
Madderty	378	Perth	Dunkeld	1701	1713
			Dunblane		1656
			Edinburgh		1582
Mains	307	Forfar	St Andrews	1635	1596
(also Strathmartine 307)			Edinburgh		1595
Makerston	797	Roxburgh	Peebles	1692	1691
			Lauder		1559
Manor	766	Peebles	Peebles	1663	1823
			Edinburgh		1583
Markinch	447	Fife	St Andrews	1635	1549
			Edinburgh		1586
			Inverness		1630
Marnoch	161	Banff	Moray	1676	1751
Maryculter	264	Kincardine	Aberdeen	1696	1746
			Edinburgh		1599

Parish	District number	County	Commissariot	OPR	Testament or inventory
Marykirk *(formerly Aberluthnot 265)*	265	Kincardine	St Andrews	1699	1635
Maryton	308	Forfar	Brechin Edinburgh	1727	1596 1586
Mauchline	604	Ayr	Glasgow Edinburgh	1670	1602 1576
Maxton	798	Roxburgh	Peebles	1689	1805
Maxwelltown *(also Troqueer 882)*	882	Kirkcudbright	Dumfries	1837	1624
Maybole	605	Ayr	Glasgow Edinburgh	1712	1555 1576
Mearns	571	Renfrew	Glasgow Brechin Edinburgh	1756	1602 1656 1578
Megget *(see Lyne & Megget 765)*	765				
Meigle *(also Persie 386b)*	379	Perth	Dunkeld Dunblane Edinburgh	1727	1638 1653 1580
Melrose	799	Roxburgh	Peebles Lauder Edinburgh	1642	1794 1560 1565
Menmuir	309	Forfar	Brechin Edinburgh	1701	1578 1576
Merton	751	Berwick	Lauder	1729	1634
Methlick	221	Aberdeen	Aberdeen	1670	1723
Methven *(also Logiealmond 375)*	380	Perth	St Andrews Dunblane Dunkeld Edinburgh	1662	1593 1653 1712 1576
Methy *(see Inverarity 292)*	292	Forfar	St Andrews		1595
Mid Calder	694	Edinburgh Midlothian	Edinburgh	1604	1567
Middlebie	841	Dumfries	Dumfries	1744	1640
Midmar	222	Aberdeen	Aberdeen	1717	1777
Mid Yell	6	Shetland	Orkney & Shetland	1723	
Migvy *(see Tarland & Migvy 242)*	242	Aberdeen	Aberdeen Inverness		1807
Minnigaff	876	Kirkcudbright	Wigtown Edinburgh	1694	1702 1577
Minto	800	Roxburgh	Peebles	1703	1681
Mochrum	892	Wigtown	Wigtown Edinburgh	1720	1706 1577
Moffat	842	Dumfries	Dumfries Lanark	1723	1627 1673
Moneydie	381	Perth	Dunkeld Edinburgh Dunblane	1655	1684 1591 1659

Parish	District number	County	Commissariot	OPR	Testament or inventory
Monifieth	310	Forfar	St Andrews	1562	1599
			Edinburgh		1580
Monikie	311	Forfar	Brechin	1613	1610
			Edinburgh		1596
			St Andrews		1599
Monimail	448	Fife	St Andrews	1656	1549
			Edinburgh		1573
Monkton & Prestwick	606	Ayr	Glasgow	1702	1607
			Edinburgh		1591
Monkland, New *(see New Monkland 651)*	651				
Monkland, Old *(see Old Monkland 652)*	652				
Monquhitter	223	Aberdeen	Aberdeen	1670	1729
Montrose	312	Forfar	Brechin	1615	1579
			Dunkeld		1676
			Edinburgh		1565
			St Andrews		1606
Monyabroch *(see Kilsyth 483)*	483	Stirling	Glasgow		1617
			Stirling		1654
			Edinburgh		1576
Monymusk	224	Aberdeen	Aberdeen	1678	1722
Monzie *(also Logiealmond 375)*	382	Perth	Dunblane	1720	1543
			Dunkeld		1731
			Edinburgh		1584
Monzievaird & Strowan	383	Perth	Dunblane	1729	1663
			Edinburgh		1599
Moonzie	449	Fife	St Andrews	1713	1596
Mordington	752	Berwick	Lauder	1721	1635
Morebattle	801	Roxburgh	Peebles	1726	1685
			Edinburgh		1576
Morham	712	Haddington E. Lothian	Edinburgh	1712	1581
Mortlach *(also Glenrinnes 155b)*	162	Banff	Aberdeen	1741	1742
Morton	843	Dumfries	Dumfries	1692	1690
Morvern	528	Argyll	Argyll	1803	1676
Moulin *(also Tenandry 394c)*	384	Perth	Dunkeld	1741	1685
			Dunblane		1655
			Edinburgh		1581
Mousewald	844	Dumfries	Dumfries	1751	1673
Moy & Dalarossie	105	Inverness	Inverness	1788	1630
			Edinburgh		1599
Muckairn	529	Argyll	Argyll	1746	1734
Muckart	385 part	Perth Kinross	Stirling also St Andrews	1698	1612
			Dunblane		1656
			Edinburgh		1580
Muiravonside	486	Stirling	Stirling	1689	1608
Muirkirk	607	Ayr	Glasgow	1659	1632

Parish	District number	County	Commissariot	OPR	Testament or inventory
Murroes	313	Forfar	St Andrews	1698	1595
			Edinburgh		1599
Muthill	386a	Perth	Dunblane	1704	1554
			Edinburgh		1589
Nairn	123	Nairn	Moray	1705	1687
Neilston	572	Renfrew	Glasgow	1688	1610
			Edinburgh		1594
Nenthorn	753	Berwick	Lauder	1715	1563
			Peebles		1691
Nesting	7/1	Shetland	Orkney &	1783	1613
(also Lunnasting 7/2, Whalsay & Skerries 7/3)			Shetland		
Nevar	300	Forfar	Brechin		1610
(see Lethnot & Nevar 300)			Edinburgh		1567
Nevay	284				
(see Eassie & Nevay 284)					
New Abbey	877	Kirkcudbright	Dumfries	1691	1628
			Edinburgh		1582
Newbattle	695	Edinburgh	Edinburgh	1618	1572
(also Stobhill 698b)					
Newburgh	450	Fife	St Andrews	1654	1591
			Dunblane		1671
			Edinburgh		1564
Newburn	451	Fife	St Andrews	1628	1550
			Edinburgh		1595
New Cumnock	608	Ayr	Glasgow	1706	1670
New Deer	225	Aberdeen	Aberdeen	1684	1725
(anciently called Auchreddie)					
New or East	500	Dunbarton	Glasgow	1691	1603
Kilpatrick			Stirling (1649–1660)		1656
			Edinburgh		1577
Newhills	226	Aberdeen	Aberdeen	1700	1725
Newlands	767	Peebles	Peebles	1677	
			Edinburgh		1576
			Dumfries		1817
New Luce	893	Wigtown	Wigtown	1695	1705
New Machar	227	Aberdeen	Aberdeen	1676	1740
			Edinburgh		1590
New Monkland	651	Lanark	Hamilton &	1693	1564
			Campsie		
			Glasgow		1652
			Edinburgh		1579
Newport-on-Tay	431				
(see Forgan 431)					
New Spynie	136	Moray	Moray	1711	1688
Newton	696	Edinburgh Midlothian	Edinburgh	1629	1600
Newton-on-Ayr	612	Ayr	Glasgow	1780	1507
(also St Quivox)					
Newtyle	314	Forfar	St Andrews	1685	1591
			Edinburgh		1570

Parish	District number	County	Commissariot	OPR	Testament or inventory
Nigg	266	Kincardine	St Andrews	1675	1614
Nigg	78	Ross & Cromarty	Ross	1730	1820
	.		Edinburgh		1589
North Berwick	713	Haddington E. Lothian	Edinburgh	1604	1576
North Bute	557	Bute	The Isles	1844	1821
North Knapdale	530	Argyll	Argyll	1779	1723
			The Isles		1787
Northmavine	8	Shetland	Orkney & Shetland	1758	1612
North Ronaldshay	22	Orkney	Orkney & Shetland	1800	1611
North Uist	113	Inverness	The Isles	1821	1782
North Yell (also Fetlar 4/1)	4/2	Shetland	Orkney & Shetland	1787	1613
Oa (Islay)	546	Argyll	The Isles	1833	
Oathlaw	315	Forfar	Brechin	1717	1662
Oban (see Kilmore & Kilbride 523)	523	Argyll	Argyll	1796	1790
Ochiltree	609	Ayr	Glasgow	1642	1605
			Edinburgh		1582
Old Cumnock	610	Ayr	Glasgow	1704	1604
Old Deer	228	Aberdeen	Aberdeen	1735	1722
Oldhamstocks	714	Haddington E. Lothian	Edinburgh	1664	1579
Old or West Kilpatrick	501	Dunbarton	Glasgow	1688	1577
Old Luce (or Glenluce 894)	894	Wigtown	Wigtown	1731	1713
Old Machar	168b	Aberdeen	Aberdeen	1641	1785
			Edinburgh		1590
Old Meldrum	229	Aberdeen	Aberdeen	1713	1725
			Moray		1695
Old Monkland	652	Lanark	Hamilton & Campsie	1695	1596
			Edinburgh		1579
			Glasgow		1652
Olrig	39	Caithness	Caithness	1699	1662
Ordiquhill	163	Banff	Aberdeen	1704	1823
Ormiston	715	Haddington E. Lothian	Edinburgh Peebles	1637	1565 1683
Orphir	23	Orkney	Orkney & Shetland	1708	1612
Orwell	463	Kinross	St Andrews Edinburgh	1688	1606 1586
Oxnam (also Edgerston 787b)	802	Roxburgh	Peebles	1700	1682
Oyne	230	Aberdeen	Aberdeen	1703	
Paisley	573	Renfrew	Glasgow Edinburgh		1552 1572

Parish	District number	County	Commissariot	OPR	Testament or inventory
Paisley High	573[1]			1788	
Paisley Middle	573[2]			1788	
Paisley Low	573[3]			1738	
Panbride	316	Forfar	Brechin	1693	1579
			Edinburgh		1576
			St Andrews		1700
Papa-Stour *(also Walls 12/1 & Sandness 12/2)*	12/3	Shetland	Orkney & Shetland	1772	1630
Papa-Westray *(also Westray 33/1)*	33/2	Orkney	Orkney & Shetland	1784	1613
Paplay *(see Holm & Paplay 19)*	19	Orkney	Orkney & Shetland		1613
Parton *(also Corsock-Bridge 862)*	878	Kirkcudbright	Kirkcudbright Edinburgh	1714	1682 1574
Peebles	768	Peebles	Peebles Edinburgh Glasgow	1622	1823 1569 1547
Pencaitland	716	Haddington E. Lothian	Edinburgh	1598	1569
Penicuik	697	Edinburgh	Edinburgh	1654	1586
Penninghame	895	Wigtown	Wigtown Edinburgh	1695	1700 1584
Penpont	845	Dumfries	Dumfries Edinburgh	1728	1627 1581
Persie *(see Blairgowrie 335 & Meigle 379)*	386b				
Perth	387	Perth	St Andrews Dunblane Edinburgh Glasgow	1561	1586 1546 1569 1744
Peterculter	231	Aberdeen	Aberdeen	1643	1730
Peterhead	232	Aberdeen	Aberdeen	1668	1722
Pettinain	653	Lanark	Lanark Edinburgh	1689	1602 1583
Petty	106	Inverness	Moray Inverness Aberdeen	1633	 1630 1743
Pharay *(see Eday & Pharay 15)*	15				
Pitsligo	233	Aberdeen	Aberdeen	1720	1735
Pittenweem	452	Fife	St Andrews Edinburgh	1611	1549 1565
Polmont	487	Stirling	Stirling	1729	1663
Polwarth	754	Berwick	Lauder Edinburgh	1652	1633 1598
Poolewe *(also Gairloch 66)*	66	Ross & Cromarty	Ross	1835	
Port-Glasgow	574	Renfrew	Glasgow	1696	1707
Port of Menteith	388	Perth	Dunblane Edinburgh	1697	1542 1600

Parish	District number	County	Commissariot	OPR	Testament or inventory
Portmoak	464	Kinross	St Andrews	1701	1550
			Edinburgh		1594
Portnahaven (Islay)	547	Argyll	The Isles	1831	
Portpatrick	896	Wigtown	Wigtown	1720	1711
Portree (Skye)	114	Inverness	The Isles	1800	1795
Premnay	234	Aberdeen	Aberdeen	1718	1732
Preston (see Bunkle and Preston 728)	728	Berwick	Lauder		1653
Prestonkirk (formerly Prestonhaugh)	717	Haddington	Edinburgh E. Lothian	1658	1570
Prestonpans (formerly Saltpreston)	718	Haddington E. Lothian	Edinburgh	1596	1568
Prestwick (see Monkton & Prestwick 606)	606	Ayr	Glasgow Edinburgh		1603 1591
Primrose (see Carrington 675)	675				
Quarff (also Bressay 1/1 & Burra 1/2)	1/2	Shetland	Orkney & Shetland	1755	
Queensferry (or Queensferry South) (also Dalmeny 665)	670	Linlithgow W. Lothian	Edinburgh	1635	1568
Queensferry, North (prior to 1855 see Dunfermline 424, since 1855 see Inverkeithing 432)		Fife	St Andrews		1718
Rafford	140	Moray	Moray Edinburgh	1682	1695 1598
Rathen	235	Aberdeen	Aberdeen Edinburgh	1704	1724 1578
Ratho	698a	Edinburgh	Edinburgh	1682	1576
Rathven (also Seafield 167)	164	Banff	Aberdeen Brechin Edinburgh	1716	1581 1594
Rattray	389	Perth	Dunkeld Dunblane Edinburgh	1606	1684 1652 1575
Rayne	236	Aberdeen	Aberdeen	1679	1738
Reay	40	Caithness	Caithness	1732	1812
Redgorton (also Logiealmond 375)	390	Perth	Dunkeld Edinburgh St Andrews	1706	1688 1579 1673
Rendall (see Evie & Rendall 16)	16	Orkney	Orkney & Shetland		1611
Renfrew	575	Renfrew	Hamilton & Campsie Edinburgh	1673	1564 1569
Rerrick	879	Kirkcudbright	Kirkcudbright Edinburgh	1736	1700 1571
Rescobie	317	Forfar	St Andrews Edinburgh	1688	1600 1597
Resolis (formerly Kirkmichael & Cullicudden 79)	79	Ross & Cromarty	Ross	1731	1816

Parish	District number	County	Commissariot	OPR	Testament or inventory
Rhu *(see Row)*	503				
Rhum	116				
(see Small Isles 116)					
Rhynd	391	Perth	St Andrews	1698	1550
Rhynie & Essie	237a	Aberdeen	Moray	1740	1687
Riccarton	611	Ayr	Glasgow	1695	1606
			Edinburgh		1569
Roberton	777	Selkirk	Peebles	1679	1823
Roberton	660	Lanark	Lanark	1691	1620
(also Wiston 660)					
Rogart	55	Sutherland	Caithness	1795	
Ronaldshay North	22				
(see North Ronaldshay 22)					
Ronaldshay South	29				
(see South Ronaldshay 29)					
Rosemarkie	80	Ross & Cromarty	Ross	1744	1804
Roseneath	502	Dunbarton	Glasgow	1722	1606
			Edinburgh		1584
Rosskeen	81	Ross & Cromarty	Ross	1783	1815
			Edinburgh		1596
Rothes	141	Moray	Moray	1717	1686
(also Dundurcas 141)			Edinburgh		1564
Rothesay	558	Bute	The Isles	1691	1661
			Argyll		1740
Rothiemay	165	Banff	Moray	1658	1687
			Aberdeen		1736
			Edinburgh		1587
Rothiemurchus	96b^2	Inverness	Inverness	1774	1630
(also Duthil 96b^1)					
Rousay & Egilshay	24	Orkney	Orkney & Shetland	1733	1612
Row *(or Rhu)*	503	Dunbarton	Glasgow	1760	1675
Roxburgh	803	Roxburgh	Peebles	1624	1683
			Edinburgh		1600
Rutherglen	654	Lanark	Glasgow	1698	1606
			Edinburgh		1581
Ruthven	318	Forfar	Dunkeld	1744	1684
			Moray		1688
			Edinburgh		1587
Ruthwell	846	Dumfries	Dumfries	1723	1638
Saddell & Skipness	531	Argyll	Argyll	1756 1783	1676
St Andrews	25	Orkney	Orkney & Shetland	1657	1612
St Andrews	142	Moray	Moray	1701	1827
(incl. Lhanbryde)					
St Andrews & St Leonards	453	Fife	St Andrews	1627	1549
			Edinburgh		1565
St Boswells	804	Roxburgh	Peebles	1692	1693
(formerly Lessudden 804)					

Parish	District number	County	Commissariot	OPR	Testament or inventory
St Cuthberts	685[2]	Edinburgh Midlothian	Edinburgh	1573	1590
(also Edinburgh 685[1] & Canongate 685[3])					
St Cyrus	267	Kincardine	St Andrews	1696	1792
(formerly Ecclesgreig 267)					
St Fergus	166	Banff	Aberdeen	1658	1823
St Kilda (Skye)	111	Inverness	The Isles	1830	
(also Harris 111)					
St Lawrence	489	Stirling	Stirling		1610
(see Slamannan 489)			Edinburgh		1598
St Leonards	453	Fife	St Andrews	1667	1550
(also St Andrews & St Leonards 453)					
St Madoes	392	Perth	Dunblane	1591	1612
			Dunkeld		1724
			Edinburgh		1594
St Martins	393	Perth	Dunkeld	1697	1586
			St Andrews		1673
			Dunblane		1658
St Monance	454	Fife	St Andrews	1628	1550
(or Abercromie)			Edinburgh		1581
St Mungo	847	Dumfries	Dumfries	1700	1657
St Ninians &	488	Stirling	Stirling	1643	1607
Bannockburn *(also Stirling 490)*			Edinburgh		1576
St Ninians, *(also known as St Ringans)*			St Andrews		1599
St Ola	21	Orkney	Orkney & Shetland		1611
(see Kirkwall & St Ola 21)					
St Quivox	612	Ayr	Glasgow	1735	1612
(also Newton-upon-Ayr 612)			Edinburgh		1599
St Ringans	488				
(see St Ninians 488)					
St Vigeans	319	Forfar	St Andrews	1669	1599
			Edinburgh		1586
Salen (Mull)	548	Argyll	The Isles	1828	1815
Saline	455	Fife	Stirling	1746	1610
Salton	719	Haddington E. Lothian	Edinburgh	1636	1578
Saltpreston	718				
(see Prestonpans 718)					
Sanday	26	Orkney	Orkney & Shetland		1613
(see Cross & Burness and Lady 26)					
Sanday	116				
(see Small Isles 116)					
Sandness	12/2	Shetland	Orkney & Shetland	1787	1630
(also Walls 12/1, Papa Stour 12/3 & Foula 12/4)					
Sandsting & Aithsting	9	Shetland	Orkney & Shetland	1733	1612
Sandwick	27	Orkney	Orkney & Shetland	1728	1612
Sandwick	3/2	Shetland	Orkney & S.	1746	1648
(also Cunningsburgh & Dunrossness 3/1 & Fair Isle 3/3)					

Parish	District number	County	Commissariot	OPR	Testament or inventory
Sanquhar	848	Dumfries	Dumfries	1693	1625
(also Wanlockhead 853)			Wigtown		1787
			Glasgow		1607
			Edinburgh		1565
Saulseat		Wigtown	Wigtown		
(incorporated with Inch in 17th century)			Edinburgh		1593
Savoch	237b	Aberdeen	Aberdeen	1852	1774
Scone	394a	Perth	St Andrews	1620	1592
			Dunblane		1652
			Edinburgh		1586
Scoonie	456	Fife	St Andrews	1675	1550
			Edinburgh		1593
Seafield	164				
(see Rathven 164)					
Selkirk	778	Selkirk	Peebles	1697	1691
			Edinburgh		1567
Shapinsay	28	Orkney	Orkney & Shetland	1632	1612
Shieldaig	58	Ross & Cromarty	Ross	1797	
(also Applecross & Kishorn 58)					
Shisken	554	Bute	The Isles	1701	
(also Lochranza 554)					
Shotts	655	Lanark	Hamilton & Campsie	1707	
			Glasgow		1606
			Edinburgh		1576
Simprim	755	Berwick	Lauder	1700	1631
(also Swinton 755)					
Skene	238	Aberdeen	Aberdeen	1746	1721
Skerries	7/3	Shetland	Orkney & Shetland	1787	
(also Nesting 7/1, Lunnasting 7/2 & Whalsay 7/3)					
Skipness	531				
(see Saddell & Skipness 531)					
Skirling	769	Peebles	Peebles	1683	1823
			Edinburgh		1594
Slains	239	Aberdeen	Aberdeen	1707	1728
Slamannan	489	Stirling	Stirling	1681	1617
(formerly St Lawrence 489)			Edinburgh		1579
Sleat (Skye)	115	Inverness	The Isles	1813	1711
Smailholm	805	Roxburgh	Peebles	1648	1682
			Dumfries		1678
			Lauder		1634
			Edinburgh		1565
Small Isles	116	Inverness	The Isles	1855	
(Rhum, Eigg, Canna, Sanday & Hyskier 116)					
Snizort (Skye)	117	Inverness	The Isles	1823	1723
Sorbie	897	Wigtown	Wigtown	1700	1730
			Edinburgh		1581
Sorn	613	Ayr	Glasgow	1692	1671
(formerly Dalgain 613)			Edinburgh		1584

Parish	District number	County	Commissariot	OPR	Testament or inventory
Southdean	806	Roxburgh	Peebles	1696	1823
(also Abbotrule 806 & Edgerston 787b)			Edinburgh		1591
Southend	532	Argyll	Argyll	1768	1725
(formerly Kilcolmkill & Kilblane)					
South Knapdale	533	Argyll	Argyll	1771	1717
South Ronaldshay	29	Orkney	Orkney &	1657	1611
& Burray *(combined in 1682)*			Shetland		
South Uist	118	Inverness	The Isles	1839	1797
(also Benbecula 118)					
Southwick	861				
(see Colvend 861)					
South Yell	6	Shetland	Orkney &	1730	
			Shetland		
Soutra	686				
(see Fala & Soutra 686)					
Speymouth	143	Moray	Moray	1654	1786
(formerly Essil & Dipple 143)			Edinburgh		1592
Spott	720	Haddington	Edinburgh	1683	1569
		E. Lothian			
Sprouston	807	Roxburgh	Peebles	1635	1681
			Edinburgh		1580
Stair	614	Ayr	Glasgow	1736	
(formed out of Ochiltree 609 in 1673)					
Staplegortoun	839				
(see Langholm 839)					
Stennes	17	Orkney	Orkney &	1732	1613
(also Firth & Stennes 17)			Shetland		
Stenton	721	Haddington	Edinburgh	1679	1581
		E. Lothian	Dunkeld		1766
Stevenston	615	Ayr	Glasgow	1700	1605
Stewarton	616	Ayr	Glasgow	1693	1548
			Edinburgh		1587
Stirling	490	Stirling	Stirling	1587	1607
(also St Ninians & Bannockburn 488)			Edinburgh		1564
Stitchel &	808	Roxburgh	Peebles	1640	1685
Hume (744)			Lauder		1560
Stobhill	698b				
(see Borthwick 674, Cockpen 676, Newbattle 695 & Temple 700)					
Stobo	770	Peebles	Peebles	1783	1684
			Edinburgh		1580
Stonehouse	656	Lanark	Glasgow	1696	1600
Stoneykirk	898	Wigtown	Wigtown	1744	1727
			Edinburgh		1592
Stornoway	88	Ross & Cromarty	The Isles	1762	1798
(Lewis)			Ross		1804
Stow	699	Edinburgh	Edinburgh	1626	1575
(also Caddonfoot 774a)					
Strathcathro	320	Forfar	Brechin	1709	1600
Strachan	268	Kincardine	Brechin	1704	1581

Parish	District number	County	Commissariot	OPR	Testament or inventory
Strachur *(also Stralachlan 534/1)*	534/2	Argyll	Argyll	1745	1685
Straiton	617	Ayr	Glasgow Edinburgh	1644	1551 1576
Stralachlan *(also Strachur 534/2)*	534/1	Argyll	Argyll	1764	1676
Stranraer	899	Wigtown	Wigtown	1695	1701
Strath (Skye)	119	Inverness	The Isles	1820	
Strathaven *(see Avondale 621)*	621	Lanark	Glasgow Edinburgh		1576
Strathblane	491	Stirling	Glasgow Edinburgh	1672	1549 1590
Strathbrock *(see Uphall 672)*	672	Linlithgow	Edinburgh		1592
Strathdon *(formerly Invernochtie, incl. Corgarff 240)*	240	Aberdeen	Aberdeen	1667	1730
Strathfillan *(see Killin 361)*	394b				
Strathmartine *(also Mains 307)*	307	Forfar	St Andrews Edinburgh	1744	1598 1600
Strathmiglo	457	Fife	Dunkeld Edinburgh St Andrews	1719	1694 1578 1595
Strichen	241	Aberdeen	Aberdeen Inverness	1672	1744 1727
Stromness	30	Orkney	Orkney & Shetland	1695	1612
Stronsay	31	Orkney	Orkney & Shetland	1743	1619
Strontian or Sunart *(also Aharacle 505/1, Arisaig 505/2 & W. Ardnamurchan 505/4)*	505/3	Argyll	Argyll	1804	1686
Strowan *(see Monzievaird 383)*	383	Perth	Dunblane Dunkeld		1601 1706
Suddy *(see Knockbain 73)*	73				
Swinton & Simprim	755	Berwick	Lauder Edinburgh	1700	1628 1583
Symington	618	Ayr	Glasgow Edinburgh	1642	1603 1579
Symington	657	Lanark	Lanark	1692	1626
Tain	82	Ross & Cromarty	Ross Edinburgh	1719	1817 1582
Tannadice	321	Forfar	St Andrews Edinburgh	1694	1595 1580
Tarbat	83	Ross & Cromarty	Ross The Isles Edinburgh	1801	1723 1581
Tarbert *(see Kilcalmonell & Kilberry 516)*	516	Argyll	Argyll Glasgow		1778 1793

Parish	District number	County	Commissariot	OPR	Testament or inventory
Tarbolton	619	Ayr	Glasgow Edinburgh	1730	1606 1576
Tarland & Migvy	242	Aberdeen	Aberdeen	1764	
Tarves	243	Aberdeen	Aberdeen	1695	1739
Tealing	322	Forfar	Dunkeld Edinburgh	1599	1688 1568
Temple (also Stobhill 698b)	700	Edinburgh Midlothian	Edinburgh	1688	1589
Tenandry (see Blair Atholl 334, Dull 346 & Moulin 384)	394c	Perth	Dunkeld Lauder		1674
Terregles	880	Kirkcudbright	Dumfries Edinburgh	1724	1624 1564
Teviothead (formed out of Hawick & Cavers in 1850)	809	Roxburgh	Peebles	1824	
Thankerton (see Covington 634)	634	Lanark	Lanark		1601
Thurso	41	Caithness	Caithness Edinburgh	1647	1662 1598
Tibbermore	395	Perth	Dunkeld Dunblane Edinburgh	1694	1688 1656 1576
Tillicoultry	468	Clackmannan	Dunblane Stirling Edinburgh	1640	1554 1610 1597
Tingwall (also Whiteness & Weesdale 10/2)	10/1	Shetland	Orkney & Shetland	1709	1613
Tinwald	849	Dumfries	Dumfries	1789	1624
Tiree (see Tyree 551)	551				
Tobermory (Mull)	549	Argyll	The Isles	1830	1803
Tongland	881	Kirkcudbright	Kirkcudbright Edinburgh	1693	1713 1577
Tongue	56	Sutherland	Caithness	1789	
Torosay (Mull) (also Kinlochspelvie 545)	550	Argyll	The Isles	1772	1730
Torphichen	671	Linlithgow W. Lothian	Edinburgh	1693	1577
Torrance (see East Kilbride 643)	643	Lanark	Hamilton & Campsie Glasgow Edinburgh		1610 1583
Torryburn	458	Fife	St Andrews Stirling	1663	1616 1664
Torthorwald	850	Dumfries	Dumfries	1696	1657
Tough	244	Aberdeen	Aberdeen	1706	1724
Towie	245	Aberdeen	Aberdeen	1751	1757
Tranent	722	Haddington E. Lothian	Edinburgh	1611	1570

Parish	District number	County	Commissariot	OPR	Testament or inventory
Traquair	771	Peebles	Peebles	1694	1823
			Edinburgh		1577
Trinity-Gask	396	Perth	Dunblane	1641	1603
			Dunkeld		1719
			Edinburgh		1577
Troqueer	882	Kirkcudbright	Dumfries	1690	1629
(also Maxwelltown 882)			Edinburgh		1583
Tulliallan	397	Perth	Dunblane	1673	1618
			Edinburgh		1578
Tullibody	465	Clackmannan	Stirling		1655
(see Alloa 465)			Edinburgh		1565
Tullibole	461	Kinross	St Andrews		
(see Fossoway & Tullibole 461)			Dunblane		1543
			Edinburgh		1592
Tullich	201	Aberdeen	Aberdeen		1750
(see Glenmuick, Tullich etc. 201)					
Tullynessle	246	Aberdeen	Aberdeen	1760	1775
(also Forbes & Kearn 246)					
Tundergarth	851	Dumfries	Dumfries	1791	1690
Turriff	247	Aberdeen	Aberdeen	1696	1731
Tweedsmuir	772	Peebles	Peebles	1644	1823
Twynholm	883	Kirkcudbright	Kirkcudbright	1694	1676
			Edinburgh		1574
Tynninghame	723	Haddington E. Lothian	Edinburgh		1564
(see Whitekirk & Tynninghame 723)					
Tynron	852	Dumfries	Dumfries	1742	1637
			Edinburgh		1569
Tyree (also Coll)	551/1	Argyll	The Isles	1766	1817
Tyrie	248	Aberdeen	Aberdeen	1710	1789
Udny	249	Aberdeen	Aberdeen	1744	1755
Uig	89	Ross & Cromarty	The Isles	1824	
Uist, North	113				
(see North Uist 113)					
Ulva	544	Argyll	Argyll	1828	
Unst	11	Shetland	Orkney & Shetland	1776	1613
Uphall	672	Linlithgow	Edinburgh	1600	1588
(formerly Strathbrock 672)					
Urquhart	144	Moray	Moray	1647	
			Edinburgh		1590
Urquhart & Glenmoriston	107	Inverness	Inverness	1739	1610
			Edinburgh		1590
Urquhart & Logie-Wester	84	Ross & Cromarty	Ross	1715	1821
			Moray		1687
Urr	884	Kirkcudbright	Kirkcudbright	1760	1790
(also Dalbeattie 864)			Dumfries		1624
Urray	85	Ross & Cromarty	Ross	1756	1812
			Edinburgh		1592

Parish	District number	County	Commissariot	OPR	Testament or inventory
Walls	12/1	Shetland	Orkney & Shetland	1771	1620
(also Sandness 12/2, Papa Stour 12/3 & Foula 12/4)					
Walls	32/1	Orkney	Orkney & Shetland	1708	1611
(also Flotta 32/2)					
Walston	658	Lanark	Lanark	1679	1621
Wamphray	853a	Dumfries	Dumfries	1709	1656
Wandell & Lamington	659	Lanark	Lanark	1656	1623
Wanlockhead	853	Dumfries	Dumfries		1748
(see Sanquhar 848)					
Watten	42	Caithness	Caithness	1714	1662
Weem	398	Perth	Dunkeld	1692	1738
Weesdale, now	10/2	Shetland	Orkney & Shetland	1727	1613
Weisdale *(also Tingwall 10/1 & Whiteness 10/2)*					
Wemyss	459	Fife	St Andrews Edinburgh	1660	1549 1568
West Calder	701	Edinburgh	Edinburgh	1645	1567
Westerkirk	854	Dumfries	Dumfries	1693	1642
West Kilbride	620	Ayr	Glasgow	1671	
West Kilpatrick	501				
(see Old or West Kilpatrick 501)					
West Linton	773	Peebles	Peebles	1656	1823
Westray	33/1	Orkney	Orkney & Shetland	1733	1615
(also Papa-Westray 33/2)					
Westruther	756	Berwick	Lauder	1657	1636
Whalsay &	7/3	Shetland	Orkney & Shetland	1787	1613
Skerries *(also Nesting 7/1 & Lunnasting 7/2)*					
Whitburn	673	Linithgow W. Lothian	Edinburgh	1719	1597
Whitekirk & Tynninghame	723	Haddington E. Lothian	Edinburgh	1695	1597
Whiteness &	10/2	Shetland	Orkney & Shetland	1727	1613
Weesdale/Weisdale *(also Tingwall 10/1)*					
Whithorn	900	Wigtown	Wigtown Edinburgh	1712	1700 1584
Whitsome & Hilton	757	Berwick	Lauder	1724	1653
Whittinghame	724	Haddington E. Lothian	Edinburgh Lauder	1627	1582 1790
Wick	43	Caithness	Caithness	1701	1661
Wigtown	901	Wigtown	Wigtown Edinburgh	1706	1700 1587
Wilton	810	Roxburgh	Peebles	1694	1610
Wiston	660	Lanark	Lanark	1694	1601
(also Roberton 660)					
Woodhouselee	687				
(see Glencorse 687)					
Wormit	431				
(see Forgan 431)					

Parish	District number	County	Commissariot	OPR	Testament or inventory
Yarrow (also Kirkhope 776 & Ettrick 774b)	779	Selkirk	Peebles	1691	1686
Yell, Mid (see Mid Yell 6)	6				
Yell, North (see North Yell (also Fetlar) 4/1)	4/2				
Yell, South (see South Yell 6)	6				
Yester, or Gifford	725	Haddington E. Lothian	Edinburgh	1654	1591
Yetholm	811	Roxburgh	Peebles	1689	

Appendix IV

Book list

GENEALOGY

Ferguson, Joan P.S., compiler *Family Histories.* (1986, National Library of Scotland, Edinburgh.)

Hamilton-Edwards, Gerald, *In Search of Scottish Ancestry.* (1983, Phillimore, Chichester.)

Sandison, Alexander, *Tracing Ancestors in Shetland.* (1985, A. Sandison, London.)

Steel, D.J., *Sources of Scottish Genealogy and Family History.* (1970, Phillimore, London & Chichester.)

Stuart, Mrs Margaret, & Paul, Sir James Balfour, *Scottish Family History.* (1930, Oliver & Boyd, Edinburgh.)

THE CHURCH

Anson, Peter F., *The Catholic Church in Modern Scotland.* (1937, Burns, Oates, Washbourne, London.)

Beckerlegge, O.A., compiler *United Methodist Ministers & Their Church.* (1968, Epworth Press, London.)

Burnet, George B., *The Story of Quakerism in Scotland.* (1952, James Clark, London.)

Couper, William J., *The Reformed Presbyterian Church in Scotland, its Congregations, Ministers and Students.* A Fasti of this church from 1743–1876. (1925, United Free Church of Scotland Publication Dept., Edin.)

Daiches, Salis, *The Jew in Scotland.* Pub. Scottish Church History Society Records III (1929) 196–209.

Ewing, William, *Annals of the Free Church of Scotland 1843–1900* 2 Vols. (1914, T. & T. Clark, Edinburgh.)

Goldie, Frederick, *A Short History of the Episcopal Church in Scotland from the Restoration to the Present Time.* (1951, S.P.C.K., London.)

Hutchison, Matthew, *The Reformed Presbyterian Church in Scotland, 1680–1876.* (1893, J. & R. Parlane, Paisley.)

Lamb, John A., *The Fasti of the United Free Church of Scotland, 1900–1929*. (1956, Oliver & Boyd, Edinburgh.)

Macdonald, Donald F. Macleod, *Fasti Ecclesiae Scoticanae* Vol. 10. Ministers of the church from 1955–1975. (1981, The Saint Andrew Press, Edinburgh.)

MacKelvie, William, *Annals & Statistics of the United Presbyterian Church*. (1873, Oliphant and Co., Edinburgh.)

Scott, Hew, *Fasti Ecclesiae Scoticanae; the succession of Ministers in the Parish Churches of Scotland from 1560*. New edition revised by W. S. Crockett and Sir Francis J. Grant (1915–1961) 9 Vols. (1961, Oliver & Boyd, Edinburgh.)

Small, R., *History of the Congregations of the United Presbyterian Church from 1733–1900*. (1904, David M. Small, Edinburgh.)

Swift, Wesley F., *Methodism in Scotland*. (1947, Epworth Press, London.)

HISTORY

Donaldson, Gordon, *Scotland, the Shaping of a Nation*. (1974, David & Charles, London.)

Donaldson, Gordon, *Scotland: Church and Nation through Sixteen Centuries*. (2nd edition 1972, Scottish Academic Press, Edinburgh.)

Donaldson, Gordon, *Scottish Church History*. (1985, Scottish Academic Press, Edinburgh.)

Donaldson, G. & Morpeth S., *A Dictionary of Scottish History*. (1977, John Donald, Edinburgh.)

Dunbar, Sir Archibald H., *Scottish Kings 1005–1625*, with notes of principal events, tables of regnal years, pedigrees, calendars etc. (1909, David Douglas, Edinburgh.)

Smout, T.C., *A History of the Scottish People 1580–1930*. (1969, Collins, London and Glasgow.)

ARMY & NAVY

Hamilton-Edwards, Gerald, *In Search of Army Ancestry*. (1977, Phillimore, London and Chichester.)

Rodger, N.A.M., *Naval Records for Genealogists*. (1984, PRO, London.)

HERALDRY

Innes of Learney, Sir Thomas, *Scots Heraldry*. (2nd edition 1956, Oliver & Boyd, Edin. and London.)

Paul, Sir James Balfour, *An Ordinary of Arms Contained in the Public Register of All Arms and Bearings. (1672-1902)*, continued as Vol. 2 by David Reid of Robertland and Vivien Wilson, covering the period 1903 to 73 (1977, Lyon Office, Edinburgh.)

CLANS

Adam, Frank, *The Clans, Septs and Regiments of the Scottish Highlands.* rev. by Sir T. Innes of Learney. (8th edn. 1970, W. & A.K. Johnston & G.W. Bacon Ltd., Edinburgh and London.)

Bain, R., *The Clans and Tartans of Scotland.* 4th edn. Enlarged and revised by Margaret O. Macdougall. (1959, Collins, London and Glasgow.)

Moncreiffe, of that Ilk, Sir Rupert Iain Kay, Bart., *The Highland Clans: Dynastic origins, chiefs and background of their clans connected with Highland history and some other families.* (1967, Barry & Rockcliff, London.)

Moncreiffe, Sir Iain and Pottinger, Don, *Map of Scotland of Old.* Shows areas of distribution of clans and families at the beginning of the seventeenth century. (1960, Bartholomew, Edinburgh.)

Munro, R.W., *Scotland, Land of Kin and Clan.* Well illustrated. (1980, Cassell Ltd., London.)

Munro, R.W., *Kinsmen and Clansmen.* Colour plates of tartans. (1971, Johnston & Bacon, Edinburgh.)

GENERAL

Black, George F., *The Surnames of Scotland, their Origin, Meaning and History.* (1946, The New York Public Library, New York.)

Camp, A.J., *Wills and their Whereabouts.* (1974, Phillimore, Canterbury.)

"Claverhouse" (M.C. Smith), *Irregular Border Marriages.* (1934, Moray Press, Edinburgh and London.)

Cox, J., and Padfield T., *Tracing your ancestors in the Public Record Office.* (1984, H.M.S.O.)

Dobson, David, *Dictionary of Scottish Settlers in North America 1625–1825.* (1985, Genealogical Publishing Inc., Baltimore.)

Donaldson, Gordon, *The Scots Overseas.* (1966, Hale, London.)

Ferguson, Joan P.S., *Directory of Scottish Newspapers.* (1984, National Library of Scotland, Edin.)

Foster, Janet, and Shepherd, Julia, *British Archives.* (1983, Macmillan, London.)

Gibson, J.S., *Wills and where to find them.* (1974, Phillimore, London and Chichester.)

Groome, Francis, *Gazetteer of Scotland* 6 Vols. 1882–1885. (1882–1885, Thomas C. Jack, Edinburgh.)

McLaughlin, Eve, *Simple Latin for Family Historians.* (1986, Federation of Family History Socs.)

Munro, R.W., ed. *Johnstone's Gazetteer of Scotland.* (1973, Johnson & Bacon, Edin. & London.)

Simpson, Grant G., *Scottish Handwriting 1150–1650*. An introduction to the reading of documents. (1973, Bratton Publishing, Edinburgh.)

Walker, Stephen P., *The Society of Accountants in Edinburgh 1854–1914*. (1987, Pub. privately.)

Whyte, Donald (ed.), *Dictionary of Scottish Emigrants to the U.S.A.* 2 Vols. (1972 and 1986, Magna Carta Books Co., Baltimore.)

Whyte, Donald (ed.), *Dictionary of Scottish Emigrants to Canada before Confederation.* (1986, Ontario Genealogical Society, Toronto.)

LAW

Bell, George J., *A Dictionary & Digest of the Law of Scotland*. 7th edn. by George Watson. (1890, Bell & Bardfute, Edinburgh.)

Bell, Robert, *A Dictionary of the Law of Scotland* (intended for the use of the public at large as well as for the profession). (1807, Printed by John Anderson, Edinburgh.) Sold by Messrs Longman, Hurst, Rees and Orme, London.

Gibb, A.D., *Student's Glossary of Scottish Legal Terms*. (1946, W. Green & Son, Edinburgh.)

Grant, Sir Francis J. (ed.), *The Faculty of Advocates in Scotland 1532–1943 with genealogical notes*. (1944, The Scottish Record Society.)

The Register of the Society of Writers to the Signet. Details of Members from the fifteenth century to the 1980s. (1983, Clark Constable, Edinburgh.)

Appendix V

Sample forms for searchers

BIRTH ENTRY

District registration and entry number ....

Name and Surname .... Sex (M/F)

Date of birth ....

Place of birth ....

Place of residence (if different) ....

Name and Surname of Father ....

Occupation of Father .... if deceased...........

Name and Surname of Mother ....

Maiden Surname (M/S) of Mother ....

Occupation of Mother .... if deceased...........

Date and place of parents' marriage ....

Name of Informant ....

Relationship to the child ....

MARRIAGE ENTRY

District registration and entry number ....

Date of marriage ....

Place of marriage ....

According to Forms/Rites of ....

Name and Surname of Groom ....

Age and Marital Status ....

Occupation ....

Usual Residence ....

Name and Surname of Father ....

Occupation of Father .... if deceased............

Name and Surname of Mother ....

Maiden Surname of Mother .... if deceased............

Name and Surname of Bride ....

Age and Marital Status ....

Occupation ....

Usual residence ....

Name and Surname of Father ....

Occupation of Father .... if deceased............

Name and Surname of Mother ....

Maiden Surname of Mother .... if deceased............

Name of Minister (etc) ....

Witnesses ....

Addresses ....

DEATH ENTRY

District registration and entry number ....

Name and Surname .... Sex (M/F)............

Age at death and Occupation ....

Date of death ....

Place of death ....

Place of residence (if different) ....

Marital Status and name of spouse ....

Name of Father ....

Occupation of Father .... if deceased............

Name of Mother ....

Occupation, M/S of Mother .... if deceased............

Cause of death ....

Name of Informant ....

Relationship to the deceased ....

Part II

A STEP-BY-STEP GUIDE TO SHOW YOU
THE EASIEST WAY TO WORK OUT
YOUR OWN FAMILY TREE,
QUICKLY AND ACCURATELY

HOW TO DRAW A DROP-LINE CHART

A Step-by-Step
Guide

To guide you through all the steps necessary in searching the records for birth, marriage and death entries after Statutory (Civil) Registration was introduced in 1855, and the Old Parish Registers before that date, I have been given permission to use the family tree of Margaret Dudgeon Young. Through finding out all about the Young and the Dudgeon families, when and where they were born, married, and died, I hope to show you the easiest way to work out your family tree, quickly and accurately.

During the course of this search we shall find ourselves going down some blind alleys, but this will serve to show some of the snags you may meet when searching our own family lines.

SEARCHING FOR A BIRTH ENTRY FROM 1855 ONWARDS

1. Choose a member of the family born in Scotland, whose parents' names, or at least one parent's name you know.

2. Decide in which *year* you want to start your search. Take out *red* index book for the appropriate year, turn to *surname* then find the *Christian* or *forename* you need. This system of using index books will be altered once all the entries have been put on computer – approximately 1993. The computer is easy to use and much quicker when searching over several years.

Probably there will be more than one entry for the name, so it will help to know the town or parish of birth. In this case I was searching for the *birth of Archibald Young* and I had been given his marriage certificate, dated 1922, as a starting point (Figure 11).

From the copy of his certificate we deduce that Archibald Young, aged 53, would have been born in 1869. He was the son of Thomas Young and Maria Long Young, maiden surname (M/S) Dudgeon. The marriage took place in Edinburgh, and, according to tradition, the family originated from that area.

In the index of births for 1869, I found six entries for the name

163

Archibald Young, but only one for Edinburgh. I wrote down in my notebook all the information from the index:

Birth Archibald Young. 1869 St Andrews Edinburgh – 326.

From the wall chart showing all the District Registration Numbers for Scotland I noted St Andrews, (District), Edinburgh, as 685^2.

I was careful to take the number for St Andrews, Edinburgh and not for St Andrews, Fife or St Andrews, Dundee, or I would have been in all sorts of trouble. Always make a note of the district registration and entry numbers for the year you require, as they are vital to the search.

I now filled in an order slip for a statutory register (Figure 12) as illustrated. When I received the register I checked the names of the parents against those recorded in the 1922 marriage entry. I then copied the information as follows:

> *Birth of Archibald Young*
> 1869 St Andrews District, Edinburgh (685^2/326) on April 10th at
>   5h. P.M. at 26 Maryfield Place, Edinburgh.
> *Archibald Young*   son of Thomas Young, Joiner (Journey-
>   man) & Maria Young, M/S Dudgeon.
> Marriage of parents   1859 June 6th Edinburgh.
> Informant   Thomas Young. Father. Present.

This 1869 birth certificate of Archibald Young contained the following information:

1. Date and time of birth.
2. An address, 26 Maryfield Place, Edinburgh, which can be used for the 1871 census return. Addresses are important as they lead to census entries which in turn show the parish of birth.
3. The marriage date and place for Thomas Young and Maria Dudgeon.
4. That both parents were alive when the baby was born.
5. That the informant was the father.
6. That Thomas Young was a joiner by trade. He was a journeyman joiner, i.e., he had passed his apprenticeship but he was not yet a master joiner.

Following item 2 on the list, I would search the 1871 census return and hope to find the Young family. This return should show the names of other brothers and sisters born between 1869, when Archibald was born, and 1859, when his parents married. The 1871 census may show a child born in 1870 or early 1871.

Following item 3, I would search for the marriage of Thomas Young and Maria Long Dudgeon in 1859, and for the purpose of this exercise I decided to do that.

SEARCHING FOR A MARRIAGE ENTRY FROM 1855 ONWARDS

Marriage index books are bound in green. In the 1859 male marriage index I found two entries for the name 'Young, Thomas . . . St George, (Edin) 84', and St George (Edin) 230. In the 1859 female marriage index an entry for the name 'Dudgeon, Maria . . . St George, (Edin) 84', from which you can see that the entry number I needed was 84. The wall chart indicated that for 1859 the district registration number for St George, Edinburgh is 685[1].

The entry in my notebook read:

Marriage of Thomas Young and Maria Dudgeon
1859 St George District, Edinburgh (685[1]/84)

Beware! District registration sub-numbers depend on the year of the event.

I again completed an order slip for a statutory register, filling in the line for a *marriage register*, and I noted all the information this certificate contained. I suggest that unless you are filling in your own pre-prepared certificate you use the following form:

Marriage of Thomas Young and Maria Dudgeon
1859 St George, Edinburgh, (685[1]/84) on June 6th 1859.
        Marriage after Banns was solemnized between us according to the Forms of the . . .

Thomas Young	Aged 23. Bachelor. Joiner.
	Usual residence, 27 Bread Street. (Edinburgh)
son of	John Young, Joiner (deceased) and Agnes Young M/S Paterson.
and	
Maria Dudgeon	Aged 19, Spinster, Servant.
	Usual residence, Drumdryan House (Edinburgh).
daughter of	Adam Dudgeon, Butcher (deceased) and Jean Dudgeon M/S Charles (deceased)
Signed	Robert Gemmell. Minister.
Witnesses	Andrew Taylor, Helen Young.
	John Graham, William McLean.

This 1859 marriage certificate contained the following information concerning the bridegroom:

1. Thomas Young, aged 23 in 1859, therefore born about 1836.

2. His father, John Young, a joiner and deceased by 1859.

3. His mother, Agnes Young, maiden surname (M/S) Paterson, alive in 1859.

4. His usual residence in 1859 was 27 Bread Street, Edinburgh.

5. Thomas Young was a bachelor at the time of his marriage, 1859.

6. Thomas Young was a joiner.

7. Thomas Young's religious denomination not known: entry incomplete. If necessary, this may be found by searching for the minister, Robert Gemmell, in *Fasti* etc.

8. One witness was Helen Young who may have been related to Thomas.

Similar information was recorded for Maria Dudgeon. Although her son Archibald gave her name as Maria Long Dudgeon when he married in 1922, she did not use this middle name in 1859.

Concerning the bride, there was the following information:

1. Maria Dudgeon, aged 19 in 1859, therefore born about 1840.

2. Her father, Adam Dudgeon, a butcher, deceased by 1859.

3. Her mother, Jean Dudgeon, M/S Charles, deceased by 1859.

4. Her usual residence in 1859 was Drumdryan House, Edinburgh.

5. Maria Dudgeon, probably in service at Drumdryan House as a maid.

6. It should be possible to find out who owned Drumdryan House and so to ascertain the names of Maria's employers.

7. Maria Dudgeon's religious denomination not known: entry incomplete, but might be found through minister, Robert Gemmell.

What Next?

At this point I made a chart to see how far the search had advanced. The squared chart (Figure 13) is an easy one to use while the search is in progress, as it shows each generation at a glance. Once siblings have been found, it is better to construct a drop-line chart as illustrated later in this chapter (Figures 18 and 21). Looking at the squared chart (Figure 13) we have the following information:

1. Thomas Young married Maria Dudgeon in Edinburgh in 1859.

2. Archibald, their son, was born in Edinburgh in 1869.

3. Thomas Young was the son of John Young (deceased by 1859) and his wife Agnes Paterson (alive in 1859).

4. Maria Dudgeon was the daughter of Adam Dudgeon (deceased by 1859) and his wife Jean Charles (deceased by 1859).

What Next?

A search of the 1871 census return revealed that the family were no longer at 26 Maryfield Place, Edinburgh, where Archibald Young was born in 1869. As the 1922 marriage certificate of Archibald Young recorded that his father Thomas was a surveyor, the next step was to search the most readily available copy of the *Post Office Directory for Edinburgh and Leith*. An entry in the 1888–9 issue showed:

Young, Thomas, ordained surveyor, 10 Brunton Ter. Edinburgh.

Having found a new address, the next step was to search the 1891 census return for 10 Brunton Terrace, Edinburgh, using the street index to obtain reference numbers:

1891/685²/Book 16/page 17 at 10 Brunton Terrace, Civil Parish of South Leith, Burgh of Edinburgh

Thomas	Young	Head	Mar.	53	Surveyor of Buildings	Born England
Maria	"	wife	"	50	–	b. Musselburgh Edinburghsh.
John	"	son	unmar	28	Surveyor of Buildings	b. Edinburgh Edinburghsh.
Agnes	"	daur.	"	26	Housekeeper	b. Wick, Caithness
Thomas	"	son	"	24	School Teacher	b. Hollywood, Dumfriesshire
Archibald	"	son	"	21	Ironmonger's Assistant	b. Edinburgh
Alexander	"	son	"	18	Dental Student	b. England
Ann	"	daur.	"	14	Scholar	b. England

As the next earliest available census return was 1881, I again searched the *Edinburgh and Leith Directory* (1881–2) for an address for Thomas Young and his family. The 1881 census may give more detail concerning the place of birth in England of Thomas, and his children Alexander and Ann. The 1881–2 Directory gave the address 26 Maryfield Place. (This is where Archibald had been born in 1869, but the family was not there in the 1871 census return.) Using the street index for the 1881 census return for Edinburgh for the reference number I found the following entry:

1881/685²/34/5 at 26 Maryfield Place, Greenside, Edinburgh

Thomas	Young	Head	mar.	43	Building Surveyor	b. England
Maria	"	wife	"	40	–	b. Musselburgh Midlothian

John	"	son	"	18 App.	"	"	b. Edinburgh
Agnes	"	daur	"	16	"	Dressmaker	b. Edinburgh
Thomas	"	son	"	14	Scholar		b. Edinburgh
Archibald	"	son	"	11	"		b. Edinburgh
Alexander	"	son	"	8	"		b. England
Annie	"	daur	"	4		–	b. England

Unfortunately, no precise places of birth were recorded here either. Also, the places of birth for Agnes and Thomas were recorded as Edinburgh whereas in the 1891 census return they had been Wick and Holywood!

What Next?

I now decided to search for the deaths of *Thomas Young* (aged 53 in 1891) and his wife *Maria Dudgeon* (aged 50 in 1891), both alive in 1922 at the marriage of their son Archibald. I searched the death index from 1922 until I found the following entries:

> *Death of Maria Young*
> 1926 North Leith, Edinburgh. (685¹⁰/40) on February 5th at 18 Dudley Terrace, Leith.

Maria Long Young	Aged 85. Married to Thomas Young. Building Surveyor. (Retired).
Daughter of	Adam Dudgeon. Cattle Dealer (deceased) and Jean Dudgeon M/S Charles (deceased).
Cause of death	Carcinoma of Pancreas. 3 Months. As Certified by A. Murray Woods, M.D.
Informant	John Young. Son. Present. 2 Bellevue Crescent, Ayr.

> *Death of Thomas Young*
> 1928 North Leith, Edinburgh (685¹⁰/15) on January 11th at 18 Dudley Terrace, Leith.

Thomas Young	Aged 90. Building Surveyor. (Retired) Widower of Maria Long Dudgeon.
Son of	John Young. Wright (Joiner) (deceased) and of Agnes Young M/S Paterson (deceased).
Cause of death	Myocarditis. Influenza. Cardiac Failure. As Certified by A. Murray Woods, M.D.
Informant	John Young. Son. Present. 2 Bellevue Crescent, Ayr.

What Next?

Since it is always advisable to work on one family name at a time, I decided to complete, as far as possible, the Young line.

The 1891 census return for 10 Brunton Terrace showed siblings for Archibald: I can now search for those who were born in Scotland and perhaps visit St Catherine's House in London to search for those born in England. Civil registration started in England in 1837, so the birth entry for Thomas Young, born in England, and aged 53 in 1891, should be there: and so should the entries for Alexander and Ann. It will be possible to identify Thomas Young as the names of his parents were given on his marriage certificate in 1859.

The 1891 census return recorded that Thomas and Maria had a son John born in Edinburgh circa 1863 (he was aged 28 in 1891); I searched the index to find the correct John Young entry.

Birth of John Young
1862 St Andrews District Edinburgh (685^2/334) on April 16th at
    8 Simes Court, Calton Hill, Edinburgh.

John Young	son of Thomas Young, Joiner (Journeyman) and of Maria Young M/S Dudgeon.
Marriage of parents	1859 June 6th Edinburgh.
Informant	Thomas Young. Father. Present.

Making use of the information contained in the above certificate, I searched the 1861 census return for 8 Simes Court, Calton Hill, Edinburgh. The street index provided the reference numbers for this address.

1861/685^2/Book 93 page 12 at 8 Calton Hill, Edinburgh

Thomas	Young	Head	married	24	Joiner J.	Born England, London
Maria	"	wife	"	20		Born Midlothian, Inveresk
Jane	"	daughter		10 mos.		Born Midlothian, S. Leith

Simes Court was omitted by the enumerator.

This census return provided some information not previously known. Thomas Young was born in London, England; Jane aged 10 months in 1861 was not listed in either the 1881 or the 1891 census return.

I searched for her birth entry (she should have been born either in 1860 or 1861 in South Leith). I did not find an entry in the birth index for a Jane Young in South Leith or in North Leith for either of those years. However, I did find two entries in Edinburgh, and on examination, one of these turned out to be correct for this search; i.e. the parents' names were Thomas Young and Maria Dudgeon.

Birth of Jane Young
1860   St Andrew, (Edinburgh) (658²/452) on May 31 at
                8 Calton Hill, Edinburgh.

Jane Young   daughter of Thomas Young, Joiner (Journeyman)
                 and of Maria Young M/S Dudgeon.
Informant   Thomas Young. Father. Present.

You will notice that *no date and place of the parents' marriage* was shown
on the above certificate. This was not recorded on birth certificates for
the years 1856–60 inclusive. (See chapter on 'Searching Registers from
1855 Onwards'.)

The information contained in the 1891 and 1881 census returns
showed that there were other children born to Thomas and Maria
Young in Scotland; so I decided to take copies of these entries to find
out where the family had been living. They were Agnes, aged 26 in
1891 born in Wick, County Caithness. Thomas, aged 24, born in
Holywood, County Dumfries. (The spelling in the census was given as
Hollywood.) Bearing in mind they may have been born in Edinburgh,
I searched the births index and found the following entries:

Birth of Agnes Paterson Young
1864   Wick, County Caithness (43/298) on December 4th at
         Alexandra Place, Wick.
Agnes Paterson Young   daughter of Thomas Young. Joiner, and
                          of Maria Young M/S Dudgeon.
Marriage of parents   [Not recorded].
Informant   Thomas Young. Father.

Birth of Thomas Young
1866   Holywood, Co. Dumfries (830/33) on October 4th at
         Newtonairds.
Thomas Young   son of Thomas Young, Journeyman
                        Joiner and of Maria Young M/S Dudgeon.
Marriage of parents   1859 June 6th St Cuthberts, Edinburgh.
Informant   Thomas Young. Father.

So the 1891 census return was more reliable than the 1881. Agnes and
Thomas were not born in Edinburgh after all. This shows the
advisability of trying to find a family in more than one census return.

The Young family certainly moved around a great deal! They had
children in Edinburgh, Wick, Dumfries and England. To have found
these entries without the help of a census would have been a
monumental task.

What Next?

Still working on the *Young* line. The 1859 marriage certificate of Thomas

Young and Maria Dudgeon recorded that Thomas's father John was deceased but that his mother, Agnes Paterson, was still alive at that date.

Although Thomas Young was born in London, England (according to the 1861 census return), he was in Scotland for his marriage in 1859, and for the births of most of his children; so it was worth searching for the deaths of his parents in Scottish records.

To search for the death of a John Young, age unknown, anywhere in Scotland between 1855 and 1860, promised to be a long haul; particularly as the death index for that period does not show ages at time of death.

It is nearly always best policy to *search for the death of the wife first*, so I started by looking for the death of Agnes Paterson, who was alive in 1859. There was a chance that she and her husband may have died in the same place.

SEARCHING FOR A DEATH ENTRY FROM 1855 ONWARDS

From 1859–65 married women are indexed (1) Under married surname with maiden surname in brackets alongside, shown as 'M/S' or '(or)'; (2) Under maiden surname with no mention of married surname. From the 1860 death index I noted: 'Young, (or Paterson) Agnes . . . Dundee (1st D.) 725; Paterson, Agnes . . . Dundee (1st D.) 725.'

Having found from the wall chart that the registration number for Dundee, 1st District in 1860, is 282[1], I ordered an 1860 death register, registration district number 282[1], entry number 725. Again I used the order slip for statutory registers, only this time filling in the line for a death entry. When I read entry 725 I found Agnes Young, widow of a *slater* and daughter of James *Paterson*, baker, London. But since death registers in Scotland from 1856 to 1861 do not record the name of the spouse I could not know for certain whether or not this was *our* Agnes Young M/S Paterson. However, since the subject of entry 725 would have been 57 years of age when her son Thomas was born, since she resided in Dundee when all the rest of the family were in Edinburgh, and since she was the widow of a slater and not a joiner, I reluctantly dismissed the entry as irrelevant. Nevertheless, this illustrates how important it is to record very carefully all the information, and not to accept an entry just because the names seem correct at first.

What Next?

I went back to the index of deaths to see if I could find the death of 'our' Agnes Young M/S Paterson. I searched under Young, Agnes, and Paterson, Agnes from 1859 up to 1892, and at last I found the correct entry! The names Agnes Young and Agnes Paterson were both in Liberton; both entries had the same age, 86, and the same entry number, 92. I ordered up the death register and copied out the information:

Death of Agnes Young
1892 Liberton Co. Midlothian (693/92) on September at Park
      Neuk, Liberton.

Agnes Young	aged 86 Widow of John Young, Joiner.
daughter of	Thomas Paterson, Builder (deceased) and of Catherine Paterson M/S Lithgow (deceased).
Cause	Old Age. Syncope caused by Diarrhoea. 1 Day. As Cert. by W. Booth F.R.C.S.E. etc.
Informant	Thomas Young. Son present. 10 Brunton Terrace, Edinburgh.

The informant on the above death certificate confirms that this time
I have the correct entry. I had already found Thomas Young at
Brunton Terrace in the 1891 census return. I searched the 1891 census
return for Liberton, but found nothing applicable to this search. Agnes
Young was not there then.

Agnes Dudgeon's husband, *John Young*, was definitely recorded as
being deceased in 1859 when his son was married, and with luck that was
correct. To try to save time I consulted the Monumental Inscriptions held
in New Register House for the parishes where the family had been, i.e.,
Edinburgh, Leith and Liberton, but found nothing applicable, so I
returned to the death index.

No ages were recorded in the death index before 1866, and as there
were so many entries for that name each year, I decided to confine the
search to those entries found in the Edinburgh area. There were twelve
of them, and on examination of those twelve entries, only one was a
married man, the rest were children or single men.

The one married man was a John Young who died in 1858, in Edinburgh, aged about 60, Slater (Master); Married; son of James Young,
Teacher (deceased) and —[blank]; Informant, William Goodlet, Brother-
in-law. Was he 'our' John Young? It seems doubtful as his occupation was
recorded as Master Slater and not as Joiner; he was married but his wife's
name was not recorded. How could I prove it one way or another?

What Next?

The next step was to search the 1851 census return for the address
given in the death certificate. So, using the street index for Edinburgh,
I ordered the census return, and when I read the microfilm I found:

1851/685[6] at 1 Gayfield Place, Parish of St Cuthberts,
Parliamentary Burgh of Edinburgh.

John	Young	Head	married	46	Master Slater	B. New Bannswick
Janet	"	wife	"	36	–	–	B. Midlothian, Edinburgh

James Young Nephew unmar   23 Slater   B. England
Janet   Wilson Servant   "   24 Dom. Servt.   B. Fife, Kirkcaldy

From this entry it was seen that John Young had a wife named Janet (although this was not shown on the 1858 death certificate) and the John I needed for this search had a wife named Agnes, so, reluctantly, this entry could not be accepted. But it took a lot of work and a great deal of time to prove that it was wrong for our search!

What Next?

I decided to go back to Margaret Young, who had been the source of my original information. I expressed to her my frustration at not finding any MIs (Monumental Inscriptions) for John Young, and was promptly told of a family grave with tombstones in Inveresk Cemetery!

We visited Inveresk and saw three tombstones; two of them had names and dates I had found, but the third was a goldmine of information, and took the family back another generation. On this stone was inscribed:

Also in Memory of his Grandfather
Alexander Young
Wright in Musselburgh
Died 1806
And his Wife
Ellen Douglas
Died 1865 (?) aged 85 (?) [not clear]
And their daughters
Jean & Euphemia

————

Also of his Father
John Young
Wright in Musselburgh
Died 1847
and his Wife
Agnes Paterson
Died 1892 aged 86 years
and their son
Alexander
Died 1839 (?) aged 4 years.

From one of the other stones it would appear that Thomas Young, son of John Young and Agnes Paterson, had had them erected. If I had found this MI earlier I would not have taken so long to search for the deaths of John Young and Agnes Paterson. All this was news to Margaret Young who had never read the tombstones and had never heard of Alexander Young!

You can see how important such a monumental inscription is. John Young died prior to 1855, and it would have been difficult to prove his parentage with any certainty.

Nothing in the search had indicated that John Young came from Musselburgh.

What Next?

A return to New Register House and to the 1841 census return and the OPRs for Musselburgh.

As John Young died in 1847, possibly in Musselburgh, I decided to search the 1841 census return for him and his family. Inveresk is not a large town, but there is a street index available for the 1841 and 1851 census returns. I ordered the microfilm for 1841 on a slip of the type shown in Figure 14. Not having an address for John Young in Mussel-burgh I had to read through the microfilm until I found him. Extending the search to the 1851 census return I also found Agnes as a widow.

To make full use of the information gained from the census returns and the Monumental Inscriptions, I searched the OPRs for Inveresk.

SEARCHING IN OLD PARISH REGISTERS' ENTRIES PRIOR TO 1855

Before searching the OPR, I listed all the events I hoped to find, thereby obviating the possibility of forgetting to search for an entry and having to re-order the microfilm.

> *OPR Inveresk, Co. Midlothian (689)*
> Search for:
>   1. Alexander Young died in 1806. Search for his marriage to Ellen Douglas, starting from that date.
>   2. Children to Alexander Young and Ellen Douglas. Jean, Euphemia and John, and possibly others.
>   3. Marriage of John Young and Agnes Paterson prior to 1838.
>   4. Children to John Young and Agnes Paterson. Alexander, Helen and Catherine, and possibly others. (Thomas had been born in England.)
>   5. Deaths of any relevant Young entries.

1. To search for the marriage of Alexander Young and Ellen Douglas, from the OPR index book I found the reference number for Inveresk I used an order slip for OPRs (Figure 16) to obtain the microfilm for Inveresk. I found the entry I was looking for in 1799, and recorded it in my notebook:

OPR Inveresk, Co. Midlothian (689/13) Marriages

1799 Alexander Young, Wright, & Helen Douglas married at Edinburgh upon the 29th day of January 1799, by the Revd. Dr Grieve, Minister.

I did not search the three Edinburgh OPRs to see if the marriage had also been recorded there, but this could be done.

2. To search for issue to the above couple I used the OPR index for Inveresk to obtain the reference number for the microfilm of births or baptisms covering the years after 1799:

OPR Inveresk, Co. Midlothian (689/8) Births/Bapts

1800 Alexander Young, Wright, Musselburgh & Helen Douglas his wife, their daughter Jean, born 9th bapt. 23 March. Witnesses: John Young and John Douglas.

1802 Alexander Young, Wright, Musselburgh & Helen Douglas his wife, their son John, born 18th July, baptized 5th August. Witnesses: John Young and Alexr. Shaw.

1804 Alexander Young, Wright, & Helen Douglas his wife, their daughter Euphemia born 17th Novr. baptized 2nd Decr. Wits: John Young and John Douglas.

I continued the search for children up to October 1807. Although Alexander Young died in 1806, there may have been a posthumous child.

3. No entry for the marriage of John Young and Agnes Paterson was found in Inveresk. Noted the fact that I had searched these records and the years covered.

4. As the 1851 census return showed two children born in Musselburgh to John Young and Agnes Paterson, I tried to find their birth entries, as well as the entry for Alexander born *circa* 1835. I covered the years 1835 to 1847, and 1854 for late entries, but found no children to John and Agnes registered in Inveresk.

5. In the search for any relevant Young deaths, I confined the search to the names known from the tombstones and census returns.

Once more I had to refer to the OPR index list to obtain the necessary reference numbers. Not many parishes recorded deaths and/or burials, but luckily Inveresk did. There is a register of deaths for the years 1750 to 1854, and entries for the years 1810 to 1854 are indexed:

OPR Inveresk, Co. Midlothian (689/14) Deaths

1806 October 14. Alexander Young, Wright in Musse[ll] was buried in the Southside of Handyside Stone.

The wording of this entry would imply that Alexander Young did not have a tombstone of his own, but was buried near the Handyside family. The Handyside stones are still there and the Young stones are next to them.

Also named on the tombstone were Jean (born 1800) and Euphemia (born 1804). As they may have died in infancy I searched the Inveresk death registers from 1800 to 1834 and noted the only other relevant entry found during the search:

> *OPR Inveresk, Co. Midlothian (689/20) Deaths/Burials*
>
> 1839   Alexr. Young, son of John Young, Wright. Died 1st March aged 3.
> 1850   Euphemia Young, daughter of Alexr. Young, Wright. Died 26th June, aged 45.
> 1854   Jean Young, daughter of the late Alexander Young, Wright, Died 22nd May, aged 54.
>   Place of death: 84 East Crosscausey, Edinburgh.

I searched the 1851 census return for the Edinburgh address, but there was no trace of Jean Young there. There was no entry in the death register for John Young who, according to the tombstone, died in 1847. He may have died in Edinburgh, but I did not extend the search at this stage.

What Next?

Although Thomas Young was born in London, I wished to see if his parents, John Young and Agnes Paterson, were married in Scotland. Not having found the entry in the Inveresk OPR, I decided to search the three Edinburgh parishes. Edinburgh OPRs are contained in three separately numbered districts: Edinburgh (685[1]), St Cuthberts (685[2]) and Canongate (685[3]).

The Edinburgh (685[1]/64) marriage register for the years 1828–35 has an index at the start of the book, but this shows only the bridegroom's name. From this index I noted the reference page numbers for all the John Young entries, wound on the microfilm, and looked at them all until I found the one I wanted, which was on page 433 in 1835 (Figure 17). John Young was a Wright by trade, so I could visit the National Library for a book on Wrights in Edinburgh; search the apprentice records held in the Scottish Record Office, in Princes Street (there are some Scottish apprentice records to be found in the GRO in Kew, Surrey), and search the Post Office and trades directory. Any of these places might yield information concerning John Young.

The 1835 marriage entry for John Young showed that he and Agnes Paterson were both residing in Grass Market, New Greyfriars Parish in

Edinburgh, but by the 1841 census return they were in Musselburgh, having had a son, Thomas, in London in 1838. So you see, the farther back the search goes, the more difficult and time-consuming it becomes; but it is all the more satisfactory when the correct entry does eventually turn up!

Now, as far as the Young family is concerned, it should be possible to undertake some more work on Inveresk records to try to take back the line there. A visit to London to St Catherine's House for the birth entry for Thomas and his children, Alexander and Ann, would be interesting. Where were they living? And what was the English connection that made Thomas return to the place of his birth?

The drop-line chart for the Young family is progressing (Figure 18).

What Next?

I decided to turn my attention to the *Dudgeon* line. *Maria Long Dudgeon* married *Thomas Young* in Edinburgh in 1859, and both her father, Adam Dudgeon, and her mother, Jean Charles, were deceased by then.

According to the 1891 census return, Maria was born in Musselburgh, County Midlothian, *circa* 1840. So the first thing to do was to search the 1841 census for Musselburgh for the Dudgeon family:

1841/689/7/29 at Smart's Wynd, Musselburgh, Parish of Inveresk

Adam Dudgeon	20	Flesher	Y.
Jane Dudgeon	20		Y.
Maria L. Dudgeon	1		Y.
William R. Hayart	6 months		Y.

We do not know who William R. Hayart was, but I imagine that Jane Dudgeon was a wet-nurse; having had her own baby recently, she probably had enough milk to feed little William too.

While winding on the microfilm searching for Adam Dudgeon, I came across another family which may have had a link with Adam (the name Archibald has been handed down in the Young family), so I made a note of it in passing:

1841/689/6/3 at High Street, Musselburgh, Inveresk Parish

Archd. Dudgeon	65	Flesher J.	Y.
Ann Dudgeon	55		Y.
Archd. Dudgeon	25	Flesher J.	Y.
David Dudgeon	15	Flesher	Y.
Marion Dudgeon	10		Y.

I then extended the search to the 1851 census for Inveresk, and found:

1851/689/2 Musselburgh/43 at Smart's Wynd, Musselburgh,
Parish of Inveresk, Co. Midlothian

Adam	Dudgeon	Head	married	32	Flesher	Born	Inveresk,	Co.
								Midlothian.
Jane	"	wife	"	31	–	"	"	"
Marian	"	daughter		10	Scholar	"	"	"
Ann	"	"		8	"	"	"	"
Archibald	"	son		5	"	"	"	"
Jane	"	daughter		2		"	"	"

Now I knew the names of more children born to Adam Dudgeon and Jane Charles. The names Jane and Jean tend to be interchangeable. Maria was recorded as Marian and she now had a brother Archibald, which made the Archibald Dudgeon of the 1841 census even more likely to be 'ours', so I noted the following entry:

1851/689/1/9 at High Street, Musselburgh, Par. of Inveresk, Co. Midlothian

Archibald	Dudgeon	Head	mar.	79	Flesher	B. Inveresk, Co.
						Midlothian.
Ann	"	wife	"	66	–	" " "
Archibald	"	son	unmar	39	Flesher	" " "

Two members of Archibald Dudgeon's family had either died or moved away; possibly married. David who was aged 15 and Marion who was aged 10 in the 1841 census were no longer with their parents in 1851.

What Next?

Adam and Jane / Jean were both deceased by 1859 when their daughter Maria married Thomas Young. Did they die between 1855 (start of statutory registration in Scotland) and 1859?

On searching the index to deaths I soon found that Jane Dudgeon (M/S Charles) had died in 1855 (Figure 19). Such an occurrence is always fortunate for genealogists because an 1855 certificate contains so much more information than that for any other year:

> *Death of Jane Dudgeon*
> *1855 Inveresk, Co. Edinburgh (689/7) on January 8th at Wonder Street, Musselburgh*
>
> | *Jane Dudgeon* | Aged 36. Born in Inveresk. Married to Adam Dudgeon, (Flesher). |
> | *Issue* | Maria aged 15 |
> | | Anna aged 12 |
> | | Helen deceased at 10 months in 1847 |

	Archibald aged 8
	Jane aged 6
Daughter of	James Charles. Shoemaker (deceased) and of Maria Charles M/S Long (deceased)
Cause	Consumption, one year as certified by A. Macdonald Sanderson, Surgeon, who saw deceased 7 Jany. 1855.
Burial place	Inveresk Churchyard. As certified by Robert Gibson, Undertaker.
Informant	Maria Dudgeon. Daughter.

Most of Jane Dudgeon's children's names were listed in the 1851 census return, but now I knew that there was another baby girl, Helen, who died in 1847 aged 10 months. Helen was not born by 1841, and she had died before 1851, so she could not appear in a census. Later death certificates do not list children's names, so this kind of information about a family is not as easily found after 1855.

The death certificate showed that Jane's parents, James Charles and Maria Long, were both deceased by 1855, and that her husband Adam Dudgeon was still alive . . . but was he . . .? These early certificates tend to be a bit suspect; it was odd to find the informant being Maria who was only 15 years old, if her father had been still alive. Adam was deceased by 1859 when his daughter Maria married, so I had only to search the death index from 1855 to 1859. This I did, and as I suspected, there was no trace of the death of Adam Dudgeon. Of course this does not *prove* that he died before 1855; he may have gone off somewhere, and died out of Scotland, but it is unlikely.

Before leaving the modern (post-1854) records, I decided to see if the deaths of Archibald and Ann Dudgeon could be found, in case they were the parents of Adam Dudgeon. Archibald was aged 79 and Ann was aged 66 in the 1851 census, so I searched the 1861 census return for Inveresk but could find only their son Archibald; from which I assumed that his parents had died. Once again I was searching in that twilight area of 1856–60 when spouses' names were not recorded in death certificates, and ages were not recorded in the index. I searched the death index from 1855 and found Ann Dudgeon's death in 1858; she was the daughter of James Leckie and Mary Hart. Although her husband's name was not recorded, Ann was recorded as 'widow of a Flesher'; her age at death (74) was correct, and the informant was her son Archibald.

Ann Dudgeon was a widow when she died in 1858, but a search for the death of Archibald Dudgeon between 1855 and 1858 failed to turn up the relevant entry. He must, therefore, have died prior to statutory registration in 1855.

What Next?

Having done as much as I could using statutory records from 1855, it was time once again to sit back, review the situation, add a few facts to the chart (Figure 20) and work out what I hoped to find in the Inveresk Old Parish Registers prior to 1855. Before starting to search the registers, however, I listed all the items I hoped to find:

OPR Inveresk, Co. Midlothian (689)

Search for:

1. Marriage of Adam Dudgeon and Jean/Jane Charles before 1841 (daughter Marian/Maria aged 10 in 1851 census).

2. Birth of Maria Long Dudgeon, given as Marion in the census return, *circa* 1840/1841.

3. Births of her brother and sisters, using the list of children from the 1855 death entry of her mother Jane Dudgeon as well as the list of children in the 1851 census return.

4. Birth of Adam Dudgeon aged 32 in 1851 census, therefore born *circa* 1819. Parents unknown.

5. If found, then search for births of siblings and marriage of the parents.

6. Death of Adam Dudgeon between 1851 and 1855.

1. To search for the marriage of Adam Dudgeon and Jean Charles, who were married prior to 1841, I ordered OPR 689/19. This microfilm contains the Inveresk marriage register for 1836–54 and an index. In 1839 I found the marriage of Adam Dudgeon and Jean Charles:

OPR Inveresk, Co. Edinburgh (or Midlothian) (689/19) Marriages

1839   Dudgeon, Adam, Flesher, residing in this Parish and Jean Charles also residing in this Parish gave up their names for proclamation of banns on 23^d March 1839 Cautioner for the man Alexander Kirk and for the woman Robert Henderson.

Note that this entry is for the proclamation of banns only, and that the actual date of the wedding is not stated.

A Cautioner (pronounced cationer as in nation) acted as a surety for the couple to ensure their good behaviour before the wedding date and also to ensure that they married within the stipulated time of forty days after the proclamation of banns.

2, 3. To search for the birth of Maria Long Dudgeon and her siblings, I again referred to the OPR index to see which reference number covered births/baptisms in Inveresk for the years around

1840. This was 689/17; so using the same procedure as when searching for the marriage, I searched for and found:

OPR Inveresk, Co. Edinburgh (689/17) Births/Baptisms

1840   Dudgeon, Adam, Flesher and Jean Charles his wife, their daughter Maria Long born 25th May and baptized [blank] 1840. Witnesses William Gilkerton and Robert Borthwick.

1842   Dudgeon, Adam, Flesher, Musselburgh, and Jane Charles, his wife, their daughter Anne, born 11th June baptized 7th August. Witnesses Robert Borthwick and William Smith.

1844   Dudgeon, Adam, Flesher, Musselburgh, and Jean Charles his wife, their daughter Helen born June 26th & baptized Septr 8th 1844. Witnesses John Veitch & Willm. Gibson.

This 1844 birth entry for Helen Dudgeon revealed an inaccuracy in the 1855 death certificate of her mother Jean, where Helen's birth and death dates were recorded as 1846–1847. This is not surprising when you remember that the informant was Maria, aged 15 at the time.

I searched extensively but in vain in Inveresk for birth or baptism entries for Archibald and Jane, both listed in the census and on their mother's death certificate. They may have been born and recorded in Edinburgh, but I did not take time to search for them farther afield.

4. To search for the birth of Adam Dudgeon the names of whose parents were unkown, I again referred to the OPR index list. My notebook showed:

OPR Inveresk, Co. Edinburgh (689/10) Births/Baptisms

Searched for the birth of an Adam Dudgeon. Started to search in the year 1819 as he was aged 32 in the 1851 census return, and found the following entry in 1816:

1816   Dudgeon, Archibald, Flesher, & Anne Leckie, their son Adam born 28th Jany. & bapt. 1st Feby. Wits. David Leckie & Wm. Dudgeon.

Was this 'our' Adam? The only way to make sure was to search for a few more years either side of 1816 to see if the birth of another Adam Dudgeon had been recorded. This I did, covering the years 1820–1812, and luckily I did not find the birth of another Adam Dudgeon registered in Inveresk. So his age in the 1851 census should have been recorded as 35 and not 32.

5. Using the names found in the index, I looked them up in the OPR, noting the different volume numbers of different years:

OPR Inveresk, Co. Edinburgh (689/9) Births/Baptisms

1804   Dudgeon, Archibald, Flesher, & Anne Leckie, his wife,
         their son George, born 14th & bapt. 26th August. Wits. D.
         Leckie & G. Dudgeon.
1806   Dudgeon, Archibald, Flesher, & Ann Leckie, his wife,
         their son James, born July 26 and bapt Augt [blank] Wits.
         James and John Leckie.

OPR Inveresk, Co. Edinburgh (689/10) Births/Baptisms

1809   Dudgeon, Archibald, Flesher, & Anne Leckie his wife,
         their son Archd. born 23rd June & bapt. 7th July. Wits.
         David & Geo. Leckie.
1818   Dudgeon, Archibald, Flesher & Anne Leckie, their
         daughter Marion, born 8th & bapt. 18th June. Wits. David
         Leckie and Wm. Dudgeon.

OPR Inveresk, Co. Edinburgh (689/16) Births/Baptisms

1820   Dudgeon, Archibald, Flesher, & Anne Leckie, their
         daughter Margaret, born 4th & bapt. 29th December. Wits
         David Leckie & James Dudgeon.
1823   Dudgeon, Archibald, Flesher, & Ann Leckie, their son
         David, born 27th November 1822, & bapt 27th Feby. 1823.
         Wits. David Leckie & James Dudgeon.
1830   Dudgeon, Archibald, Flesher, & Ann Leckie his wife, had
         their daughter Menie, born 1st January & bapt. 2nd May
         1830. Wits. D. Moodie and Charles Webster.

There are some points to be noted from the above birth entries. Ann
was sometimes Anne; the witnesses' names would tend to suggest that
they were members of the family, perhaps uncles to the children; and
the 1823 entry for David showed that he had been born in the
November of the previous year, 1822.

Archibald Dudgeon and Anne Leckie had their first child in 1804, so
I searched for their marriage from that date. From the index for the
Inveresk OPR it can be seen that marriages were not indexed as early
as 1803; so I ordered OPR 689/13, which contained marriage entries
between 1785–1819, and read all the entries from 1804 until I found
the one I needed.

OPR Inveresk, Co. Edinburgh (689/13) Marriages

1803   Dudgeon, Archibald, Flesher & Ann Leckie, both in this
         parish were married at Edinr. on the 9th May by the Revd.
         John McClaurin, Minister of the Gaelic Chapel of Glasgow.

This is is an interesting entry. Both Archibald Dudgeon and his bride Ann Leckie lived in Musselburgh, Parish of Inveresk, but they were married in Edinburgh, and not only that, they were married by the Minister of the Gaelic Chapel of Glasgow! I wonder what connection they had with the Revd. John McClaurin, and why, if he came through to Edinburgh to marry them, he did not go to Musselburgh which is only between five or six miles away. It is highly unlikely that the Dudgeon family were Gaelic speakers as they lived in the south of Scotland, but perhaps Anne Leckie's family came from a Gaelic-speaking area. It would be interesting to search the OPR for Edinburgh to see if the marriage entry was recorded there, and if so, if any more detail about the couples was given in that register.

6. Before leaving Inveresk I searched the OPR for Dudgeon deaths:

OPR Inveresk, Co. Edinburgh (698/20) Deaths

1845   May 14 Helen Dudgeon, daughter of Adam Dudgeon, Flesher, Aged 1, Died at Wonder Street, Newbigging, Musselburgh.

1853   July 30 Adam Dudgeon, Flesher, aged 34, died at High Street, Musselburgh.

1853   Septr. 18 Archibald Dudgeon, flesher, aged 84, died at High Street, Musselburgh.

Unlike the Young family, the Dudgeons did not have a tombstone.

This seemed a good place at which to stop this search in the OPRs – for the time being anyway. There is always more to be done; I could certainly try to take back the Dudgeon line, and the Charles line (Jane Dudgeon who died in 1855 was the daughter of James Charles and Maria Long), and so it goes on . . . and on . . . and on!

What Next?

The next step was to visit the Scottish Record Office to search for wills and deeds to see what could be found for the *Young* and for the *Dudgeon* families. There is no charge for searching records in the SRO, so it is better to plan your research so as to stay in New Register House until you have used up your search pass there – one day, or one week or for whatever period you have paid.

I searched the index of testaments (wills) and inventories, in the Edinburgh commissariot, for the Young family. There was nothing for John Young and his wife Agnes Paterson, but I did find wills and inventories for their son, Thomas Young, and his wife, Maria Dudgeon.

'At Edinburgh the First day of March Nineteen hundred and twenty six, the following Inventory of the Personal Estate of Mrs

Maria Dudgeon or Young, and Deed relating to the disposal
thereof, were presented by Alex. Ross, S.S.C., 108 George Street,
Edinburgh: 'Inventory of the moveable or personal estate and
effects, wheresoever situated, of the late Mrs Maria Dudgeon or
Young, wife of and who resided with Thomas Young, at Number
18 Dudley Terrace, Leith, Edinburgh, who died at 18 Dudley
Terrace, aforesaid, on the fifth day of February 1926.'

There followed a list of sums of money, cash in the house, cash in the
bank, bonds and the value of her personal effects. In her will she made
the following bequests:

'I Mrs Maria Dudgeon or Young, Wife of and residing with
Thomas Young at number eighteen Dudley Terrace, Leith being
desirous of settling the succession to my means and estate after
my death Do Hereby asign and Dispone and Bequeath to my
daughters Agnes Paterson Young and Annie Dudgeon Young,
my whole means estate and effects heritable and moveable which
shall belong to me at the time of my death subject to the following
legacies viz: To my eldest daughter Agnes Paterson Young, my
diamond gold ring; To my youngest daughter Annie Dudgeon
Young my diamond gold brooch and gold watch and chain; and
any Jewellery, Silver plate, Linen and China equally divided
between my two daughters before mentioned: I also bequeath to
my daughter-in-law Isabella Paterson Young the sum of Ten
Pounds Sterling to be paid after my death free of Legacy Duty:
And I nominate and appoint my sons John Young, two Bellevue
Crescent Ayr and Thomas Young one hundred and six Comiston
Drive Edinburgh and the survivor of them to be my Executors
and Executor. In Witness Whereof these presents written on this
page are subscribed by me at Edinburgh on the eighth day of
June Nineteen hundred and twenty before these witnesses
Robert Somervell Campbell, Solicitor Supreme Courts
Edinburgh and James Haxton Banks Clerk to Messrs Alexander
Campbell and Son, Solicitors Supreme Courts, Edinburgh.'

For *Thomas Young*, the husband of *Maria Dudgeon*, I found an
inventory and a will. The inventory listed money in the same way as the
inventory of his wife, but there was also a value of the house and effects,
and an amount due to Thomas by his son Thomas. From the
genealogical point of view, the will was more interesting than the
inventory.

'At Edinburgh the Seventeenth day of January One thousand
nine hundred and twenty eight the DEED herinafter engrossed

was presented for registration in the Books of Council and Session for preservation and is registered in the said Books as follows:

I, Thomas Young residing at Number eighteen Dudley Terrace, Leith, being desirous of settling the succession to my means and estate after my death do hereby nominate my sons John Young, Number two Bellevue Crescent, Ayr, Thomas Young, One hundred and six Comiston Drive, Edinburgh, and Archibald Young, Number Seven Cargil Terrace, Edinburgh, to be my Trustees and Executors and I assign, dispone, devise and bequeath to them as Trustees under these presents and the survivor of them the whole means and estate heritable and moveable real and personal wherever situated which shall belong to me or over which I may have the power of disposal at the time of my death in trust for the following purposes videlicet (First) for payments of my debts funeral expenses and the expenses of executing the Trust hereby created (Second) I direct my Trustees to deliver the following legacies (1) to my son the said John Young the portraits of myself and my late wife and also my bureau (2) to my son the said Thomas Young my gold chain and appendages, gold sleeve links and studs and silver watch, and (3) to my son the said Archibald Young, my gold watch (Third) I direct my Trustees to convey my house and pertinents at Number eighteen Dudley Terrace, Leith, to my son the said John Young and my daughters Agnes Paterson Young and Annie Dudgeon Young equally between them (Fourth) I direct my Trustees to deliver to my daughters the said Agnes Paterson Young and Annie Dudgeon Young the whole household effects belonging to me at the time of my death equally between them (Fifth) I direct my Trustees to convey to my sons the said John Young, Thomas Young and Archibald Young equally between them my heritable properties situated at number Fifty two Maryfield, Edinburgh, and Number Twelve Brunton Terrace, Edinburgh, and to pay to them equally between them the sum of Five hundred pounds Sterling and (Sixth) I direct my Trustees to pay assign or convey the whole residue of my means and estate to my daughters the said Agnes Paterson Young and Anne Dudgeon Young equally between them share and share alike And I confer on my Trustees all requisite powers for carrying out the purposes of this Trust in particular I empower them to sell any part of my means and estate by public roup or private bargain And I consent to registration hereof for preservation: IN WITNESS THEREOF these presents written on this page are subscribed by the said Thomas Young at Leith upon the Fourteenth day of April Nineteen hundred and twenty seven before these witnesses Mrs. Janet Miller Innes, Twenty Dudley Terrace Leith, and Mrs. Mary Agnes Preston, Typist to Alexander Ross, Solicitor Supreme Courts, Edinburgh, (Signed) Thomas Young, Janet M. Innes. Witness, M. A. Preston, Witness.'

I also searched the register of sasines and found who had bought the property belonging to Thomas Young. I did not, however, search for apprentice records of John Young. I searched for wills for Archibald Dudgeon and for his son, Adam, but could find nothing for them at all. So there I called a temporary halt to the search.

Alexander Young who married in 1799 was probably born about 1775, and *Archibald Dudgeon* who died in 1853, aged 84, was probably born about 1769. His wife, *Ann Leckie*, died in 1858, aged 74, and her parents, *James Leckie* and *Mary Hart*, are *Margaret Dudgeon Young's* great-great-great-grandparents (Figure 21).

I did not complete either line, but I am sure that if I were to continue the search I might find their births and the marriages of their parents . . . and their births . . . and . . .!

This search took me about ten days, working for six hours a day.

Index

Fictitious names used as examples throughout the text, and names
found in 'Step by Step' are not included in this index.
F.H.S. = Family History Society.

Registery Office (Births Deaths Marriage
Genealogy Dept
22, Park Circus — 0141 - 249 - 4500
£12-00 - per day.